# The Challenge of
# Institutional Reform
# in Mexico

# The Challenge of Institutional Reform in Mexico

edited by
Riordan Roett

LYNNE
RIENNER
PUBLISHERS

BOULDER
LONDON

Published in the United States of America in 1995 by
Lynne Rienner Publishers, Inc.
1800 30th Street, Boulder, Colorado 80301

and in the United Kingdom by
Lynne Rienner Publishers, Inc.
3 Henrietta Street, Covent Garden, London WC2E 8LU

**Library of Congress Cataloging-in-Publication Data**
Roett, Riordan, 1938–
    The challenge of institutional reform in Mexico / Riordan Roett.
    Includes bibliographical references and index.
    ISBN 1-55587-545-9 (alk. paper)
    1. Mexico—Politics and government—1988–  2. Mexico—Economic
policy—1970–  3. Mexico—Social policy. I. Title.
JL1224.R64  1995
303.48'4'097209049—dc20                                      95-3465
                                                             CIP

**British Cataloguing in Publication Data**
A Cataloguing in Publication record for this book
is available from the British Library.

Printed and bound in the United States of America

        The paper used in this publication meets the requirements
   ∞    of the American National Standard for Permanence of
        Paper for Printed Library Materials Z39.48.1984.

    5  4  3  2  1

# Contents

**PART 2   PUBLIC POLICY REFORMS AND CHALLENGES**

**PART 3 CONCLUSIONS**

# Tables

# Preface

## Guadalupe Paz

Mexico is changing, rapidly and fundamentally. Liberalization of the nation's economic and political affairs has led to a reassessment of state relations with key political and social actors—labor, the peasantry, political parties, the business community, the church—which, in turn, has resulted in further institutional reform. New forces have emerged in the country's political process; new constituencies have found a voice and are being heard; reestablishing stability—economic and political, as well as social—has become a major government concern; and international interest in Mexico, particularly on the part of the United States, has heightened foreign scrutiny of the country's transition process.

The following collection of essays, which represents the views of eleven scholars from both Mexico and the United States, describes the background, nature, and extent of Mexico's recent institutional reforms; assesses the extent to which the reforms have been implemented; and explores the likely long-term effects of these changes. The authors also address a variety of dilemmas arising from the restructuring of state-society relations and offer proposals for adjusting and supplementing the reform process as Mexico strives to adapt to changing domestic and international realities.

A timely volume, *The Challenge of Institutional Reform in Mexico* is the fourth in a continuing series coordinated by the Program on U.S.-Mexican Relations at the Paul H. Nitze School of Advanced International Studies of the Johns Hopkins University. The program is sponsored by the William and Flora Hewlett Foundation, whose generous support has made possible the publication of this and the previous volumes in the series—*Mexico and the United States: Managing the Relationship* (1988), *Mexico's External Relations in the 1990s* (1991), and *Political and Economic Liberalization in Mexico: At a Critical Juncture?* (1993)—which have been published in Mexico and the United States.

As the two countries are becoming increasingly interdependent—particularly since the North American Free Trade Agreement was signed—

there is renewed interest on each side of our shared border to learn more about the other. The goal of our U.S.-Mexico series is to enhance understanding of the bilateral relationship by making a variety of policy perspectives accessible to a broad audience in both countries. The commendable efforts and continued interest of the contributors and all those who in some way participated in the publication of this volume are an integral factor in helping us attain this goal.

*Guadalupe Paz*
*Coordinator, SAIS Program on U.S.-Mexican Relations*

# Acknowledgments

I wish to express my sincere appreciation to those individuals and institutions that made this publication possible. First, I would like to extend my thanks to my fellow authors, especially for their valuable contributions to this volume, but also for their understanding and cooperation during the editing and publication process. Special thanks go to those whose efforts resulted in the successful completion of this volume: Wendy Campbell, for her exceptional work editing the English-language manuscript; Guadalupe Paz, the coordinator of the Program on U.S.-Mexican Relations, for her dedication to this project and for overseeing the numerous details involved; Sergio Aguayo Quezada, for his unfailing support in coordinating and editing the Spanish-language manuscript; Anne McKenzie, for her cheerful and willing support at all times; and Anne McKinney, for her advice and her continued interest in the program. I would also like to thank Charles Roberts, for his translation of the chapters originally written in Spanish, and Bertha Ruiz de la Concha, for the translation of the English-language manuscript into Spanish.

As always, my deepest gratitude goes to Clint Smith and the William and Flora Hewlett Foundation for their ongoing support in the study of U.S.-Mexican relations.

Riordan Roett

# Acronyms

| | |
|---|---|
| AMCB | Asociación Mexicana de Casas de Bolsa (Mexican Association of Brokerage Houses) |
| AMIS | Asociación Mexicana de Instituciones de Seguros (Mexican Association of Insurance Institutions) |
| ANIT | Asociación Nacional de Industriales de la Transformación (National Association of Manufacturing Industries) |
| ANMEB | Acuerdo Nacional para la Modernización de la Educación Básica (National Agreement for the Modernization of Basic Education) |
| Bancomext | Banco Nacional de Comercio Exterior (National Bank for Foreign Trade) |
| Canacintra | Cámara Nacional de la Industria de la Transformación (National Chamber of Manufacturing Industries) |
| CCE | Consejo Coordinador Empresarial (Business Coordinating Council) |
| CEM | Conferencia del Episcopado Mexicano (Conference of Mexican Bishops) |
| CEPS | Comisión Episcopal de Pastoral Social (Social Pastoral Commission) |
| CMHN | Consejo Mexicano de Hombres de Negocios (Mexican Council of Business Executives) |
| CNA | Consejo Nacional Agropecuario (National Agricultural Council) |
| CNAE | Consejo Nacional de Autoridades Educativas (National Council of Educational Authorities) |
| CNC | Confederación Nacional de Campesinos (National Confederation of Peasants) |
| CNOP | Confederación Nacional de Organizaciones Populares (National Confederation of Popular Organizations) |

| | |
|---|---|
| CNPA | Coordinadora Nacional del Plan de Ayala (National "Plan de Ayala" Coordinating Committee) |
| CNTE | Coordinadora Nacional de Trabajadores de la Educación (National Coordinator of Education Workers) |
| COECE | Coordinadora de Organizaciones Empresariales de Comercio Exterior (Coordinating Body of Foreign Trade Business Associations) |
| COFIPE | Código Federal de Instituciones y Procedimientos Electorales (Federal Code for Electoral Institutions and Procedures) |
| Conamin | Confederación Nacional de la Microindustria (National Confederation of Microindustries) |
| Conasupo | Comisión Nacional de Subsistencias Populares (National Commission for Popular Subsistence) |
| Concamin | Confederación de Cámaras Industriales (Confederation of Chambers of Industry) |
| Concanaco | Confederación de Cámaras Nacionales de Comercio, Servicios y Turismo (Confederation of National Chambers of Commerce, Services, and Tourism) |
| Coparmex | Confederación Patronal de la República Mexicana (Employers' Confederation of the Republic of Mexico) |
| CROC | Confederación Revolucionaria de Obreros y Campesinos (Revolutionary Confederation of Workers and Peasants) |
| CROM | Confederación Regional de Obreros Mexicanos (Regional Confederation of Mexican Workers) |
| CRSE | Coordinación de Representaciones de la SEP en los Estados (Coordinator of SEP Representatives in the States) |
| CSP | Councils of Social Participation |
| CTM | Confederación de Trabajadores de México (Confederation of Mexican Workers) |
| DFS | Dirección Federal de Seguridad (Federal Security Bureau) |
| EZLN | Ejército Zapatista de Liberación Nacional (Zapatista National Liberation Army) |
| FDN | Frente Democrático Nacional (National Democratic Front) |
| FESEBS | Federación de Sindicatos de Empresas de Bienes y Servicios (Federation of Unions of Goods and Services Companies) |
| GATT | General Agreement on Tariffs and Trade |
| IFE | Instituto Federal Electoral (Federal Electoral Institute) |
| ILO | International Labour Office |
| INEGI | Instituto Nacional de Estadística, Geografía e Informática (National Institute of Statistics, Geography, and Information) |
| ISI | import substitution industrialization |

| | |
|---|---|
| LGE | Ley General de la Educación (General Law of Education) |
| Mimexa | Asociación de Microempresarios Mexicanos (Association of Mexican Microentrepreneurs) |
| NAFTA | North American Free Trade Agreement |
| PAN | Partido Acción Nacional (National Action Party) |
| PARM | Partido Auténtico de la Revolución Mexicana (Authentic Party of the Mexican Revolution) |
| PCM | Partido Comunista Mexicano (Mexican Communist Party) |
| PDM | Partido Democrático Mexicano (Mexican Democratic Party) |
| PEMEX | Petróleos Mexicanos (Mexican Petroleum [Company]) |
| PFCRN | Partido del Frente Cardenista para la Reconstrucción Nacional (Party of the Cardenista Front for National Reconstruction) |
| PGR | Procuraduría General de la República (Office of the Attorney General) |
| PMS | Partido Mexicano Socialista (Mexican Socialist Party) |
| PMT | Partido Mexicano de los Trabajadores (Mexican Workers' Party) |
| PPS | Partido Popular Socialista (Popular Socialist Party) |
| PRD | Partido de la Revolución Democrática (Party of the Democratic Revolution) |
| PRI | Partido Revolucionario Institucional (Institutional Revolutionary Party) |
| PRM | Partido de la Revolución Mexicana (Party of the Mexican Revolution) |
| PRT | Partido Revolucionario de los Trabajadores (Workers' Revolutionary Party) |
| PROCAMPO | Programa de Apoyos Directos al Campo (Program of Direct Support to the Countryside) |
| PRONASOL | Programa Nacional de Solidaridad (National Solidarity Program) |
| PSD | Partido Socialdemócrata (Social Democratic Party) |
| PST | Partido Socialista de los Trabajadores (Socialist Workers' Party) |
| PT | Partido del Trabajo (Work Party) |
| PVEM | Partido Verde Ecologista de México (Green Ecologist Party of Mexico) |
| SARH | Secretaría de Agricultura y Recursos Hidráulicos (Secretariat of Agriculture and Water Resources) |
| Secofi | Secretaría de Comercio y Fomento Industrial (Secretariat of Commerce and Industrial Development) |
| SEP | Secretaría de Educación Pública (Secretariat of Public Education) |

SNTE        Sindicato Nacional de Trabajadores de la Educación
            (National Union of Education Workers)
STC         Scholastic Technical Council
STRM        Sindicato de Telefonistas de la República Mexicana
            (Union of Telephone Workers of the Mexican
            Republic)
TELMEX      Teléfonos de México (Mexican Telephone [Company])
UNORCA      Unión Nacional de Organizaciones Regionales
            Campesinas (National Union of Regional Peasant
            Organizations)

# 1

# The Challenge of Institutional Reform in Mexico: An Introduction

## Riordan Roett

This fourth volume in the School of Advanced International Studies series on U.S.-Mexican relations examines the dynamic challenge of institutional reform in Mexico. We have chosen two general themes to demonstrate the progress—and the complexity—of the reform process: the institutional changes taking place in state-society relations; and the public policy reforms that have been either introduced or proposed and the continuing challenge to deepen reform.

The complexity of the process of institutional reform in Mexico has been amply dramatized by the events of 1994. The January uprising in Chiapas, the series of kidnappings of prominent businessmen, the assassination of the ruling party's presidential candidate Luis Donaldo Colosio, followed by that of the Institutional Revolutionary Party (PRI) secretary-general José Francisco Ruiz Massieu, and the unprecedented international—and domestic—interest in the transparency of the August national elections have all served not merely to intensify scrutiny of the reform process but also to illuminate the pressing need for vigorous analysis and adaptation as the individual reforms move forward.

Several implications for bilateral relations between the United States and Mexico are obvious. With the signing of the North American Free Trade Agreement (NAFTA) in 1993, the relationship has begun a new and uncertain phase in its long evolution. What is clear is that the economic opening between the two countries has heightened U.S. interest in the ability and the willingness of Mexico's leaders to address social and political issues as an important complement to the success of the economic and financial modernization process carried out during the *sexenio* (six-year term) of President Carlos Salinas de Gortari (1988–1994).

Public interest in and commitment to institutional reform is also on the rise among the Mexican citizenry. The impressive proliferation of nongovernmental organizations (NGOs) in Mexico, giving voice to a wide variety of social and political persuasions, attests to an empowerment of civil

1

society to a degree unimagined just a decade ago. Whether in response to that civic mobilization, or in an attempt to retain control, the governing PRI has promulgated a broad range of electoral reforms culminating in the decision to permit "foreign visitors" to observe the elections on August 21, 1994. The Federal Electoral Institute (IFE) now oversees a highly computerized and newly renovated set of institutional mechanisms to protect the secrecy of the ballot on election day. Other institutional arrangements, again unpredicted just a few years ago, are in place in the hope of avoiding the postelection challenges that have accompanied the two most recent national elections.

But the election of a new president in Mexico does not signal the end of institutional change. The next administration will have to confront a formidable array of institutional challenges in both the social and the political arenas. Nor does the backdrop of economic stabilization guarantee social and political change. Reform in those arenas will require national consensus and leadership from the next administration as it takes office in December 1994. The chapters in this volume, as outlined below, seek to highlight priorities for institutional change as well as the challenges inherent in Mexican society in doing so successfully.

## State-Society Relations and Institutional Change

The central role of labor in Mexican political life is emphasized in the chapter by James G. Samstad and Ruth Berins Collier. Reviewing the Salinas administration's efforts to refashion the state-labor alliance with a project of "new unionism," the authors conclude that the government has failed to substantially alter the institutional framework it inherited in 1988—"a corporatist political structure and state-labor alliance often at odds with the government's free-market orientation." But given the dramatic reorientation of the Mexican economy, beginning in the Miguel de la Madrid sexenio (1982–1988) and continuing today with the implementation of NAFTA, a redefinition of labor's ties to the state and society must be a top priority of the next administration. The authors provide a thorough review of the inherent contradictions in the current institutional arrangements and provide a blueprint for the changes that need to be undertaken to modernize—and liberalize—Mexican labor.

The Mexican peasantry is the backbone of the revolutionary tradition in Mexico. Merilee S. Grindle's chapter cogently explores the changing tempo in relations among peasants, the market, and the state. Indeed, one of the most dramatic institutional changes undertaken by the Salinas administration was to modify Article 27 of the Constitution of 1917 and the agrarian code that regulated *ejidos,* land communally held by legally incorporated groups of peasants. As Grindle points out, "This legislation

. . . set the scene for major changes in the economic relationships that existed in the agrarian sector and seriously undermined the traditional political relationship between the state and the peasantry." Does the revision of Article 27 open the possibility for new freedom for the Mexican peasantry? Or does it reflect another example of authoritarian liberalization? The author examines both of these important questions in her chapter, as well as the likely course of peasant-state relations in the future.

From the perspective of Jorge Alcocer V., the political party system in Mexico is at a historic turning point. Political reform, which began in 1978, rapidly accelerated during the Salinas sexenio. In 1990 Congress enacted a new electoral code, and a variety of additional electoral safeguards were instituted as late as May 1994. Campaign spending is now regulated, the Federal Electoral Institute is now autonomous and has new authority to oversee electoral procedures, and a new federal electoral registry issues tamper-proof voter identification cards. The electoral roll has been updated and verified. Special procedures have been put in place to insure ballot secrecy and transparent voting on election day. As noted earlier, foreign observers have been allowed for the first time, with the electoral proceedings in full view of the international community. While these reforms are important, what Alcocer finds of greatest significance is the realignment of the party system to reflect a newfound diversity in Mexican society and to permit an orderly transfer of power from the PRI to another political party when the Mexican people choose to do so.

One of the most dynamic changes in institutional arrangements in recent years has been that between the state and the private sector. Leaving behind the traditional command economy in which the state played a major role, the free-market reforms of recent years have provided an unprecedented opportunity for the transformation of Mexican entrepreneurs. Matilde Luna's chapter examines the transition from a corporatist set of relations to the new and still evolving role of business and banking in Mexico. NAFTA has accelerated the shift in relations, but business opportunities both within Mexico and across the country's borders have emboldened the business community to seek greater degrees of autonomy and political influence. Luna details the changing role of the business community and its evolving relationship with the modernizing state, both of which will play a significant part in the broader institutional change now under way in Mexico.

It can readily be argued that for the first time since the Revolution of 1910 the Roman Catholic church has again become an institutional player in Mexico. The decision by President Salinas in September 1992 to establish formal diplomatic relations with the Vatican was one important aspect of this reversal. But the assassination of Cardinal Juan Jesús Posadas Ocampo, the archbishop of Guadalajara, in May 1993 raised a series of disturbing questions about the willingness of Mexican society to accept a new and more open role for the church. Moreover, the emergence of Bishop Samuel Ruiz as one of the principal interlocutors in the Chiapas uprising in early 1994 demonstrated the growing complexity of the role of the church in modern Mexico. Roberto J. Blancarte's chapter discusses the emergence of a more critical church, one now willing to analyze more pragmatically the societal implications of political, economic, and social change in Mexico. The author illustrates the variegations in this new leaf in state-church relations and the internal tensions within the church that are likely to lead to further institutional changes in the years ahead.

## Public Policy Reforms and Challenges

Guillermo Trejo's chapter on the politics of educational reform argues that the reform "represents one of the major social policy initiatives" of the Salinas administration. The reform process during the Salinas sexenio aimed at changing the structure and distribution of power throughout the educational system. The educational reform package of 1992–1993 has opened the possibility for further institutional changes if the balance between the center and the periphery in Mexican society can be altered. But the author argues that "the reform has opened a Pandora's box." Will local authorities be able to capitalize on the reform process? Will the centralized authorities share power with state and local entities? The scene is set in coming years for a reallocation of authority for determining the educational outcomes of the Mexican system. The outlook is uncertain—because of the traditional weaknesses of the states and localities—but the reform initiative does provide a fundamentally altered framework for institutional change in the future.

In his chapter on social policy issues Wayne A. Cornelius addresses the problem of the medium- to long-term sustainability of Mexico's restructured economy, that is, the ability of the national government to cushion the populace from the social costs of economic reform while at the same time pursuing the fiscal constraints of the new economic model. The events in Chiapas and social unrest elsewhere in the society are "clear danger signals" indicating that "the economic reforms of the 1985–1993 period remain vulnerable to mounting social problems that, if unchecked, could cause an unraveling of the broad coalition that has thus far supported radical economic restructuring in Mexico." Through various examples of government efforts to alleviate social problems such as poverty—the National Solidarity Program being one of the major initiatives—the author demonstrates that even if carefully designed and appropriately funded, these programs will "work only where powerful political and economic interests do not prevent them from reaching their target populations." Cornelius concludes that the government needs to break long-standing power alliances in order to attain a broader political opening that will be consistent with Mexico's market-driven economic policies.

The stunning episodes of civil unrest in recent years—the peasant uprising in Chiapas, political and drug-related assassinations, and the upsurge in kidnappings of business leaders—form the backdrop for Martin Edwin Andersen's timely analysis of civil-military relations and the role of the police in Mexico. His chapter raises uncomfortable questions about the oft-neglected issues of public safety and national defense. What legacy does the Salinas administration leave on security issues? What factors influence the public's perception of military threats and civil insecurity? How has the military's role in internal security affected the armed forces themselves, as well as the police with whom they are in frequent, and sometimes tragic, competition? Although necessarily speculative, the questions posed in this analysis go to the heart of the nation's emerging democratic pluralism and speak to the misguided tendency to continue to expand the military's mission at a time when public safety concerns call for a well-functioning police force in Mexican communities. The author concludes that the government needs to demilitarize its internal security apparatus by professionalizing the police, and that the state must clearly distinguish between national defense and internal security.

## Conclusion

Together these chapters set forth an ambitious set of institutional priorities for the next presidential sexenio (1994–2000). Viewed in the context of Mexico's ongoing economic and financial liberalization, the challenges, though often conflicting, are urgent. Basic institutional relations need to be reassessed and redefined. The role of the traditional pillars of the Revolution—the peasants and the workers—must be carefully reexamined. The need for a modern educational system and the requirements of a newly competitive private sector are related yet distinguishable. The political party system and the democratic process are under pressure for further institutional changes that will guarantee transparency in elections and fairness in representation. The role of the military and the police as extensions of the state and the role of the Catholic church in society, both largely unexplored for decades, are now increasingly critical in alleviating the civil tensions that were inevitably to follow on the heels of the nation's recent economic and political openings.

The agenda for institutional reform in Mexico is not impossible to achieve. It will require determined political leaders with a commitment to negotiation and consensus building. The next government in Mexico will want to continue to question the old institutional values and relationships but without the penchant to discard them without good reason. Societies change slowly. Institutional arrangements in place have strong antecedents and powerful current defenders. The challenge of institutional reform in Mexico, as elsewhere, is to know when and where to move to pragmatically accomplish new societal goals. The institutional changes discussed in this volume will require many years of debate and complex forms of interaction between the state and society. But the dynamic nature of institutional change is a reality in today's Mexico and can be avoided only at the peril of a future institutional stalemate, with its obvious social and political costs.

# — PART 1 —
## State-Society Relations and Institutional Change

# 2

# Mexican Labor and Structural Reform Under Salinas: New Unionism or Old Stalemate?

## James G. Samstad & Ruth Berins Collier

When President Carlos Salinas de Gortari entered office at the end of 1988, many observers believed that his commitment to a new economic model would soon bring an end to a defining feature of Mexican politics: the traditional corporatist relation between the state and organized labor. The previous six years had already brought a radical transformation of the country's economic strategy. Having ushered in the Third World debt crisis in 1982 by announcing its inability to pay, Mexico adopted a short-term stabilization program that, within a few years, became a long-term commitment to a thoroughgoing restructuring of the economy: from a protectionist and interventionist model of growth to a more liberal orientation based on free trade and international competitiveness. Yet, the long-standing political alliances in Mexico had been consummated and reinforced in the context of the old economic model, and the question now was whether those alliances would be compatible with the new pattern of economic decisionmaking and distribution of wealth and influence. If economic policy could be changed with almost breathtaking speed, political institutions were characterized by greater stickiness.

This question was perhaps most germane in the case of organized labor, one of the pillars of Mexico's postrevolutionary coalition. As in the rest of Latin America, the Mexican state had intervened extensively in the economy to protect workers from an untrammeled labor market in the broader context of a model of import substitution industrialization (ISI). That model underwrote a class compromise based on the contribution of rising real wages to an expanding domestic market. The new, neoliberal model, by contrast, called for a reduction in the state's protection of labor, an emphasis on keeping wages competitively low, greater flexibility in the organization of work, and a greater reliance on market discipline in industrial relations. Under these conditions, the perpetuation of the historic position of Mexican labor as a major constituency within the governing coalition was called into question. The new economic policies seemed to deprive the government of a material basis for retaining this constituency, structurally represented by its central organizational position in the ruling Institutional Revolutionary Party (PRI).

Tension between the new economic direction and the old political structures had already become evident during the presidency of Miguel de la Madrid Hurtado (1982–1988), but no alternative to the existing state-labor alliance was articulated during that period. A political crisis came into full public view in 1988 when the PRI, which had historically won three-quarters of the vote, proved unable to win a simple majority without recourse to widespread electoral fraud. Salinas was thus confronted with a dilemma upon entering office: At a time of political weakness, when he seemed most dependent on generating political support, his own economic policy goals were threatening one of the party's most important constituencies. The new president attempted to resolve this dilemma through a political and economic project he termed "new unionism."

This chapter explores the attempt to work out the contradictions between the old political structures and the new economic model on the part of a cross-pressured government and a labor movement divided in its response. After first defining the traditional alliance, we analyze the tensions that arose under De la Madrid. We then focus on Salinas's political-economic project of new unionism as an effort to restructure state-labor relations in a manner consistent with the new economic orientation, as well as three major responses by labor: (1) concurrence, by those unions that in whole or in part adopted Salinas's project; (2) confrontation, by those that opposed his neoliberal policies and favored greater distance and autonomy from the government, and (3) retrenchment, by those that strategically cooperated with the economic policies, hoping to preserve the old political structures and hence their position within the governing coalition and their ability to negotiate within it on behalf of their long-term political and economic interests. Given labor's response and the government's own ambivalence, no definitive break with the traditional pattern had occurred by the end of the Salinas presidency.

## The Traditional State-Labor Alliance

Through most of the twentieth century labor played a central role in Mexico's ruling coalition by legitimating the government, providing it with an important base of voters, and facilitating decisionmaking and implementation of government policies. The "corporatist" alliance between labor and the state was formed during the period of radical populism that characterized politics for much of the two decades following the Mexican Revolution (1910–1917). During that time organized labor had substantial clout because of the government's difficulty in consolidating its power, its need, in turn, to establish a base of political support, and the unique political resources of an organized labor movement in a postrevolutionary context in which institutions were being created anew. In this context the governing political elites and organized labor formed a series of alliances during the 1920s and 1930s: a brittle one under President Alvaro Obregón (1920–1924), a more solid one under Plutarco Elías Calles (1924–1928), and an even stronger one under Lázaro Cárdenas (1934–1940). Under Cárdenas the alliance became institutionalized in the restructured governing party, the Party of the Mexican Revolution (PRM), with the major labor confederations serving as collective members of the party's labor or popular sector.[1] In the forties the alliance was solidified, surviving even a major reordering of power relations that substantially subordinated the labor movement to a now much more conservative state. This reordered alliance found its institutional expression in a second restructuring of the governing party in 1946, when the PRM became the PRI. The party, with its union membership and related structures, provided the government with considerable political resources to control labor, moderate its demands, and avoid class conflict and polarization.

The terms of the reordered alliance, substantially less favorable to labor than the original ones of the 1920s and 1930s, provoked continual attempts by the stronger and the more progressive unions and labor factions to establish a dissident labor movement, more autonomous from the state than what became known as the "official" labor movement. The best known of these attempts took place in the late 1940s, the late 1950s, and the 1970s. In each case, however, the state, using the political resources stemming from its alliance with the official labor movement, as well as strong-arm measures when necessary, was successful in marginalizing, containing, and essentially defeating the dissident movements and hence in reproducing the alliance on an ongoing basis.[2]

In fact, the government had various mechanisms to ensure support from the Confederation of Mexican Workers (CTM), the Revolutionary Confederation of Workers and Peasants (CROC), the Regional Confederation of Mexican Workers (CROM), and the other labor organizations that were incorporated into the governing alliance. Many of the resources at its command derived from formal party-union linkages, which channeled the electoral and political activities of the unions within the party and provided the state with a vehicle to dispense favors and benefits to union officials and members. More specifically, over the years the government was able to exercise a high degree of influence over leadership positions in the unions and coopt union leaders through the extensive material and political rewards commonly associated with machine politics.[3] Second, the government had the capacity to channel benefits with discretion, thereby benefiting cooperating unions and punishing those it saw as acting too militantly or too independently of the state's goals.[4] Third, the government and the PRI often financed labor organizations, creating a degree of economic dependency on the state. Fourth, the government had the power to declare strikes illegal, or, more commonly, "nonexistent." Finally, corrupt leaders (*charros*) of national labor federations often acted to control dissidence among the rank and file.[5]

In addition to the political resources enjoyed by the state, the state-labor alliance was underwritten by the import substitution industrialization model of economic growth. ISI relied on the domestic market as the outlet for nationally produced industrial goods. As the wage level is a central factor in determining the size of a domestic market, this model provided the conditions for a class compromise between labor and management: rising real wages, which expanded the market, and protectionist measures, which insulated domestic producers from stringent cost and efficiency considerations. Economic indicators illustrate this class compromise and the participation of the working class in the benefits of economic growth. After a deep plunge in real wages that occurred with the new conservative direction of President Manuel Avila Camacho (1940–1946), real wages rose, with few exceptions, every year from the late forties to the mid-seventies.[6] Moreover, with the Constitution of 1917, the Federal Labor Law of 1931, and other legislation, workers in Mexico had, on paper if not in fact, some of the strongest statutory protections in the developing world, including mandatory Christmas bonuses of fifteen days' wages, vacation and maternity leaves, seniority rights, and protections against arbitrary or discriminatory dismissals.[7]

Postrevolutionary state-labor relations, then, are best seen as a "pact" (albeit one on unequal terms) in which labor leaders delivered both electoral and organizational support to the government in exchange for material gains, not only for the leaders, but to some extent for the rank and file as well. Although the traditional alliance afforded the state substantive control over labor, that control was maintained through an ongoing process of negotiation and conciliation in which the state was obliged to engage in extensive cooptive activities and give at least some minimal level of protection to labor.

## Tensions Under De la Madrid

The economic crises of 1976 and, most important, 1982 put severe strains on the corporatist state-labor relationship.[8] Accelerating inflation in the early 1970s culminated in a dramatic currency devaluation in 1976, the first in twenty-two years, marking the start of a breakdown of the old economic model. Only temporarily revived with the vast expansion of oil exports during the *sexenio* of José López Portillo (1976–1982), the populist policies and the ISI model on which they depended were delivered a coup de grace by the onset of the debt crisis in August 1982. Initially, however, President De la Madrid did not definitively break with the old model, conceiving his orthodox economic stabilization program as merely a short-term corrective. By 1985 his policies were converted into a long-term strategy of economic restructuring and the adoption of a new economic model of export-oriented industrialization, with an emphasis on efficiency, competitiveness, and economic liberalization. Tensions between the new economic direction and the old political structures soon became evident. In the next couple of years rising inflation and the emergence of a credible electoral opposition on the left increased the perceived need to maintain at least some type of alliance or social pact with labor. Thus cross-pressured, the president articulated no clear alternative political project; at the same time, the strategy of most union leaders was to retain labor's position in the governing alliance, even as the rank and file showed signs of restlessness.

A striking feature of the Mexican regime in the years following the 1982 debt crisis was its capacity, made possible by the state-labor alliance, to achieve some understanding with labor on macroeconomic policy and thereby to implement an orthodox stabilization policy and impose economic hardship in the short run. The purchasing power of wages plummeted, the share of wages in national income dropped dramatically, from 42.6 percent in 1981 to 32.5 percent in 1984, and contractionary policies threw many workers out of their jobs.[9] Yet the traditional understanding with labor was again worked out, as it had been in earlier crises. Government policymakers initially projected a difficult two-year period during which inflation and the debt-servicing burden would be brought under control and after which a recovery would begin. On that basis, an understanding was reached that gave the state a somewhat longer time horizon than in many other debtor countries—an understanding in which labor would acquiesce to temporary belt-tightening in exchange for anticipated future gains and continued inclusion in the governing alliance.

After 1985 the strains in state-labor relations intensified as the government moved more decisively toward long-term economic liberalization and restructuring. The new policies clashed with the long-standing tradition of labor protection (however limited it may have been in practice). Specifically, policies that promoted competitiveness, efficiency, privatization, and market mechanisms were at odds with the artificial maintenance of real wage, employment, and unionization levels as well as social welfare policies. At the same time, the new export orientation meant that unless Mexican firms were reorganized to become more efficient, they would be destroyed by international competition when trade and foreign investment restrictions were phased out; but such a reorganization would still require renegotiating collective bargaining agreements, which in turn would heighten opposition from labor leaders anxious to preserve hard-won contractual benefits and protections. Ultimately, both a new technocratic policymaking style and the new policies themselves were undermining the social pact with organized labor.

With its new economic orientation the government came to view labor less as a political ally and more as an obstruction to the goal of structural economic reform. The incompatibility of the new economics and the old politics could be observed on a number of fronts. Labor demands ran counter to the government's attempt to fight inflation (which in 1986 and 1987 reached new and alarming heights), counter to its attempt to reduce spending (which, after 1985, included a new willingness to trim social programs), and counter to its efforts to reduce subsidies on basic consumption goods (stimulated not only by deficit reduction, but also by the state's commitment to a free market).[10]

Wage policy also changed. Labor increasingly came to be seen not as a source of demand for domestic industry but as a cost in a highly competitive global economy. Accordingly, after the 1982–1985 squeeze real wages did not experience their customary recovery. As shown in Table 2.1, both the official minimum wage and the average manufacturing wage plunged in real terms during De la Madrid's first year in office, falling 16.8 percent and 26.6 percent, respectively. Those declines were significantly greater than the decline of 6.5 percent in real per capita gross domestic product the same year, indicating that wage earners in the formal economy were disproportionately suffering the cost of the initial adjustment to the debt crisis. Wage decline was not merely the result of a short-term adjustment to the initial crisis but would be the rule throughout the De la Madrid period. Real minimum and average manufacturing wages fell every year during the sexenio except 1985 and (in the case of average manufacturing wages only) 1987. In contrast with an average annual decline in real per capita GDP of 2.1 percent during the sexenio, manufacturing wages fell an average of 7.0 percent annually, for a total six-year decline of 37.8 percent, while the minimum wage fell 8.5 percent, for a total decline of 42.4 percent.

The government also found its policy of privatization at odds with labor interests. On the one hand, it saw privatization impeded by the terms of labor contracts that resulted from the "special relationships" most state enterprises had developed with their workers. On the other hand, privatization policy also represented a retreat from the government's former employment policies: Whereas public sector employment had previously been used to curb joblessness, now the willingness to dismantle that sector marked quite a different set of priorities.[11]

Indicative of the new attitude was the way the government handled some of the important strikes of the period. In February 1986, in apparent violation of Article 123 of the Constitution, the government declared illegal a strike for higher wages by autoworkers at the Dina and Renault plants and sent the strike leaders to jail for seven days.[12] A year later the

Table 2.1    Trends in the Real Minimum Wage, Manufacturing Wage, and Per Capita Gross Domestic Product in Mexico, 1982–1992

| Year | Real Minimum Wage[a] Index (1982=100) | Annual Change | Real Manufacturing Wage[b] Index[c] (1982=100) | Annual Change | Real GDP Per Capita Index[d] (1982=100) | Annual Change[e] |
|------|------|------|------|------|------|------|
| 1982 | 100.0 |        | 100.0 |        | 100.0 |        |
| 1983 | 83.2  | –16.8% | 73.4  | –26.6% | 93.5  | –6.5   |
| 1984 | 77.5  | –6.8   | 70.5  | –3.9   | 94.6  | 1.2    |
| 1985 | 81.8  | 5.5    | 71.0  | 0.6    | 94.8  | 0.2    |
| 1986 | 70.1  | –14.3  | 63.8  | –10.1  | 89.2  | –5.9   |
| 1987 | 65.9  | –6.0   | 65.9  | 3.3    | 88.8  | –0.5   |
| 1988 | 57.6  | –12.6  | 62.2  | –5.6   | 87.9  | –1.0   |
| 1989 | 54.1  | –6.1   | 63.7  | 2.4    | 88.8  | 1.0    |
| 1990 | 49.1  | –9.3   | 64.6  | 1.3    | 90.7  | 2.2    |
| 1991 | 47.0  | –4.3   | 66.4  | 2.9    | 92.0  | 1.4    |
| 1992 | 44.8  | –4.6   | 67.2  | 1.1    | 92.5  | 0.6[f] |

| Sexenio | Cumulative Change | Average Annual Change | Cumulative Change | Average Annual Change | Cumulative Change | Average Annual Change |
|------|------|------|------|------|------|------|
| De la Madrid (1982–88) | –42.4% | –8.5% | –37.8% | –7.0% | –12.1% | –2.1% |
| Salinas[g] (1988–92) | –22.3 | –6.1 | 7.9 | 1.9 | 5.3 | 1.3 |
| Total (1982–92) | –55.2 | –7.5 | –32.8 | –3.5 | –7.5 | –0.7 |

*Sources:* Indices calculated from nominal minimum wage data obtained from National Development Bank (Nafinsa), *La economía mexicana en cifras, 1992,* 13th ed. (Mexico City: Nafinsa, 1992), p. 23; and National Institute of Statistics, Geography, and Information (INEGI), *Estadísticas históricas de México,* vol. 1 (Mexico City: INEGI, 1985), pp. 167–168. Nominal manufacturing wage data from International Labour Office (ILO), *Year Book of Labour Statistics* (Geneva: ILO, various years). All real wages calculated based on national average annual consumer price index data from Hugo Ortiz Dietz, *México: Banco de datos, Año VIII* (Mexico City: El Inversionista Mexicano, 1990), p. L-3; and Nafinsa, *La economía mexicana,* p. 149. Per capita GDP data from United Nations, Economic Commission for Latin America and the Caribbean (ECLAC), *Statistical Yearbook for Latin America and the Caribbean* (Santiago de Chile: United Nations, various years).

a. Based on a yearly average of the legal minimum wage of each official geographic region. For those years in which the minimum wage changed, the data represent a weighted average based on the number of days each wage level was in effect.

b. Based on a yearly average.

c. In 1985 the International Labour Office changed the methodology for calculating nominal wages. Since both figures were available for 1985, this index has been constructed by joining the two series.

d. Index calculated from the annual percentage-change data presented in the next column.

e. Based on average annual rates and constant market prices.

f. Preliminary estimate.

g. Data for the Salinas period are based on the first four years only; hence, cumulative change data for the De la Madrid and Salinas periods are not directly comparable.

government broke a strike among electrical workers by declaring it "nonexistent." While it had become nearly routine for the government to move against industrial action by workers in dissident unions, this episode represented a move against an important member of the national Labor Congress (an umbrella organization largely dominated by pro-government leadership) in a strike that had very wide support and that had as its aim an increase in wages comparable to that already granted for the minimum wage.[13] In July 1987 a strike at Ford ended with the dismissal of 3,200 workers, as the company developed plans to automate.[14] In 1986–1987, then, relations between the government and labor deteriorated, as the government committed itself to a project of economic restructuring that emphasized low wages, efficiency, firm flexibility, market discipline of the labor force, nonunion labor in the booming *maquiladora* sector, and a streamlining of employment in traditional sectors.[15]

As the tensions between the state and organized labor intensified, one could discern the outlines of an attempt by the government to adopt a new political project to dislodge labor from its central political position.[16] The state's alliance with the lower classes—workers and peasants—had become too costly in the context of its commitment to economic restructuring. The more technocratic government leaders were no longer as willing to protect groups from the market and were starting to recognize the demographic changes making Mexico a more urban and middle-class society as rendering obsolete the PRI's traditional constituency and its "overreliance" on labor and peasant support. At the very least the project of the "modernizers" or "reformers" in the federal government envisioned an alliance that would be substantially altered and a party that would be more centrally based in the growing urban middle classes.

How did labor respond? Its reaction generally followed the lead of Fidel Velázquez, head of the CTM since the 1940s. In 1983 Velázquez had been an outspoken critic of government policy, denouncing it as favoring industry at the expense of the working class. As the 1985 interim elections neared, however, the veteran labor leader turned his attention to what he perceived as the greater threat posed by the rightist opposition party, the National Action Party (PAN), and the "electoral advances of the reaction."[17] After those elections and with the new government commitment to economic restructuring, Velázquez became increasingly harsh in his criticism. In early 1986 he became persistent in calling for an emergency wage increase, and a rift with the government again opened. In the words of the newsweekly *Proceso,* Velázquez became "radicalized" in his pronouncements, and in November 1986 he declared the government's program "unacceptable" as it "puts into danger the viability of our national project."[18]

Those last words hold the key to an interpretation of Velázquez's position during the De la Madrid period: opposition to the new economic orientation and a defense of the status quo ante, in both its political and its economic aspects. Most labor leaders seemed intent on fighting a rear-guard action to preserve the old alliance in the face of an assault from the right—not only from the PAN, which in 1986–1987 still appeared to be the major opposition to the PRI, but also from within the PRI and the government. In other words they were presented not only with an unfavorable economic policy but also with the possibility of a new political project, one that would exclude labor from the governing coalition and would abandon labor to the discipline of market forces. In this situation the move to open confrontation over economic policy was particularly tricky for these labor leaders, who wanted to preserve their privileged position and advantages derived from the historic pattern of bargaining within an inclusionary coalition. While CTM and other powerful labor leaders could tactically threaten a rupture, in the end they could not really risk one.

Thus, despite occasional strikes and heated rhetoric as the 1988 presidential election approached, most of the Mexican labor leaders chose to work within the existing political structures, trying to influence the choice of the party's presidential candidate for the 1988 elections and particularly to prevent the naming of Carlos Salinas de Gortari, secretary of budget and planning and a key author of much of the government's restructuring program. He was vigorously opposed by both Velázquez and Joaquín Hernández Galicia (popularly known as "La Quina"), head of the powerful oil workers' union, who associated Salinas with the (then largely unsuccessful) attempts to restructure the petroleum sector and weaken the union.[19] Their opposition strategy failed. In October Salinas received the PRI nomination.

Despite all these strains the state-labor alliance was not abandoned. Quite the contrary, many labor leaders remained reluctant to break with the government, and it became apparent that the government would have a difficult time dispensing with the support and cooperation of labor. In November and December 1987 the Mexican economy took a sharp turn for the worse, with a stock exchange crash following that of the world's major markets, a halting of the debt-equity swap program, a disappointing outcome of negotiations with the United States over trade and investment, renewed capital flight, a devaluation of the peso, and a resurgence of inflation.[20] With the election about to take place and the PRI's presidential candidate the author of an economic program that in many ways seemed to be coming apart, the government entered into negotiations with labor and business representatives and engineered an agreement on an anti-inflationary package with wage and price guidelines.

This Economic Solidarity Pact illustrated the main contradictions the PRI faced in marginalizing labor economically and politically as the government continued to rely on labor to control inflation, particularly at election time. The pact also illustrated the way key labor leaders tenaciously clung to the old strategy, rejecting an oppositionist role and instead continuing to bargain and negotiate from within the governing coalition to the point of signing a pact that furthered the slide in real wages.

Labor leaders' consent to De la Madrid's economic policy did not, however, ensure consent by their rank and file, let alone by the Mexican populace as a whole. The left-of-center presidential candidacy of Cuauhté-moc Cárdenas, his criticism of the economic program, and the unprece-dented support he garnered in the 1988 election produced one of the most serious challenges to the political dominance of the PRI. Indeed, his can-didacy raised the ante in the state's efforts to redefine its alliance with labor. The unions continued to be among the largest organized groups in civil society, and PRI leaders clearly feared the consequences should labor defect to Cárdenas, especially since the ruling party was having trouble re-constructing its coalition to include new constituencies that might be more supportive of conservative economic policies.

With the highly contested, and suspect, election of Salinas, the De la Madrid presidency ended on an ambivalent note. Economically, Salinas's succession represented the ongoing commitment of the government to eco-nomic policies that seemed to imply the exclusion of labor; yet with the wage-price pact the government had again found it necessary to rely on labor cooperation to control inflation. Politically, labor support seemed more important than ever, given the hair's breadth by which Salinas man-aged a majority vote even in the official returns, not to mention the wide-spread electoral fraud that delegitimated those returns and potentially even his presidency. Yet the Mexican government continued to be committed to changing the social base of the state and to disarticulating, though not completely severing, the state-labor alliance.

## Salinas and the Project of "New Unionism"

The fraud-ridden election of Salinas seemed to bring to center stage the question of the contradictory nature of the state-labor alliance—the politi-cal advantages it afforded both state and labor, combined with its incom-patibility with the new economic direction, which was favored by the gov-ernment and opposed by labor. To resolve the contradiction, Salinas might have backed off from the new economic policies. Far from retreating, however, he pushed them further, as seen most dramatically in the 1990 decision to begin negotiations over a North American Free Trade Agree-ment (NAFTA). Since NAFTA would intensify the need to make Mexican industries more competitive by global standards, it became all the more critical for Salinas to promote a model of labor relations that would miti-gate labor's power to oppose and obstruct firms' ability to reorganize pro-duction. Accordingly, the president moved very early in his term to artic-ulate a new formula for state-labor relations along the lines he dubbed "new unionism."

At a May Day rally in 1990, Salinas outlined, before some 200,000 workers in attendance, eight points that would characterize new unionism:

1. Strong and representative unionism with an interlocutory capacity
2. The necessity to abandon the confrontational strategy of the beginning of this century
3. Establishment of formulas for cooperation between labor and management
4. Preservation of the historic alliance between the labor movement and the state
5. Respect for union autonomy as a matter of governmental policy
6. Improvement of labor relations with obligations for both management and unions
7. The urgency of workers' understanding and implementing efforts to increase productivity, lower costs, and cooperate to conquer markets both in and outside the country
8. Management commitment to establishing a culture of motivation and communication that gives incentives, encouragements, and rewards to the work force[21]

This project can be summarized as focusing on three areas of change: the internal workings of unions, state-labor relations, and union-management relations. Internally unions were to become more representative, but not more militant (points 1 and 2). With regard to state-labor relations, labor's historic alliance with the state would be continued, although with increased autonomy for unions (points 4 and 5). Finally, labor-management relations would be based on greater cooperation and communication, with workers recognizing the primacy of increasing productivity and with the company providing an indeterminate set of obligations and incentives to workers to increase productivity (points 3, 6, 7, and 8).

The first set of goals—for more representative unions—was designed to meet Salinas's political needs as well as his economic program. It was hoped that those unions able to garner greater rank and file support internally could also secure greater political support for the ruling party than had the traditional, oligarchic unions. A few days after Salinas's speech Luis Donaldo Colosio, the president of the PRI, suggested that union democratization and greater worker participation in the internal life of unions was "essential" for reorganizing and revitalizing the PRI itself.[22] In fact, the party's candidates from the labor sector had fared poorly in the 1988 election, leading to the widespread perception that the main labor centrals could no longer deliver the votes they once had.[23] Better labor mobilization obviously had a new urgency for Mexico's political leaders.

Much of the focus of new unionism, however, was concerned not with political goals but with securing greater flexibility for enterprises in restructuring their operations, raising their productivity, and generally improving their international competitiveness without meeting resistance from powerful labor interests. The core concept here was the notion that workers identify with what was traditionally viewed as the realm of management: the planning and implementing of efforts to increase productivity. Elsewhere in his May Day address Salinas underlined the importance of worker participation, calling the "participatory firm" the model of companies in the 1990s and emphasizing that more cooperative labor relations should extend "not only within the firm, but also within the departments and work areas of each firm."[24] This goal borrowed from worker participation schemes being implemented elsewhere in the industrialized world to improve productivity. In addition greater union representativeness and "interlocutory capacity" might also boost productivity if they meant that union leaders could more effectively identify production problems on the shopfloor and perhaps be more responsive to management's desire to reorganize and raise production. The participatory union, then, was conceived as one that was reoriented toward firm-level issues of production and away from national-level negotiations that involved the extraction of state concessions and protection, the pattern in which the traditional labor bureaucracy was vested.

The project was fraught with contradictions. Left unclear was how the goal of greater representativeness was to be made consistent with the other goals of political support and firm restructuring. Salinas's own recognition of this problem seems to have been reflected by his use of the term "representative" rather than "democratic" unionism, even though at the time Colosio explicitly emphasized that union democracy was implied by the new unionism project.[25] Yet union democracy, or even representativeness, had the undesirable potential to produce a more militant leadership that might in turn challenge firm restructuring, seek greater independence from the PRI, or confront the state's neoliberal policies. Nor was it clear what motivation there would be for undemocratic or unrepresentative labor leaders to risk losing their power by allowing greater rank and file participation or to shift their sphere of influence from the national to the firm level.

For all its many contradictions, Salinas's program of new unionism demonstrated the degree to which he, unlike his predecessor, explicitly tried to transform the pattern of state-labor relations in a direction more consistent with neoliberalism. New unionism was an attempt to reduce the influence of organized labor in national politics, ensure effective labor mobilization for the PRI without as much reliance on traditional corporatist structures, and allow the implementation of more flexible production methods without running into opposition from organized labor. Not all union leaders would concur with his project, however. While a few did, others chose a strategy of direct confrontation with the government, and most fell in line behind a policy of retrenchment adopted by their centrals that made broad concessions to the president's economic policies while vigorously defending the primary structural sources of their power and attempting to hold fast to the traditional alliance.

## Pockets of Union Concurrence

The few unions that concurred with the new unionism project were marked by an unusual set of circumstances: they were relatively democratic unions that lacked militant internal opposition, had earlier established a degree of autonomy from the government, and faced economic conditions that made their firms more open to negotiating concessions regarding worker dislocations due to firm restructuring. The most prominent union leader in this group was Francisco Hernández Juárez, head of the Union of Telephone Workers of the Mexican Republic (STRM), who in large measure had anticipated the model that Salinas would subsequently adopt as the new unionism. The congruence of the paths and interests of Salinas and Hernández Juárez meant that the latter would become one of the most visible and influential labor leaders in Mexico.

The particular features of Hernández Juárez and the STRM were fortuitous indeed for Salinas, who had promised during his presidential campaign that "telecommunications will become the cornerstone of the program to modernize Mexico's economy."[26] The indebted Mexican state had few resources to invest in the expansion and technological improvement of its antiquated telecommunication services, and Salinas sought to gain the necessary capital by privatizing the state-owned telephone monopoly, Teléfonos de México (TELMEX). Hernández Juárez's willingness and ability to negotiate change with the support of the rank and file smoothed the way for privatization and productive restructuring at a time when such changes were a high priority of the government.

A special condition of the STRM was that it early came to be characterized by democratic procedures combined with a lack of serious internal opposition. With a 1976 rank-and-file revolt that replaced the union's old leadership and elected Hernández Juárez, the telefonistas established internal representativeness early on, but questions of the union's relationship with the government and TELMEX would remain uncertain for years to come. Initially Hernández Juárez sought to increase the union's political autonomy but without completely severing ties with the government or the official labor movement. One of his first acts was to change the union's statutes and disaffiliate from the PRI, at the same time that he also chose to work with other, more traditional labor leaders by remaining in the Labor Congress, arguing that proposals to leave it were "irrational leftism."[27] Initially, the presence of a strong, militant opposition faction made a cooperative relationship with the government and TELMEX difficult.

Under pressure from that faction, Hernández Juárez at first adopted a highly confrontational labor strategy, with the union striking four times in the two years between April 1978 and April 1980.[28] Yet the power balance within the union soon changed. A 1982 attempt to modify the collective bargaining agreement in a limited manner to permit digitalization provoked an illegal strike by union dissidents. With the support of the Labor Congress, the CTM, and the government, Hernández Juárez crushed the strike, in the process discrediting his internal opposition.[29] Henceforth, in spite of secret ballot voting and other democratic procedures, the union became marked by a complete lack of serious internal opposition.

With the rout of the militant faction, Hernández Juárez was in a position to maintain internal democratic procedures and at the same time acquiesce in firm restructuring and proceed with developing cooperative relations with the government. He proceeded to negotiate the introduction of digital technology, a process begun in 1983 that by 1986 led to limited contract revisions and a more expansive 1987 accord that permitted modernization.[30] With ambitions to play a leadership role in the national labor movement, Hernández Juárez sought the presidency of the Labor Congress in February 1986, only to have his election blocked by labor leaders concerned about his and his union's lack of membership in the PRI. Throughout 1986 he worked to strengthen his relationship with the government and the CTM, and in January 1987 he succeeded in winning the Labor Congress presidency. A month later, taking advantage of his new political power, Hernández Juárez led the telephone workers on their only strike since 1982, this time in protest against a government decree limiting salary increases in state industries to 20 percent. Rather than choose a more confrontational approach by pushing for salary increases for all state enterprise workers (as the electrical workers had unsuccessfully tried to do a short time earlier), Hernández Juárez used his strategic position as the head of the Labor Congress to negotiate with the government over a salary increase for his workers only. After just eight days he successfully won the telefonistas a salary increase totaling between 83 percent and 95 percent.[31] By this point Hernández Juárez clearly understood the advantages of having a strong political relationship with the government. Just two months after the strike he emphasized in a May Day speech the importance of an alliance with the state that still allowed for autonomous union decision-making. In August 1987 he publicly announced his personal membership in the PRI and in the following year became one of Salinas's strongest backers in his campaign for president.

By the opening days of the Salinas administration, then, the telefonistas had already met the conditions of new unionism, with democratic internal procedures, semiautonomous cooperation with the government, and successful negotiation with management over firm restructuring. During the Salinas years Hernández Juárez became a model of the new union leader: At the firm level he negotiated even more profound productivity and organizational changes at TELMEX, and, as noted below, at the national level he became a leader of a new organization that held the promise of forming the organizational nucleus of the new unionism.

In 1989 the union and TELMEX signed an agreement expanding the 1987 accord to modernize the company technologically and organizationally. Even more dramatically, that same year the STRM consented to privatization of the company, a process completed in 1991. During this reorganization and privatization the union preserved many of its contractually granted benefits, at a time when many other unions were losing theirs. Most importantly, the STRM negotiated a guarantee of employment security during the modernization process.[32] The privatization agreement also allowed the union (with government financial aid) to acquire 4.4 percent of TELMEX stock, worth, by 1992, in excess of $700 million.[33] Both the productivity agreements and the privatization were implemented smoothly, with the representative union leadership able to negotiate accords with the state and management that met with rank-and-file approval.

With this cooperative stance with management and the government, Hernández Juárez took on an increasingly influential role on the national stage, becoming the head of the new Federation of Unions of Goods and Services Companies (FESEBS).[34] Founded in 1990, FESEBS served as a power base for several self-styled "new unions" to rival the influence of the CTM and the other established labor confederations. Fidel Velázquez personally attacked the nascent organization as having no right to exist and accused Hernández Juárez of trying to divide the Labor Congress.[35] This opposition delayed government recognition for a while, but FESEBS gained official status in 1992.

Notwithstanding Hernández Juárez's success as the prototypical "new union leader," the overall impact of new unionism was limited. The STRM model must be seen as an unusual confluence of several factors: not only the unique mix of internal democracy and nonmilitance, but also the unusual market condition of a critical national utility (the telecommunications industry) facing an expanding market that allowed the company greater leeway to make concessions to labor.[36] Other unions that did try to adopt the model tended to share many of the STRM's traits: they were concentrated in government-connected industries, suggesting that the private sector was more reluctant than the state to cooperate with the new unionism project; and they were unions that had representative but moderate leadership. Yet even the other unions that formed the FESEBS (electrical workers, airline pilots and flight attendants, film production workers, and streetcar workers),[37] which other than the telefonistas had some of the best claims to new union status, had a much more difficult time negotiating successful terms for increases in productivity and achieving the same political position of an alliance with the state based on greater union autonomy. As a result most Mexican unions chose to oppose Salinas's new unionism project. For some this was an all-out confrontation with the president; for others it was a more strategic and measured opposition.

## Union Confrontation and Government Reprisals

Those unions that pursued a strategy of confrontation, rejecting new unionism and the neoliberal economic model that underlay it, were the clearest losers. A diverse group, these unions generally fell into two broad subcategories. First were democratic unions, or democratic movements within unions, that were small and politically weak. These unions confronted their firms and the government over a restructuring that the rank and file feared would lead to layoffs, lower wages, and reduced benefits. The second subgroup consisted of very powerful and decidedly undemocratic unions whose leaders saw Salinas and his plans to reorganize their respective industries not only as harmful to workers but also as a direct threat to their own power. What the two subgroups had in common was their effort to impede the restructuring of important sectors, a move that the government saw as "obstructionist" at the firm level and that often came to include political opposition to Salinas and his economic project at the national level.

The response of the smaller and more democratic group underlined a key contradiction of Salinas's stated labor project. While the official model of new unionism promoted the ideas of union representativeness, autonomy, and worker participation, strict limits were placed on what the government would tolerate in terms of militancy or political opposition. This underlying tension most often flared into open conflict when firms with democratic unions (or internal democratic movements) attempted to reorganize. Responding more directly to rank and file demands than their less democratic counterparts, these unions were necessarily concerned not only with the prospects of speed-ups and weaker contractual protections, but, most important, with possible layoffs if higher productivity were achieved. The resulting conflicts often had a political as well as an economic dimension. These unions tended to oppose the government's economic policy and challenged PRI dominance of the labor movement. Furthermore, they resisted the undemocratic control exercised by the CTM and other federations over the majority of organized labor, particularly since those labor centrals willingly allied with the government against these unions and served as key agents in breaking more democratic and confrontational movements among their own affiliates.

In 1990, the year of Salinas's new unionism speech, major labor conflicts at Modelo, Ford, and Tornel demonstrated the limits of the political system's tolerance of union militance and democracy. In February a strike at the Modelo brewery by a CTM affiliate demanding greater benefits led to accusations by Fidel Velázquez that the workers were being manipulated by Cuauhtémoc Cárdenas's political party, a reference to some of the union's outside legal advisors.[38] A short time later the federal arbitration council declared the strike to be politically motivated and therefore "nonexistent." Another CTM affiliate, at the Ford automobile plant in Cuautitlán, also collided with government policies by trying to block the reelection of the Velázquez-backed general secretary in retaliation for his failure to protect workers' rights during a modernization process. On January 8, 1990, one worker was killed and many others were injured when a strike planned by plant workers to force a democratic union election was violently broken up by armed thugs who appear to have been hired by the CTM and Ford and for whom the CTM actually paid bail.[39] An attempted vote in August of that year by Tornel tire factory workers in Tultitlán seeking to switch from the CTM to the CROC was also broken up violently by a group linked to the CTM.[40] In the aftermath the company fired some six hundred workers. In a second vote three months later the government declared the CTM the winner, in spite of voting irregularities.

Perhaps the most telling example of the limits placed on union democracy and militance was a conflict with Volkswagen in Puebla. Ironically, the VW union earlier seemed to meet many of the criteria of new unionism by being a representative, autonomous union that had been participating in an ongoing process of firm restructuring.[41] What proved troublesome was its lack of political ties to the government (the union had left the CTM in 1972) and worker militance that had emerged from its highly democratic internal procedures. The union came onto a collision course with the firm and the government in July 1992 when the union's leader, Gaspar Bueno, signed a productivity accord that increased wages overall but greatly changed the structure of wage scales and job classifications.[42] An opposition movement within the union struck, demanding that a vote be held both to rescind the agreement and to remove Bueno. Management, in turn, responded by declaring bankruptcy, closing the firm, and reopening it immediately afterward as technically a new company that did not recognize the previous union contract. The Federal Arbitration Council sided with the VW management, declaring in August that the company's actions were legal and subsequently permitting the firing of six hundred union activists.[43] Immediately after that decision, and presumably at Salinas's behest, Hernández Juárez intervened personally and helped negotiate a new, weaker contract for the union that included clauses allowing for modernization—an action that to many discredited the telefonista leader.[44] Shortly after his intervention the VW union officially joined Hernández Juárez's FESEBS federation.[45]

The second category of unions that resisted firm restructuring and in the process ran afoul of the government was the group of more traditional

charro unions in key state sectors. The most prominent examples concerned the government's attempt to restructure the oil industry and education. In one of his first acts in office Salinas arrested much of the leadership of the oil workers' union, including its most important leader, La
Quina. The arrest of La Quina, long thought to be politically untouchable,
was a signal that blocking industrial reorganization or displaying disloy-
alty and opposition would not be tolerated even among the most powerful
union leaders. La Quina had ruled his union, and to some extent PEMEX
(Petróleos Mexicanos) itself, for twenty-seven years in a corrupt and authoritarian manner.[46] Officially he was charged with the illegal importa-
tion of arms and later murder, but it was obvious there were economic and
political reasons why, of all the corrupt union leaders in Mexico, La Quina
was singled out. As noted earlier, he had had serious conflicts previously
with then-Budget Secretary Salinas over the issue of PEMEX restructuring. While prior to the 1988 election La Quina had closely aligned himself
with the PRI, he surreptitiously opposed Salinas's presidential candidacy
and lent support to Cárdenas, who went on to win in virtually every significant petroleum region. With La Quina's subsequent arrest, the union's
new leader, Sebastián Guzmán Cabrera, quietly consented to a major restructuring of PEMEX that resulted in the firing of more than thirty thousand oil workers by 1991.[47]

On the heels of La Quina's arrest, Salinas's ouster of Carlos Jonguitud
Barrios as head of the powerful National Union of Education Workers
(SNTE) further demonstrated the limits of allowable opposition to the
state's goals of restructuring. Ruling the teachers' union in an authoritarian manner since 1972, Jonguitud and his Revolutionary Vanguard movement[48] within SNTE emphasized a traditional nationalist ideology which
by the mid-1980s was increasingly at odds with Mexico's new neoliberal
political leadership.[49] In particular, although Mexican officials clearly
viewed educational reform as critical to upgrading the labor force, Jonguitud was able to veto significant change.[50] When a well-organized dissident
movement mobilized in 1989 calling for internal democracy in SNTE,
Salinas pressured Jonguitud to resign, breaking the power of the Vanguard. As explained in Chapter 7, less than three years later the new SNTE
leader, Elba Ester Gordillo, agreed to sign with then-Secretary of Education Ernesto Zedillo Ponce de León a National Agreement for the Modernization of Basic Education that restructured and decentralized the Mexican educational system in a manner that threatened to reduce the SNTE's
power at the national level.[51]

If the Modelo, Ford, Tornel, and Volkswagen conflicts were initiated
by dissidents in relatively small unions with little political clout, La
Quina's capture and the removal of Jonguitud were instead the silencing of
extremely powerful, long-time political insiders. Together the actions of
private firms, the Salinas government, and even traditional labor leaders

severely limited the space available for confrontation by both types of more independent union movements. That employers resisted such labor action is not surprising, while the resistance of the Salinas government points to the inconsistencies within the model of new unionism. We turn next to the role of traditional labor leaders.

## The Strategy of Retrenchment

Many of the most important labor leaders had benefited from the traditional pattern of Mexican unionism and thus rejected any fundamental change in the corporatist structures. These were primarily the leaders of national federations and confederations, who had been most directly involved in the old pattern of national bargaining and had much to lose if the arena of labor struggle were shifted from the national policy level to the firm level. In addition, new unionism and its emphasis on union representativeness, perhaps even democracy, directly threatened the charros and their undemocratic privileges and patron-client pattern of controlling the disbursement of workers' promotions and benefits.[52]

These leaders were caught in a difficult situation. Since the main thrust of their strategy was to preserve the state-labor alliance, they were limited in the degree to which they could overtly confront government economic policy they opposed. Furthermore, their attempt to maintain the alliance was particularly difficult to achieve because virtually all the major labor organizations had opposed Salinas's nomination for the PRI candidacy and had later apparently failed to deliver labor's vote in the election. Thus, in contrast to the more heated rhetorical conflicts of the De la Madrid period, labor leaders during the Salinas sexenio acquiesced in economic policy to a greater degree and concentrated instead on blocking any measure that would challenge the structural power of labor, particularly any moves to change existing federal labor law or to eliminate labor's privileged position as a sector within the ruling party. This strategy drove a wedge between economic policy, to which Salinas was primarily committed and to which labor leaders could concede, and the political or structural aspects of the new unionism, which they opposed as a fundamental threat and which, even from the government's perspective, was fraught with its own contradictions.

One of the clearest examples of the strategic nature of labor's concessions to Salinas was its public stance with regard to NAFTA. In contrast to their counterparts in the United States and Canada, Mexican labor leaders early on decided not to oppose Salinas on what was undoubtedly his most important economic project. In sharp contrast to his opposition to De la Madrid's 1985 decision to join the General Agreement on Tariffs and Trade (GATT), as early as 1990 Velázquez endorsed the principle of a free-trade agreement in order "to make national companies more competitive."[53] Subsequently, the CTM and other labor organizations were notably silent with regard to the treaty in spite of its potentially great impact on jobs and working conditions in Mexico. "It does not fall to workers to speak about and debate NAFTA but only to make it a useful tool for Mexico," Velázquez commented shortly after the negotiated proposal was made public.[54] By not opposing the president on NAFTA, labor leaders avoided a showdown between labor and the government that might have led Salinas to seek formal, institutional changes to reduce the power of labor.

As in the De la Madrid sexenio, labor leaders also participated in a wage-price agreement, although a recovering Mexican economy allowed at least a partial recovery of manufacturing wages. As data on Salinas's first four years in office show (Table 2.1), manufacturing wages increased in real terms every year, averaging a 1.9 percent increase annually. Those increases were even slightly higher than the average annual increase in gross domestic product per capita of 1.3 percent during the same years. The advance in wages represented only a partial recovery of the previous sexenio's wage loss (by 1992 real manufacturing wages still were only 67.2 percent of what they had been in 1982); yet the Salinas period seemed at least to mark an end to the further deterioration of wages in manufacturing. At the same time, however, the wage squeeze continued for workers earning the lowest wages, as the minimum wage continued to decline, on average, 6.1 percent per year for a four-year total of 22.3 percent. Labor leaders continually protested the minimum wage losses but ultimately consented to them by continuing to sign the periodic wage-price pacts.

Along with their neutrality on NAFTA and their consent to wage controls, key union leaders also limited strike actions even in those cases in which their members faced layoffs due to restructuring or privatization. As discussed earlier, the CTM even went so far as to play an active role in crushing strikes and militant internal movements in the conflicts at Modelo, Ford, and Tornel. Similarly, during Salinas's first year in office, the head of the national mine workers' union, Napoleón Gómez Sada, repeatedly criticized strikes by locals in his own organization[55] and failed to support workers who struck when the government closed the state-owned Cananea copper mine in Sonora,[56] leaving thousands laid off and the remaining miners largely unable to achieve their demands.

In contrast to acquiescence in these areas, these labor leaders were ready to do battle against attempts to change the labor law and topple labor from its privileged position within the party. The labor law conflicted with the administration's growing emphasis on seeking foreign investors, who were wary of powerful unions and costly labor regulations. Although Mexico's labor laws were often violated, their mere existence acted as a constraint and thus came under attack. Key business associations pushed to overhaul the labor law, including the long sacrosanct Article 123 of the Constitution.[57] As private sector pressure grew, Hernández Juárez, in a move that would further alienate him from the rest of the labor movement, echoed the calls for labor law changes, arguing that they were required for successful competition under NAFTA and the real danger would be the formulation of new labor policy without the participation of workers.[58] Virtually every other major labor leader strongly opposed any modifications. The coordinator of the CTM's deputies declared that the labor central would defend existing labor law "to the death,"[59] and the Labor Congress made opposition to any change in labor law the theme of its 1992 May Day march, an event that was traditionally and unambiguously progovernment.[60] Although labor leaders would admit, sometimes publicly, that portions of the law could be brought up-to-date, from the labor movement's perspective a period of economic liberalization was clearly not the safest time for reforms to be written. When asked when would be a better time, Velázquez responded, "when the country's economic crisis has disappeared completely and the economy has normalized. Then they can reform the law."[61]

After an initial retreat on the issue and numerous official declarations to the contrary at various points,[62] the Salinas administration seemed to renew its intention to modify labor law in the early 1990s, but in the end failed to act.[63] The last attempt came just days before the November 28, 1993, *destape* (unveiling) of Luis Donaldo Colosio as the PRI's presidential candidate—the final opportunity to make changes before the start of the 1994 electoral campaign. The specific proposal was to eliminate the federal labor arbitration councils (constitutionally mandated bodies composed of a government official and equal numbers of business and labor representatives that resolve labor-management disputes), as well as the statutory system of "blind" promotions (mandating that promotions be determined by seniority, familial economic situation, and unionized status).[64] The same day the proposal was reported in the press, Velázquez privately met for more than two hours with CTM deputies and senators, later reiterating his strong rejection of any such changes and expressing his confidence that the president would "maintain his promise not to reform the labor law."[65] The next day the Secretary of Labor publicly announced that there would be no proposals to change labor law and that it would be "madness" to eliminate the arbitration councils.[66]

Labor leaders were equally adamant in their opposition to proposals to reorganize the internal structure of the PRI and eliminate the labor sector, although with more mixed results. Many within the government and the PRI had come to see the traditional organization of the official party, with its labor, peasant, and popular sectors, as inhibiting efforts to attract middle-class support.[67] Unsuccessful attempts to open up the party and make it more representative had become sexenial events since the 1960s. At the sixtieth anniversary of the PRI on March 4, 1989, both Salinas and party president Luis Donaldo Colosio again emphasized the importance of internal party reform.[68] Although an internal democratization of the party's Fourteenth National Assembly in September 1990 had been promised, little structural reform occurred, and party dissidents charged that the traditional PRI elites continued to exercise undemocratic control.[69] One of the only concrete changes to emerge from that assembly was a reorganization of the PRI's popular sector organization, the forty-seven-year-old National Confederation of Popular Organizations (CNOP), as Une ("Unite") in the hope of attracting greater middle-class participation.

In the months prior to the next national meeting of the PRI (the Fifteenth National Assembly, which was held in March 1992), observers expected Salinas to use the opportunity to reorganize the party radically, perhaps even eliminating the sectors altogether in favor of an organization of individual members.[70] In a thinly veiled threat to leave the PRI if the latter were the case, the CTM announced a week before the assembly that if the sectors' role in the party were constrained, the PRI could lose support to the opposition parties.[71] Although, to the surprise of many, the Fifteenth Assembly failed to result in any modification of the PRI's structure, the issue remained alive. Finally, in March 1993 a compromise was reached that the PRI would keep, but reorganize, its sectoral structure.[72] Adopted with the support of the leaders of each existing sector, the compromise resulted in three new sectors: a "Popular Urban Territorial Movement" of individual members who would join geographically defined local units of the PRI; a "National Front of Organizations and Citizens," essentially a re-reorganized CNOP/Une; and a "Worker-Peasant Alliance" that combined the old labor and peasant sectors.[73] The compromise, worked out through hard negotiations, made more room for middle-class and individual affiliates at the expense of labor and collective affiliates, which were nevertheless retained.

With the PRI nomination of Colosio, the CTM seemed to believe it had successfully weathered the storms of austerity and neoliberalism, while retaining much of labor's structural power. In stark contrast to the cold reception he had given Salinas six years earlier, the ninety-three-year-old Velázquez, described in the press as "a kid with a new toy," promised to campaign throughout the country for Colosio and pledged to contribute CTM funds to his campaign.[74] Colosio's assassination in March 1994 and the successor candidacy of Ernesto Zedillo did little to change labor's strategy. In spite of the fact that Zedillo was more consistently associated with Salinas's neoliberal technocratic elite than Colosio had been, Velázquez and other labor leaders were intent on proving their continued electoral value to the ruling party. The CTM leader campaigned hard to ensure that his organization's claimed membership of 5.5 million voted for the PRI, and he successfully secured the commitment of the Labor Congress as a whole to back Zedillo.[75] While it is impossible to gauge accurately the exact number of labor votes delivered to the PRI, the traditional centrals appeared to regain some of their electoral importance. While in 1988 the CTM candidates running on the PRI ticket for electoral office suffered unprecedented losses, in the 1994 election, fifty of the fifty-one CTM candidates were victorious.[76]

Whether these contributions to the PRI's victory will be enough to prevent the newly elected president from trying to restructure the old state-labor alliance, however, is difficult to predict. Only days after the election results were officially announced, Velázquez's own fear of possible moves by Zedillo to change the old corporatist system was underlined when the CTM leader met with the central's newly elected legislators to instruct them to block any labor law modifications.[77] The future position of labor in the Mexican political system remained unsettled.

## Conclusion

With his project of new unionism Salinas sought to refashion the state-labor alliance that had underlain the hegemony and stability of the postrevolutionary regime but that, after 1982, had become incompatible with the new economic policies. Salinas called for a labor movement that, at the macro level, would maintain its alliance with the government, refrain from militant action, and foster a more representative union leadership to facilitate mobilization of the rank and file in order to garner greater legitimacy for the ruling party. At the micro level unions were asked to participate in firm-level efforts to enhance productivity. Overall, union influence was to shift from macro- to micro-level participation, with greater cooperation to increase efficiency and with diminished union influence in setting the national economic program.

Economically, new unionism came down unambiguously in favor of restructuring both the national economy and the labor process within firms and industries. Indeed, this was the prime motivation behind the project. The political goals of the project were ambiguous, however, betraying an ultimate contradiction that was never worked out. With respect to internal union matters Salinas seemed to have been influenced by the model of flexible, team-oriented workers who participate in shopfloor organizational decisions to raise productivity, troubleshoot problems, and air grievances. With respect to state-labor relations, a more representative union was seen as a better interlocutor in terms of generating working-class support for the government. But the Salinas project was never able to square representative or participatory unionism with the possibility that a democratic union, responsive to rank-and-file demands, might threaten the restructuring process itself or support one of the opposition parties.

Labor leaders who concurred with the new unionism were those whose unions were not fundamentally threatened by firm or sectoral restructuring but instead were able to adapt to it and even benefit from any resulting strengthening or revitalization of the sector. Politically, those unions escaped the inherent contradiction in the project because they were already relatively democratic and did not face an internal, militant faction that opposed restructuring. Furthermore, those same unions had already established a semiautonomous position vis-à-vis the state: They had opted out of the corporatist ties to the party, but their leaders supported the government as individuals and demonstrated a capacity to perform the desired interlocutory function.

Not many unions fit that profile, however. Confrontation with employers and the government arose in sectors directly threatened by the new economic project, especially where it led to firm or sectoral restructuring. These other unions tended to oppose not only restructuring itself but the economic policies promoting it. They also often began to question the existing terms of the state-labor alliance. Some had longer histories of political opposition and autonomy, while others moved in that direction as the changing economy brought new threats to their members. On the issue of internal governance, this group of unions was not uniform: Some were relatively democratic internally, while others were bureaucratic and oligarchic.

The labor groups characterized by a strategy of retrenchment were primarily national federations and the confederations, which were a level removed from firm or sectoral concerns and hence did not directly face issues of restructuring. These labor organizations (and their leaders) were among those that had most benefited from the political connections of the old alliance and the particular way in which Mexican labor had been inserted into the political system. First and foremost these leaders were interested in retaining the state-labor alliance as institutionalized in the PRI and in defending the legal base of labor rights. To these ends they were willing to accede to the main outlines of national economic policy and demonstrate their political inclusion and indispensability, as evidenced by the wage-price pacts. Their stance with respect to firm restructuring was also subordinated to the priority they placed on preserving the state-labor alliance: In some noteworthy cases the labor centrals opposed member unions in confrontation with the state over restructuring, thereby again trying to demonstrate their political indispensability to the government. Yet these leaders did not adopt new unionism, since their power had been centrally based on a clientelistic flow of benefits, and they saw internal representativeness and democracy as a threat to this source of personalistic power. They were also heavily invested in their role in the PRI. Ultimately, these leaders succeeded in blocking significant change to the structure of Mexican state-labor relations as embodied in labor law and labor's position in the party.

By the end of the Salinas presidency, no definitive restructuring of state-labor relations had occurred. Despite the proposal for a new unionism, the government itself continued to find the old model useful in negotiating a social pact around wage-price policies, and the route to a new reliable constituency that would still deliver political support was never clear, especially in an electorally more competitive context. For its part the labor movement was divided into groups that supported the new unionism, groups that supported the old model, and groups that rejected both. Not only did support for the new unionism seem to require quite special union and sectoral conditions, but by 1992 the labor leader who had seemed positioned to spearhead the new model on a national level (Hernández Juárez) faced declining credibility among many unionists as he made his way through the ongoing dilemmas entailed in both supporting the government and representing the rank and file of the larger labor movement. In the end, the ambivalence of the government and the support of powerful labor leaders for the old model meant that Salinas had failed to substantially alter the contradictory situation he inherited: a corporatist political structure and state-labor alliance often at odds with the government's free-market orientation.

## Notes

1. Individuals became members of the party through their membership in labor unions, peasant groups, and other organizations that were affiliated with one of the party's sectors. The PRM established four sectors that were later reduced to three: labor, popular, and peasant.

2. See Ruth Berins Collier and David Collier, *Shaping the Political Arena: Critical Junctures, the Labor Movement, and Regime Dynamics in Latin America* (Princeton, N.J.: Princeton University Press, 1991), pp. 196–250 (on the early years of the state-labor alliance); pp. 403–420 (on the alliance in the 1940s); pp. 410–416 and 596–604 (on the dissident labor groups); and pp. 580–583 (on the state's mechanisms for influencing labor).

3. See also Ian Roxborough and Ilán Bizberg, "Union Locals in Mexico: The 'New Unionism' in Steel and Automobiles," *Journal of Latin American Studies* 15, no. 1 (May 1983): 117–135; Mark Thompson and Ian Roxborough, "Union Elections and Democracy in Mexico: A Comparative Perspective," *British Journal of Industrial Relations* 20, no. 2 (July 1982): 201–217.

4. For example, government control of union registration was often manipulated to put pressure on union leaders, as in 1983 when the PRI government aided a unionization effort of CROC when its rival, the CTM, publicly threatened a general strike. Kevin J. Middlebrook, "The Sounds of Silence: Organized Labour's Response to Economic Crisis in Mexico," *Journal of Latin American Studies* 21, no. 2 (May 1989): 195–220.

5. Collier and Collier, *Shaping the Political Arena,* pp. 584–587. Literally "cowboy," the term *charro* has become a label for union leaders who are often corrupt, pro-government bosses of undemocratic unions. For further discussion of the term, see Ian Roxborough, "The Analysis of Labour Movements in Latin America: Typologies and Theories," *Bulletin of Latin American Research* 1, no. 1 (1981): 81–95.

6. Jeffrey Bortz, "Política salarial en México: Evolución de los salarios mínimos desde la posguerra hasta la crisis económica actual," in *Industria y trabajo en*

*México,* ed. J. W. Wilkie and J. Reyes Heroles González Garza (Mexico City: Autonomous Metropolitan University, Azcapotzalco, 1990), pp. 315–332; Esthela Gutiérrez Garza, "De la relación salarial monopolista a la flexibilidad del trabajo: México, 1960–1986," in *La crisis del estado del bienestar, vol. 2, Testimonios de la crisis,* ed. E. Gutiérrez Garza (Mexico City: Siglo XXI, 1988), pp. 129–173.

7. Rodney D. Anderson, "Mexico," in *Latin American Labor Organizations,* ed. G. M. Greenfield and S. L. Maram (New York: Greenwood Press, 1987), pp. 511–548.

8. The following discussion draws extensively on Ruth Berins Collier, *The Contradictory Alliance: State-Labor Relations and Regime Change in Mexico* (Berkeley: International and Area Studies, University of California, Berkeley, 1992), in particular, pp. 80–92.

9. Cited in Robert R. Kaufman, *The Politics of Debt in Argentina, Brazil, and Mexico: Economic Stabilization in the 1980s* (Berkeley: Institute of International Studies, University of California, Berkeley, 1988), pp. 92–99.

10. In these years official figures registered the first triple digit inflation. The 106 percent inflation of 1986 represented a failure of previous stabilization attempts, though not a dramatic increase over the previous high in 1982. However, the rise to 159 percent in 1987 revealed a process out of control. Inflation figures from Hugo Ortiz Dietz, *México: Banco de datos, Año VIII* (Mexico City: El Inversionista Mexicano, 1990) p. 2–3.

11. A case in point was the closing of a state-owned steel foundry in Monterrey in May 1986 and the consequent elimination of ten thousand to fifteen thousand jobs. This act was a stark abandonment of the government's priority on jobs, which was precisely the commitment it had acted upon a decade earlier when it had originally taken over the foundry. See Wayne A. Cornelius, "Mexico," in *Latin America and Caribbean Contemporary Record, vol. 5,* ed. A. F. Lowenthal (New York: Holmes and Meier, 1987), p. B348.

12. Article 123, Part A, Section XVIII, for example, states that "strikes shall be considered unlawful only when the majority of strikers engage in acts of violence against persons or property or in the event of war, when the workers belong to establishments or services of the government."

13. *Proceso,* March 9, 1987.

14. *Latin American Weekly Report,* October 8, 1987; Kevin J. Middlebrook, "Dilemmas of Change in Mexican Politics," *World Politics* 41 (October 1988): 120–141.

15. Raúl Trejo Delarbre, "La parálisis obrera," *Nexos* (April 1987): 37–64. The *maquiladora* program, located in northern Mexico, allows factories to assemble products with duty-free foreign components and raw materials, and then to export the products with duty charged only on the value added in Mexico.

16. For a more elaborated description of this project, see Collier, *The Contradictory Alliance,* pp. 119–129.

17. *Proceso,* May 25, 1987.

18. Ibid.

19. George Grayson, *Oil and Mexican Foreign Policy* (Pittsburgh: University of Pittsburgh Press, 1988).

20. *Latin American Weekly Report,* November 12 and 19, December 3 and 10, 1987.

21. Cited in Luis Méndez and Othón Quiroz Trejo, "Organización obrera: Nuevos rumbos, ¿nuevas perspectivas?" *El Cotidiano* 36 (July-August 1990): 48. Authors' translation.

22. *La Jornada*, May 14, 1990, pp. 1 and 8, and May 17, 1990, p. 3.

23. Some of the country's best known labor leaders lost deputy and senatorial elections that year, including such CTM stalwarts as Arturo Romo, Venustiano Reyes López, and Joaquín Gamboa Pascoe; see Javier Aguilar García and Lorenzo Arrieta, "En la fase más aguda de la crisis y en el inicio de la reestructuración o modernización, 1982–1988," in *Historia de la CTM, 1936–1990, vol. 2,* ed. J. Aguilar García (Mexico City: National Autonomous University of Mexico, 1990), pp. 657–731. Overall, about a third of all CTM and Labor Congress candidates for the PRI lost in 1988; see Juan Reyes del Campillo, "El movimiento obrero en la Cámara de Diputados (1979–1988)," *Revista Mexicana de Sociología* 52, no. 3 (July–September 1990): 139–160.

24. *Excélsior*, May 2, 1990, p. 49.

25. *La Jornada*, May 14, 1990.

26. Gabriel Székely, "Mexico's Challenge: Developing a New International Economic Strategy," in *Changing Networks: Mexico's Telecommunications Options, Monograph Series 32,* ed. P. F. Cowhey, J. D. Aronson, and G. Székely (La Jolla: Center for U.S.-Mexican Studies, University of California, San Diego, 1989), p. 81.

27. Jorge Basurto, *En el régimen de Echeverría: rebelión e independencia, vol. 14, La clase obrera en la historia de México,* ed. P. González Casanova (Mexico City: Siglo XXI, 1983), pp. 35–37; Mario Rangel Pérez, *Los telefonistas frente a la crisis y la reconversión* (Mexico City: Editorial Nuestro Tiempo, 1989), p. 178.

28. Raúl Trejo Delarbre, *Crónica del sindicalismo en México (1976–1988)* (Mexico City: Siglo XXI, 1990), pp. 327–328.

29. Roberto Borja and Fabio Barbosa, "El movimiento del 8 de marzo en el sindicato de telefonistas," in *Educación, telefonistas y bancarios, vol. 4, Los sindicatos nacionales en el México contemporáneo,* ed. J. Aguilar García (Mexico City: GV Editores, 1989): 11–54; María Xelhuantzi López, *El Sindicato de Telefonistas de la República Mexicana: Doce años (1976–1988)* (Mexico City: Sindicato de Telefonistas de la República Mexicana, 1988), p. 184.

30. Rosario Ortiz and Rodolfo García, "Concertación en Teléfonos de México," in *Negociación y conflicto laboral en México,* ed. G. Bensusán and S. León (Mexico City: Fundación Friedrich Ebert, 1990), pp. 229–238.

31. These events are related in Xelhuantzi López, *El Sindicato de Telefonistas,* pp. 283–289, 308–310, and 318.

32. María Xelhuantzi López, "Relaciones laborales, actores sociales y modernización: El caso del Sindicato de Telefonistas de la República Mexicana y la empresa Teléfonos de México," in *Relaciones laborales en las empresas paraestatales,* ed. G. Bensusán and C. García (Mexico City: Fundación Friedrich Ebert, 1990), p. 36.

33. *La Jornada*, September 18, 1992, p. 13.

34. In the past often referred to as FESEBES.

35. *Unomásuno*, September 11, 1992, p. 10.

36. For a more extensive discussion of the political and economic requisites of new unionism, see James G. Samstad, "Reestructuración productiva, democracia sindical y la transformación de las relaciones laborales" (paper presented at the conference "Tercer Coloquio sobre 'Reestructuración Productiva y Reorganización Social,'" University of Xalapa, Veracruz, October 7, 1992).

37. In addition to the STRM, the initial membership of FESEBS consisted of the Alliance of Mexican Streetcar Workers (ATM), the Labor Association of Air-

line Pilots (ASPA), the Labor Association of Airline Flight Attendants (ASSA), the Mexican Union of Electrical Workers (SME), and the Union of Technical and Manual Workers in Studios and Laboratories of Cinematographic Production and Allied Workers of the Mexican Republic (STyM). Later two more unions joined the federation, the Independent Union of Workers in the Automotive Industry and Allied Workers, "Volkswagen of Mexico" (SITIAVW), and the National Union of Workers in Financial Services, Services in General, Commerce, and Allied Workers of the Mexican Republic (SNTSFSGSCRM). In addition, in December 1992 the CROC officially formed an alliance with FESEBS to work together to restructure the Labor Congress (see Luis Méndez and José Othón Quiroz Trejo, *Modernización estatal y respuesta obrera: Historia de una derrota* (Mexico City: Autonomous Metropolitan University, Azcapotzalco, 1994), p. 307.

38. Luis Méndez, "La Cervecería Modelo: Vergonzosa muestra de modernización laboral," *El Cotidiano* 35 (May–June 1990): 59–65; Raúl Trejo Delarbre, *Los mil días de Carlos Salinas* (Mexico City: El Nacional, 1991).

39. Trejo Delarbre, *Los mil días*, p. 306; Pilar Vásquez Rubio, "¿Habrá final feliz en el conflicto de la Ford?" *El Cotidiano* 34 (March–April 1990): 61–64.

40. Trejo Delarbre, *Los mil días*, pp. 317–318.

41. Yolanda Montiel, *Proceso de trabajo, acción sindical y nuevas tecnologías en Volkswagen de México* (Mexico City: Center for Research and Higher Studies in Social Anthropology, 1991).

42. Ludger Pries, "Volkswagen: ¿Un nudo gordiano resuelto?" *Trabajo,* no. 9 (March 1993): 7–23.

43. *La Jornada,* August 18, 1992, pp. 1 and 16, and September 8, 1992, p. 16.

44. Hernández Juárez officially participated in his capacity as an advisor to Bueno and the Volkswagen union, although many in Mexico suspected he acted with government encouragement. See *Proceso,* August 31, 1992, p. 28, and Méndez and Quiroz Trejo, *Modernización estatal,* pp. 288–289.

45. *Restaurador 22 de abril,* January 1993, p. 3.

46. Salvador Corro and José Reveles, *La Quina: El lado oscuro del poder* (Mexico City: Planeta, 1989).

47. Fabio Barbosa Cano, *La reconversión de la industria petrolera en México* (Mexico City: Institute for Economic Research, National Autonomous University of Mexico, 1993), pp. 100–103.

48. Jonguitud had formed the Vanguard in 1974.

49. Auroro Loyo, "Los ámbitos de la negociación del magisterio," in *Negociación y conflicto laboral en México,* ed. G. Bensusán and S. León (Mexico City: Fundación Friedrich Ebert, 1990), pp. 229–238.

50. Ibid.

51. Luis Hernández Navarro, "SNTE: La transición difícil," *El Cotidiano,* no. 51 (November–December 1992): 54–70.

52. Ilán Bizberg, "La crisis del corporativismo mexicano," *Foro Internacional* 30, no. 4 (April–June 1990): 695–735. See also Kevin J. Middlebrook, "The Politics of Industrial Restructuring: Transnational Firms' Search for Flexible Production in the Mexican Automobile Industry," *Comparative Politics* 23, no. 3 (April 1991): 275–297.

53. *Unomásuno,* June 18, 1990, p. 2.

54. *La Jornada,* September 14, 1992, p. 33.

55. At the metallurgical plant of Altos Hornos in Monclova, Coahuila, and Siderúrgica Lázaro Cárdenas–Las Truchas in Michoacán.

56. *La Jornada,* September 14, 1992, p. 33.

57. A 1989 Coparmex (Employers' Federation of the Mexican Republic) proposal represents probably the most thorough, and most controversial, of these efforts; see Confederación Patronal de la República Mexicana, "Propuestas preliminares que la Confederación Patronal de la República Mexicana presenta para la discusión del anteproyecto de una nueva ley federal del trabajo (L.F.T.): Marco conceptual," unpublished report (Mexico City: Coparmex, June, 1989). Along with Coparmex virtually all of the most important business associations—including representatives of Canacintra (National Chamber of Manufacturing Industries), Concamin (Confederation of Chambers of Industry), and even the umbrella organization for Mexico's business groups, the Business Coordinating Council (CCE)—publicly called for making changes in the law to coincide with the implementation of NAFTA; see *El Financiero,* September 2, 1992, p. 1; *La Jornada,* January 24, 1992, p. 11, and September 19, 1992, pp. 1 and 35; and *Unomásuno,* February 16, 1992, p. 8.

58. *La Jornada,* January 31, 1992, pp. 1 and 12.

59. *La Jornada,* June 17, 1992, p. 18.

60. *La Jornada,* March 30, 1992, p. 13.

61. *La Jornada,* January 29, 1992, p. 15.

62. *La Jornada,* November 9, 1991, p. 15, April 10, 1992, p. 10, June 27, 1992, p. 4, and August 20, 1992, pp. 1 and 12; *Unomásuno,* January 25, 1992, pp. 3 and 9, and July 21, 1992, p. 7.

63. In 1990, for example, the government instituted the Revisory Commission of the Federal Labor Law to draft such legislation, but the commission quickly became inactive and to date has not produced a single proposal. See Sara Lovera, "Las reformas de la Ley Federal del Trabajo," *La Jornada Laboral,* January 31, 1992, pp. 1 and 8.

64. *La Jornada,* November 24, 1993, p. 1.

65. *La Jornada,* November 25, 1993, pp. 1 and 18.

66. *La Jornada,* November 26, 1993, p. 1.

67. For a more general discussion of a new political project that began to take shape in the 1980s, see Collier, *The Contradictory Alliance,* pp. 121–129.

68. Trejo Delarbre, *Los mil días,* pp. 233–234.

69. Collier, *The Contradictory Alliance,* pp. 145–146.

70. *Proceso,* March 2, 1992, p. 18.

71. *El Financiero,* February 25, 1992, pp. 1 and 30.

72. *Unomásuno,* April 14, 1992, p. 1.

73. *La Jornada,* June 24, 1992, pp. 1 and 11, and June 27, 1992, p. 3.

74. *La Jornada,* December 13, 1993, pp. 1 and 12; *Reforma,* December 14, 1993, p. 4A.

75. *La Jornada,* August 14, 1994, p. 13.

76. In 1994 the CTM won forty-one deputy and nine senate seats, losing only a single deputy seat to a PAN candidate in the state of Jalisco. The PRI's labor sector as a whole won seventy federal deputy seats, the same number it had after its recuperation in the 1991 elections. See *La Jornada,* August 25, 1994, p. 24, August 31, 1994, p. 19, September 1, 1994, p. 19.

77. *La Jornada,* August 31, 1994, p. 19.

# 3

# Reforming Land Tenure in Mexico: Peasants, the Market, and the State

## *Merilee S. Grindle*

In 1917 the Mexican state guaranteed access to land to its rural population through a constitutionally mandated agrarian reform. Article 27 enabled organized groups of peasants to have rights to communally held land through an institution known as the *ejido*. In 1991 the Constitution was amended to permit privatization of ejido land and its sale or rental to individuals or corporations. The declared purpose of this significant change in rural property rights was to increase the incentives for investment in agriculture. More fundamentally, however, the constitutional revision set the stage for an end to an agrarian system in which the state stood between peasants and the market in almost all economic transactions and seriously limited the peasants' political autonomy.

The old system, in the view of those who led the initiative to redefine rural property rights, not only discouraged entrepreneurship within the ejidos, but it also left non-ejido farmers in a state of permanent insecurity. The reformers anticipated that the new system would distance the peasantry from any special status vis-à-vis the state and allow for the efficient operation of land, labor, and capital markets in rural areas. It would also, they hoped, destroy the power of the rural bosses who had exploited the peasants' economic and political vulnerability. At the same time, however, the reformers expected considerable opposition to the change because to alter the ejido system was also to challenge long-standing mores and fundamental characteristics of the rural economy as well as deeply embedded political beliefs and bureaucratic relationships.

There was strong rural resistance to the new, market-oriented legal and regulatory structures—and to the incorporation of Mexico's rural areas into the North American Free Trade Agreement (NAFTA)—but it came two years *after* the legal basis for economic liberalization in the countryside had been introduced. The gap between the introduction of change in a fundamental aspect of Mexico's revolutionary nationalist heritage and reaction to it can be explained in part by the highly centralized and presidentialist system of decisionmaking that virtually excluded the participation of the affected rural population. From this perspective, peasants could participate only through their reaction to change.

Equally important in explaining the gap between the state-led initiative and reaction to it was the clear failure of the original agrarian reform of 1917, as pursued after 1940, to provide for the economic and political well-being of Mexico's rural poor. By the 1980s the ejido system had few defenders. Would the new system offer any more to those who had long been excluded from most of the benefits of the country's economic development? The rural rebellion in the southern state of Chiapas that erupted on January 1, 1994, indicates that many peasants seriously question the possibility.

This chapter considers the political and economic results of Mexico's earlier agrarian reform and the conditions that led to a historic redefinition of the relationship between the state and the peasantry in the early 1990s. That the initiative for reform came from the state is stark testimony to the extent to which the country's peasants had been reduced to almost silent dependence on the regime. The consequences of the change, however, will be largely determined by the peasantry's ability to respond to market forces and to organize effectively for political participation in the future.

## The Ejido Tradition, 1917–1970

Article 27 of the Constitution of 1917 guaranteed Mexico's landless peasant population access to communally held land by means of new federal rights to expropriate land and water resources and to specify the beneficiaries of land redistribution. It established the legal basis for the ejido, a grant of use-rights to land communally held by legally incorporated groups of peasants, or *ejidatarios*. At the same time, the Constitution guaranteed the right to private ownership of noncommunal lands and to communal ownership of land in traditional indigenous communities.[1] Modeled on conceptions of pre-Hispanic land tenure systems, the communal property institutions were designed to protect the peasant population from a repetition of the loss of lands that had followed the liberal reform laws of 1857 and the expansion of agrarian capitalism in the decades leading up to the Revolution of 1910.[2]

Article 27, as well as the federal agrarian code subsequentially developed to implement it, provided that an ejido be organized when a group of twenty or more peasants petitioned the state for land and carried out a complex set of legal and administrative procedures. Once chartered by the state, each ejido was to be governed by a general assembly composed of ejidatarios. The general assembly, in turn, was to elect a commission of three to oversee the affairs of the community and represent it to the local, state, and national governments.[3] Each ejido could determine if its land would be exploited individually or collectively; in fact, in 1990 the vast majority (87.5 percent) of the country's twenty-eight thousand ejidos were divided among the individual ejidatarios.[4] Ejidatarios enjoyed protection from loss of their land because its sale or mortgage was prohibited. Until the early 1980s rental of ejido land was also illegal, although often practiced.[5]

In the immediate aftermath of the Revolution of 1910, little systematic implementation of the agrarian reform provisions took place. Those who managed to consolidate power after the Revolution were not the peasants who had played a major role in the conflict but northern landowners and industrialists, who were generally uninterested in the plight of the peasantry—then as now concentrated in the central and southern states. This situation changed with the presidency of Lázaro Cárdenas (1934–1940). Motivated by a plan to create a base of political support among peasants and workers, a vision of a prosperous rural economy rooted in a distinctly Mexican landholding system, and a desire to pursue the more radical goals of the Revolution, Cárdenas spearheaded a massive land redistribution initiative and encouraged peasant mobilization around political demands for land and justice. Cárdenas also encouraged collectively farmed ejidos, established the Ejidal Bank to provide credit, and expanded social and physical infrastructures in rural areas. By the end of his presidency nearly nineteen million hectares of land, or over 9.1 percent of Mexico's surface, had been redistributed as ejido grants to petitioning groups of some 815,000 peasants.

Table 3.1 shows the extent of land redistributed as ejidos from 1900 to 1988. The total, over 105 million hectares, represents nearly 50 percent of the country's agricultural, grazing, and forest land and benefited over 3 million ejidatarios by 1988.

From Cárdenas through the administration of Miguel de la Madrid Hurtado (1982–1988), the regime of the Institutional Revolutionary Party (PRI) reaped a large political windfall from the ejido system. Those years were also marked by government manipulation and deception, and by increasing rural poverty, but the ejidatarios consistently legitimized the regime with their support and votes. Peasants who failed in their petitions for ejido status rarely lost hope that, with persistence, loyalty, and the right political godfathers, they would someday succeed. The PRI further cemented its rural support through extensive economic linkages between ejidos and the state. The Ejidal Bank was key, because the ejidatarios, proscribed from mortgaging their land, could not borrow money through commercial sources.[6] In 1937 a state marketing agency—eventually known as Conasupo (the National Commission on Popular Subsistence)—was established to ensure the supply of basic foodstuffs through a state-run monopoly of markets for corn, beans, and other staples. The peasants, then, eventually came to look to the state not only for access to land and

Table 3.1    Total Land Redistributed as Ejido Grants in Mexico, 1900–1988,
             by Presidential Administration

| Period | Land Redistributed (Hectares) | % of Total Area Redistributed by 1988 |
|---|---|---|
| Pre-Cárdenas (1900–1934) | 11,738,328 | 11.2% |
| Cárdenas (1934–1940) | 18,786,131 | 17.9 |
| Avila Camacho (1940–1946) | 7,277,697 | 6.9 |
| Alemán Valdés (1946–1952) | 4,590,381 | 4.4 |
| Ruiz Cortínez (1952–1958) | 6,056,773 | 5.8 |
| López Mateos (1958–1964) | 8,870,430 | 8.4 |
| Díaz Ordaz (1964–1970) | 24,738,199 | 23.5[a] |
| Echeverría Alvarez (1970–1976) | 12,773,888 | 12.1 |
| López Portillo (1976–1982) | 6,097,005 | 5.8 |
| De la Madrid Hurtado (1982–1988) | 4,167,588 | 4.0 |
| TOTAL | 105,096,420 | 100.0% |

*Source*: John R. Heath, "Enhancing the Contribution of Land Reform to Mexican Agricultural Development," World Bank Working Paper no. 285 (Washington, D.C.: World Bank, February 1990), p. 60. Based on official statistics.
a. Much of this distribution resulted from final legalization of already distributed land.

credit, but also for agricultural inputs, markets for their products, and even consumer goods. Their political ties to the government also became highly structured. In 1938 the ejidatarios were incorporated into the National Confederation of Peasants (CNC), one of the three corporate pillars of the PRI.

Gradually, as the machine-like clientele networks of the PRI expanded, ejido commissioners were transformed into brokers between government and peasants, trading their ability to deliver the votes of ejidatarios for the patronage and protection of the regime. By the late 1940s and 1950s the national PRI was firmly linked to the state-level officials and regional strongmen who controlled the ejido commissioners; they, in turn, delivered the rural vote to the PRI in local, state, and national elections. Peasants who resisted this system found it difficult to maintain their access to land, credit, social services, and other goods and services provided by the state. Although groups of peasants did organize independently from time to time to make demands on the government, they were generally coopted or repressed by the formidable power and resources available to the various power brokers throughout the system.[7]

Ultimately, the peasant sector became the most loyal and least autonomous base of support for the ruling party. Table 3.2 shows that, even in recent periods when overall support for the PRI was flagging, rural votes continued to provide the greatest cushion for the party in presidential elections. The fact that many of those votes were fraudulently cast or extorted from peasant communities by local or regional bosses only underscores the extent to which the independent political voice of the peasantry was severely limited. As long as the government retained the right to determine legal access to land and wielded control over credit, inputs, development investments, and jobs, it was in a position also to determine the political relationship of the countryside to the state.

Table 3.2    **Support for the PRI Candidate in Presidential Elections, 1979–1988, by Urban, Mixed, and Rural Congressional Districts**

| | Percentage of District(s) Voting for PRI Candidate | | | | |
|---|---|---|---|---|---|
| Districts, by type | 1979 | 1982 | 1985 | 1988 | Average 1979–1988 |
| Federal District | | | | | |
| (Mexico City) | 46.7% | 48.3% | 42.6% | 27.3% | 41.2% |
| Other Urban[a] | 53.4 | 56.2 | 51.1 | 34.3 | 48.8 |
| Mixed[b] | 67.9 | 66.2 | 59.2 | 46.4 | 60.0 |
| Rural[c] | 83.5 | 80.9 | 77.3 | 61.3 | 75.8 |

*Source*: Wayne A. Cornelius and Ann L. Craig, *The Mexican Political System in Transition* (La Jolla: Center for U.S.-Mexican Studies, University of California, San Diego, 1991), p. 70.

a. Urban districts are those in which 90 percent or more of the population lived in communities of 50,000 or more inhabitants. Total number: 96 (40 in the Federal District and 56 in other urban areas).

b. Districts in which 50 percent or more but less than 90 percent of the population lived in communities of 50,000 or more inhabitants. Total number: 44.

c. Districts in which less than 50 percent of the population lived in communities of 50,000 inhabitants. Total number: 160.

But if the ejido was a political boon to the regime, it was an economic tragedy for the countryside itself, especially when viewed in the light of the Cárdenas vision of a prosperous, communally based peasantry. Initially, a number of ejidos—those farming productive, irrigated land—competed effectively with capitalist landholdings. The vast majority of ejidos, however, were established on land that peasants had been pushed onto in earlier decades by large landholders and state authorities; it was generally the least productive available. Moreover, only 21 percent of ejido land became cultivated, the rest was forest or pasture, and only about 15 percent of ejido land was irrigated by 1990.[8]

Despite pervasive official rhetoric about the centrality of the ejidos to the nation's development, policies in the 1940s and 1950s began to discriminate against them, and their productivity began to decline.[9] A variety of federal policies designed to stimulate rapid industrial and agricultural development encouraged the emergence of large-scale, commercial, and export-oriented agriculture on Mexico's most productive land.[10] In particular, the state invested heavily in irrigation and transportation systems that benefited large farmers; made credit available to encourage mechanization and the adoption of "green revolution" technologies; and sponsored research and extension programs to expand the use of miracle seeds and other technologies by the modern farm sector. The productivity of the large, private farms increased, helping to form not only a prosperous export-oriented agroindustrial sector but also a powerful new class of modern capitalist farmers, particularly in the north. Fully in tune with the modernizing development of the country, those farmers were to reap the benefits of most of the government's attention to agriculture from the 1940s through the 1970s.

The peasants, who produced staple crops for the domestic market, were far less advantaged and eventually became the most obvious orphans of the country's rapid development. On land of poor quality, they were dependent on erratic rainfall and government pricing policies that were biased in favor of urban consumers. Their access to credit was limited to local moneylenders and state-owned banks whose lending policies were tied to specific products and at times to specific technologies for growing them. The latter form of credit was never available in sufficient quantity to meet the demand, and as with many other state-provided goods and services, its allocation was frequently tied to the PRI patronage machinery. Agricultural research and extension services, investment in irrigation, and access to green revolution technology were scant and also limited by the political and economic agendas of the regime.

All told, it is little wonder that by 1970 the productivity of the ejido sector compared unfavorably to that of the large farm sector and even to that of the small private landholding peasantry. At that time per person output on private farms was about four times greater than that on ejidos.[11] Significant differences in output per unit of land were also an indictment of the ejido system, as shown in Table 3.3. Census data for 1970 indicate that 72.8 percent of all productive agricultural units—most of them within ejidos—fell into the categories of subsistence or infrasubsistence (less than subsistence) production.[12] Although a few ejidos, mainly those in northern regions that could deploy irrigation and mechanization, were able to remain competitive, the vast majority of ejidatarios faced ever more stringent barriers to providing subsistence for their families.

Peasant households remained tied to the ejido through legislation requiring them to cultivate at least once every three years, but many families also had to turn to other ways of making a living. By the 1960s and 1970s temporary labor migration to cities, other rural areas, and the United States were commonplace in thousands of peasant communities.[13] At the same time, incentives to produce for the market declined as the prices of agricultural inputs rose and prices for crops remained controlled by government.

Table 3.3    A Comparison of Irrigation and Output on Private and Ejidal Farms, 1970

| Farms, by Type | Irrigation as % of Arable Land | Value of Crop Output per Arable Acre (in pesos) | Value of Livestock Output per Animal Unit (in pesos) |
|---|---|---|---|
| Private | 24.4% | — | 721 |
| Over 12.5 acres | — | 589 | — |
| Under 12.5 acres | — | 514 | — |
| Ejidal | 15.1 | 393 | 284 |

*Source*: Lamartine P. Yates, *Mexico's Agricultural Dilemma* (Tucson: University of Arizona Press, 1981), pp. 71, 134, 135.

In the mid-1960s Mexico began importing ever larger amounts of staples to feed its burgeoning and increasingly urban population.

## Precursors to Change, 1970–1990

Lagging productivity and mounting concerns about food security, as well as evidence of rural unrest and a resurgence within government and intellectual circles of a nationalist commitment to the ejidos, encouraged a significant rebirth of attention to the sector in the early 1970s. Extensive investment in rural development began under the presidency of Luis Echeverría Alvarez (1970–1976) and reached massive proportions in the oil boom years under the presidency of José López Portillo (1976–1982).[14] The investment was concentrated on providing rural infrastructure, direct support to production, and expanded social welfare institutions for rainfall-dependent areas.

Despite this shift in both policy and programs, productivity in the ejido sector remained low. Nor was accelerated land distribution pursued, except for episodic responses to rural political tensions. Instead, temporary labor migration and diversification of income-generating strategies increased in rural areas, signaling the ongoing inability of ejido households to subsist from the land alone. And the renewed state investments came to an abrupt halt in 1982, when Mexico's debt crisis forced the government to focus almost all of its attention on managing the debt and macroeconomic instability. Between 1982 and 1989 the countryside was virtually forgotten by Mexico's policymakers.

Intellectual debate about the ejido, if not government action, continued, however. Concern over the problems in the sector began to grow in the 1970s, as policymakers, scholars, and others pointed to its persistent underproductivity and unrelenting poverty. Much of the criticism at the time was leveled at the federal government for both its industrial and agricultural development policies and its failure to invest in the alleviation of rural poverty.[15] Several scholars illuminated the ways in which government pricing and credit policies discriminated against small farmers and particularly against the ejidatarios, who still had no access to commercial credit or open markets for their crops. They also pointed out the extent to which the peasant population was politically bound to the government through the corruption of the PRI machine and its network of rural bosses.[16]

Other scholarly criticism, however, began to recognize the structure of the ejido itself as the main impediment to higher productivity. According to this view, the constraints on land, labor, and credit markets created by the ejido system were directly at odds with the incentives needed to stimulate entrepreneurial peasants to invest in their land and increase their productivity.[17] With credit limited and tied to specific crops and technologies, with prices for crops controlled by the government, with no capacity to mortgage land, with many of the decisions about when and what to plant made by ejido leaders rather than individual farmers, and with no legal right to rent or sell land or to hire outside labor, ejidatarios had little incentive to invest in irrigation, improved technology, increased production, or even new crops.

Gradually, evidence about the economic failure of the ejido sector mounted, and voices singling out its structure as the strongest impediment to increased productivity became more insistent. But until the administration of Carlos Salinas de Gortari (1988–1994), the political success of the ejido eclipsed its economic failure. Deeply rooted in the mythology of Mexico's pre-Hispanic past, imbued with the nationalistic vision of Mexico's uniqueness, not to mention centrally important as a bedrock of support for PRI electoral success, the ejido system was a political sacred cow.

### Changing the Rules, 1988–1994

In the short time between late 1989 and late 1991, not only was the sacred cow questioned, it was fundamentally undermined by a small group of planners in the Salinas administration who worked, largely in secret, to revise Article 27 of the Constitution and the ponderous agrarian code that had grown up to regulate the ejido sector. Under the system of rural property rights they introduced, ejidatarios could convert their land to private property and rent or sell it and their labor through the market. The same legislation increased the security of tenure on private property holdings and allowed ejidatarios to form associations, to contract with domestic and international investors, and to hire non-ejido labor.[18] Land redistribution was declared at an end, and agrarian tribunals were set up to adjudicate outstanding land claims and conflicts. Land would no longer have to be cultivated to maintain valid claims to it. This legislation, passed by the

Mexican Congress in December 1991 and February 1992, set the scene for major changes in the economic relationships that existed in the agrarian sector and seriously undermined the traditional political relationship between the state and the peasantry. How did this historic change come about?

The Salinas administration's ability to alter the legal structure of land tenure relationships in the countryside took most people by surprise. The initiative emerged within the government as part of the broader set of state-led efforts during the De la Madrid and Salinas administrations to liberalize the Mexican economy. There was virtually no discussion with those who would be affected most directly by the change, the ejidatarios, and only limited consultation with organizations representing the peasants; the peasants' confederation (the CNC) and the PRI were directly informed of the government's intentions only after they had been decided upon. Nor were representatives of the large landholding sector or the international financial agencies negotiating economic restructuring with Mexico involved. The change was the work of a small group of technocrats who were able to count on the political support of a highly technocratic and centralized administration. Indeed, the process of decisionmaking for a fundamental change in the Constitution merely highlighted the extent to which the peasants had become effectively disenfranchised in the years after the Cardenista reforms.[19]

Discussions about the need for change had begun quietly in late 1989 in the small and newly created Office of Deregulation in the Secretariat of Commerce and Industrial Development (Secofi). This office, whose job it was to spearhead technical analysis of domestic economic liberalization and negotiate any pertinent policies of the administration, was given the mandate to assess any and all sectors of the economy that appeared to be hampered by overregulation. Based on this mandate, officials in the office began considering the legal and regulatory constraints on Mexican agriculture. When apprised of their work, President Salinas indicated interest and asked for more analysis of the issues. In January 1990 the president also established a small working group in the Secretariat of Agriculture and Water Resources (SARH) to assemble data and consider how the government should approach "the agrarian question."

The resulting undersecretariat for planning in SARH was small and composed of young, technocratically oriented lawyers and economists. Several of them had been involved in the initial studies of agricultural deregulation in Secofi. In charge of the new planning group was Luis Téllez Kuenzler, a young economist with a Ph.D. from the Massachusetts Institute of Technology, who had been Director of Economic Planning at the Secretariat of Finance and Public Credit in prior years and had impressed the president and the architects of the country's economic reform program. The task of his group was to find ways to improve the productivity of the agricultural sector, particularly that of peasant producers. The ejido was a particular focus of attention. The data were unambiguous: The ejido was not an economically productive institution, and most ejidos and ejidatarios were poverty stricken and powerless both economically and politically. The discussion quickly led to a pair of opposing solutions. As one member of the planning group explained:

> On the one hand, you had those who focused on the asphyxiating role of the state in the rural economy and its authoritarian political relationships with groups in the countryside. For these people, the solution was to get the state out, period. On the other hand, you had those who argued for the state's maintaining its supportive role. . . . This situation boiled down to those who wanted the magic of the marketplace and those who said, "Don't abandon them."[20]

Initially, the planning group considered questions of prices and credit availability for the ejido and small farm sectors. Before long, however, the analysts became convinced that the real constraints on the peasant agricultural sector were much more fundamental. They were the constraints posed by land tenure relationships and the legal structure of the ejido itself. In a series of closed meetings the group gradually focused its attention on three key issues: (1) the lack of a land market under existing law; (2) the need for security of land tenure for both peasants and large landholders; and (3) the extensive legal restrictions on the use of land. All three of these issues required legal reform of property rights in the countryside if they were to be addressed effectively.

Yet even while focusing on legal concerns, members of the group had strong reservations about whether such a sweeping set of reforms could be taken on by the government. When Salinas had assumed office in late 1988, the legitimacy of the PRI regime was at an all-time low; the president had won an election with the lowest margin of victory of any president since the party was formed in 1929. Many observers at the time believed that the 50.7 percent of the vote he garnered was achieved only through widespread fraud at the polls. And for the first time the dominant party had failed to return the 67 percent majority to Congress necessary to *pass* a constitutional amendment. According to one member of the SARH planning group, "There was a sense that it was all just for discussion, that the issue was so big that no action would ever really be taken on it."[21] Nevertheless, by spring 1991 the group was meeting with the president and had begun to confer with top officials in several of the secretariats that would be affected by any change in rural property rights. The possibility of revising Article 27 was also discussed in cabinet meetings.

Other impediments to altering property rights in the countryside were formidable. The planners tried to anticipate the nature of the likely opposition as they shaped the content of the reform. To make the initiative more palatable to those who defended the special relationship between the state and the peasantry, the decision about whether to reorganize ejidos as private property would be left to the individual ejidos to make. Even so, the planners expected that when the initiative became public, they would have to face strong resistance from both inside the government—from the Secretariat of Agrarian Reform and the Secretariat of Agriculture itself— and outside—from the CNC and other peasant organizations, the political left, and intellectuals who had long celebrated Mexico's agrarian roots and sense of nationalism.

The congressional elections of August 1991 gave an important boost to the prospects for change. The PRI returned enough deputies to restore its two-thirds majority. As the government openly acknowledged the pending legislation, President Salinas met with peasant leaders, who were particularly concerned about having been excluded from the decisionmaking process. In response the president issued a document, "The Ten Points," that clarified peasant rights under the new law. The discussions with the peasants came too late in the day to shape the policy, however, and their outcome was more political than substantive in nature.[22] Once the amendment moved handily through Congress, the SARH planning group was in a better position to move on to the more challenging task of revising the lengthy agrarian code, described by one of them as "an incredible nightmare of regulations and stipulations."[23] In early 1992 their changes again moved quickly through Congress.

Most observers were astounded by the speed and extent of the changes and by the virtual absence of public dissent about them, even after they had become known and passed by Congress. The changes would, after all, strip some three million peasant families of the protection they had had from open land and labor markets for more than seventy years. However much that protection had made them vulnerable to exploitation by rural bosses and institutions of state authority, however much it had locked them in poverty, it did ensure their access to land. The politically potent ejido commissioners, local bosses, and governors would lose the basis of their ability to control the rural population when they could no longer deliver land, jobs, development investments, and other forms of state patronage. And the Secretariat of Agrarian Reform, which had the right to interpret the agrarian code and considerable influence in rural politics, would lose its historic mandate.

In fact, however, when the changes were introduced, few were willing to defend the only known alternative to the proposed plan—the old system. There were few ejidatarios who could not relate dozens of stories about corruption, broken promises, and exploitation in their experiences with the CNC, the PRI, and state institutions. Although the "tyranny of the market" loomed as an unknown threat to many ejidatarios, and some observers predicted that many would lose their lands because of their poverty and likely increases in land prices, the farmers were not willing to go to the barricades to defend the old system. Indeed, many seemed interested in finding ways to interact more effectively with the state and the market. In the years leading up to the legal reform, most peasants were not political activists and tended to pursue their political demands through the PRI's patronage system. But some organizations had emerged that shared an interest in redefining the old relationship of dependence between the peasantry and the state. A "new peasant movement" had emerged that insisted on independence from the corporatist CNC and denounced the power of rural bosses and corrupt leaders of the CNC and the PRI.[24] Broad alliances such as the National "Plan de Ayala" Coordinating Committee (CNPA) and the National Union of Regional Peasant Organizations (UNORCA) brought together local and regional groups to heighten the rural population's profile in national politics. These groups demanded greater autonomy from the government, greater government accountability and responsiveness, better prices for agricultural commodities, access to markets and credit, development of production infrastructure and basic services, and control over inflation.[25] And in mobilizing as producers, consumers, and citizens—rather than as petitioners for land—some peasants began to find interests in common with other groups that also felt alienated from the government. Those interests were not likely to be mobilized in defense of the old system.

Effective opposition to the new legislation was hard to mobilize from other sectors as well. The country's nationalist intellectuals, who had long believed in the peasantry's special relationship to the market mediated by the state, had no practical alternative to offer that would address the ejidos' problems of poverty, underproductivity, and economic and political disenfranchisement. Again, the CNC had not taken part in the negotiations or discussions until the initiative was almost ready to go to Congress. Even then, the CNC leadership was brought in primarily to be informed and convinced of the need for the change, not to be bargained with in terms of its content. The rural political bosses were simply excluded from the discussions, and during a period in which the technocratic political establishment was holding the old bosses of the PRI at arm's length, they had few links to the center of power that they could exploit. Even the Secretariat of Agrarian Reform was marginal to the discussions that shaped the reform.

Those who argued for the demise of the corporate basis of land tenure and for expanding markets for land, capital, and labor in Mexico's rural areas had a number of advantages that helped them capture the initiative in promoting policy change. Certainly the secrecy and centralization of the planning process had given the revisionists the upper hand. They also commanded extensive data and analyses to buttress their assessment of the problems of rural Mexico. In an administration headed by "probably the most economically literate group that has ever governed any country anywhere," the language of economic analysis they used resonated well with the president and his cabinet.[26] This gave the SARH planning group important credibility in arguing its case. Moreover, they were unambiguous in their proposals. "What you need for a market economy in the countryside is clear—property rights, clear rules of the game, and macroeconomic stability."[27] This perspective compared favorably with the decidedly more complex philosophical, historical, and nationalist arguments of those who questioned the change. In the end the opposition was not able to offer a convincing alternative, especially since the tight fiscal policies of the administration's economic recovery program would rule out any alternative requiring extensive government investment. Furthermore, given the complexity of the agrarian law, the revisions to it, and the technical language in which it was discussed, few outside of government were likely to have understood fully what the revisions meant.

## Implementing Change: How Much? How Fast?

If making new policy to restructure rural property rights proceeded relatively easily, implementing that policy would be a much more daunting process.[28] Under the new laws and regulations, each ejido could decide whether or not its members would receive individual property rights. For such a decision to go into effect, however, a vast number of outstanding ejido claims would have to be settled. There were, in fact, few ejidos in the entire country that did not have disputed boundaries with adjoining ejidos or private landholders.[29] There were fewer still, perhaps only some two thousand five hundred, in which internal disagreements over plot allocations and size were not a major impediment to privatization. Moreover, if a market in land were to be developed, the rights of ejidatarios as individuals needed to be clarified and the value of agricultural land had to be assessed. According to one official source, this would require "a massive effort to regularize, register, and title the estimated 4.6 million agricultural parcels and 4.3 million house plots currently used by residents of ejidos and communal lands."[30]

The reform initiative included establishing an extensive system of land courts, but their procedures and powers needed to be clarified and understood by the ejidatarios and government officials involved in implementing change. The ejidatarios themselves, who were generally the least educated of all Mexicans, needed to be informed of their rights under the new legislation. In 1992, when the new system took effect, it was not clear how many of the ejidos would elect to institute private title to the land, once effective procedures for privatization were developed, although it was expected that most would vote to disband. Not only did the ejidos vary widely in their social solidarity and experiences with corrupt leadership, but the peasants themselves, as we have seen, were pursuing a variety of income-generating activities both on and off ejido lands. After the new law had been in effect for a year, some 10 percent of ejidos had registered in the program that would allow them to obtain individual title to the land.

The expected economic results of expanded property ownership in rural areas would not be seen in the short term either. Raising agricultural productivity was central among the reasons for the change, but production systems on newly privatized land would take time to emerge. Since the 1960s agriculture in Mexico's large landholdings had incorporated substantial expansion of the livestock industry, the globalization of markets, and the introduction of new technologies. But it was not at all clear how far those trends would extend into the small farm and ejido sectors, with the exception of lands with good productive potential that might witness increased investment from domestic and foreign sources, perhaps with a growth in contract agriculture. Foreign investment in the wake of NAFTA was expected to concentrate in other areas of the economy and in only those agricultural sectors in which it was already an important source of financing, such as fruit and vegetable production.[31] There was considerable discussion of the potential for extensive concentration of landholdings and the destruction of rural communities, as poor farmers became forced to sell viable lands and abandon the rest for wage labor, but the dimensions of this could not be anticipated. Finally, the ultimate impact on the rural sector of altered property rights would be complicated by the concurrent elimination of price supports for basic crops and by NAFTA itself.

The political outcomes of the redefined property rights were also unpredictable. By ceasing to be virtual wards of the state, peasant farmers had greater potential to develop autonomous political organizations. This potential became evident in the immediate wake of the Chiapas rebellion of early 1994, as groups all over the country, but particularly in the poverty-stricken southern regions, underscored the demands of the Chiapas-based Zapatista National Liberation Army (EZLN) for "jobs, land, housing, food, health, education, independence, freedom, democracy, justice and peace."[32] The EZLN had also demanded a repeal of NAFTA and the revised Article 27, as well as a redistribution of large landholdings. The demands of peasant groups were taken up by a broad spectrum of local, regional, professional, and nongovernmental organizations, all pressuring the government to open the political system to more just and democratic elections, decisionmaking processes, and policies.

The January uprising in Chiapas illustrates how closed and authoritarian decisionmaking processes—the failure to consult—and repressive responses to citizen demands can widen the gulf between making new laws and actually implementing them. Nevertheless, there was little evidence that the widespread demands for democratic opening and a more responsive government would inhibit the government's promulgation of NAFTA or curtail its efforts to effect economic liberalization in the countryside through Article 27.

Over the longer term, particularly if the bases are laid for a more democratic political system, peasants who survive the introduction of the market and have the potential to increase their productivity under the new system may find new interests and principles around which to organize and relate to the state. They might, for example, become active in existing or newly created crop-specific producer organizations or associations of consumers of agricultural inputs. Through affiliations such as these they might develop the capacity to act through lobbying groups to influence national and more local politics. It is certainly possible that many rural communities and organizations would actively support opposition political parties that promise greater attention to the problems of rural poverty and injustice, as some did in supporting the presidential aspirations of Cuauhtémoc Cárdenas Solórzano—son of Lázaro Cárdenas—in the 1988 presidential election. It will take time, however, to assess the capacity of peasant communities and organizations to operate under the new conditions and to negotiate effectively with the regional and national leaders of the opposition parties.

In the meantime, will the rural bosses and regional strongmen, and those who wielded national political power in the past, find new mechanisms in a market economy and a more open political context to manipulate the rural poor? And how willing is the regime to relinquish its important base of support in rural areas? Repeatedly the technocrats of the Salinas administration demonstrated their dependence on the PRI's ability to deliver the vote that would enable them to carry out their vision of a new market-oriented and internationally competitive Mexico. The use of state resources dedicated to the country's social adjustment program, the National Solidarity Program (PRONASOL), to pull in the vote in 1991, for example, suggested that traditional clientelist political relationships were still a cornerstone of the government's leadership style. In 1993, less than a year before the next presidential election, President Salinas initiated an extensive rural income support program, the Program of Direct Support to the Countryside (PROCAMPO), targeted to producers of basic staples. This program would give peasant producers an economic cushion to adjust to lower prices for commodities once NAFTA was fully implemented. At the same time it promised to be a politically convenient way to shore up rural electoral support. The government's initial response to the peasant uprising in Chiapas further attested to the extent to which old mechanisms of control were still in use. Together these experiences suggest that historic patterns of behavior that have served the regime well in the past would continue to be employed.

Of course, in attempting to establish a political peace in Chiapas and restore legitimacy to the PRI regime, the government has been forced to make concessions to the national, regional, and local demands for reform.

Those concessions have lessened the imbalance of power between the government and the PRI, on the one hand, and those who sought more democratic debate, decisionmaking, and elections, on the other. They meant much greater leeway to contest the right of the PRI to monopolize political power in the future. But the question for the peasants and the organizations formed to represent their interests is the extent to which they will be able to occupy this space, remain organized for political demandmaking over the long term, and compete effectively with other voices and other interests. In the final analysis, then, it is the peasants who will have to be the driving force for altering the conditions that have traditionally bound them to the state.

## Notes

1. Article 17 also established the legal basis of *comunidades,* or agricultural communes of indigenous peoples who had traditionally held land in common. Comunidades are few, and the distinction between them and ejidos is often blurred legally and practically. For the purposes of this chapter, all communally based land-tenure units are referred to as ejidos.

2. The 1857 reforms had allowed for the state's expropriation not only of the large landholdings of the Catholic church but also the communal lands of indigenous villages and other corporately held lands. Further legal changes in the 1880s made it easier for private companies to survey and claim traditional lands. By the eve of the Revolution of 1910, some 90 percent of indigenous communities had lost their lands. The result of a half-century of agrarian capitalism was an extensive system of large landholdings that produced for national and international markets using both wage and feudal or even quasi-slave labor: only a few thousand landowners held almost all of Mexico's arable land. It was these conditions that led to the peasant revolts that accompanied the Revolution. For a vivid description of agrarian conditions before 1910, see John Womack, *Zapata and the Mexican Revolution* (New York: Vintage Books, 1968).

3. Each ejido commission was to be complemented by a vigilance committee, whose job was to ensure that the commissioners were fulfilling their responsibilities to the ejidatarios both legally and equitably.

4. See Billie R. DeWalt and Martha N. Rees, *The End of Agrarian Reform in Mexico: Past Lessons, Future Prospects* (La Jolla: Center for U.S.-Mexican Studies, University of California, San Diego, 1994), p. 4.

5. DeWalt and Rees (ibid.) present an excellent summary and analysis of land use and its determinants in Mexico.

6. In 1976 all rural banking institutions owned by the state, including the Ejidal Bank, were reorganized into the National Rural Credit Bank (BANRURAL).

7. See Arturo Warman, *"We Come to Object": The Peasants of Morelos and the National State* (Baltimore: Johns Hopkins University Press, 1980), on this tradition of rural protest. For a more recent analysis, see Jonathan Fox, "Democratic Rural Development: Leadership Accountability in Regional Peasant Organizations," *Development and Change* 23, no. 2 (1992): 1–36.

8. According to a 1990 agricultural census, 17 percent of ejido land was forest or jungle, 57 percent was pasture, and 4 percent was "other." See DeWalt and Rees, *The End of Agrarian Reform,* p. 10.

9. The policy-based attack on the collective farms is detailed in Gerardo Otero, "The New Agrarian Movement: Self-Managed, Democratic Production," *Latin American Perspectives* 15, no. 4 (1989): 28–59.

10. The increasing bifurcation between peasant agriculture and large-scale commercial agriculture is discussed in Merilee S. Grindle, *State and Countryside: Development Policy and Agrarian Politics in Latin America* (Baltimore: Johns Hopkins University Press, 1986).

11. See Merilee S. Grindle, *Searching for Rural Development: Labor Migration and Employment in Mexico* (Ithaca, N.Y.: Cornell University Press, 1988), p. 59.

12. See CEPAL (Comisión Económica para América Latina), *Economía campesina y agricultura empresarial* (Mexico City: Siglo XXI, 1983).

13. See Grindle, *Searching for Rural Development*, for an analysis of rural poverty and labor migration in Mexico.

14. See ibid., chap. 5 for a discussion of these initiatives.

15. For a review of criticism of Mexico's national development strategy, see Otero, "The New Agrarian Movement." See also CEPAL, *Economía campesina y agricultura empresarial*. Roger Bartra, ed., *Caciquismo y poder político en el México rural* (Mexico City: Siglo XXI, 1975), analyzes the relationship of the peasants to structures of exploitation.

16. The political relationship between peasants and the PRI is well presented in Roger Hansen, *The Politics of Mexican Development* (Baltimore: Johns Hopkins University Press, 1971), and Bartra, *Caciquismo y poder político*. See also Ann L. Craig, "Legal Constraints and Mobilization Strategies in the Countryside," in *Popular Movements and Political Change in Mexico*, ed. Joe Foweraker and Ann L. Craig (Boulder, Colo.: Lynne Rienner Publishers, 1990).

17. Lamartine P. Yates, *Mexico's Agricultural Dilemma* (Tucson: University of Arizona Press, 1981), presents one of the most thoroughly documented arguments against the economic rationale embedded in the structure of the ejido.

18. Lynn Stephen, "Certifying the Future: Reception of Article 27 in Three Oaxacan *Ejidos,* A Preliminary Assessment," (Boston: Department of Anthropology and Sociology, Northeastern University, 1993), provides a useful overview of the legislation.

19. The following discussion draws on Merilee S. Grindle, *Challenging the State: Crisis and Innovation in Latin America and Africa*, forthcoming, chap. 4.

20. Confidential interview, Mexico City, June 22, 1993 (translation by the author).

21. Confidential interview, Mexico City, January 19, 1992 (translation by the author).

22. See Jonathan Fox, "Political Change and Mexico's New Peasant Economy," in *The Politics of Economic Restructuring in Mexico,* ed. Maria Lorena Cook, Kevin Middlebrook, and Juan Molinar Horcasitas (La Jolla: Center for U.S.-Mexican Studies, University of California, San Diego, 1993).

23. Confidential interview, Mexico City, June 19, 1992.

24. See especially Fox, "Democratic Rural Development."

25. See especially Jonathan Fox and Gustavo Gordillo, "Between State and Market: The Campesinos' Quest for Autonomy," in *Mexico's Alternative Political Futures*, ed. Wayne A. Cornelius, Judith Gentleman, and Peter H. Smith (La Jolla: Center for U.S.-Mexican Studies, University of California, San Diego, 1989).

26. "Free-Market Mexico: The Rhythm of the Future," *The Economist,* December 14, 1991, p. 19.

27. Confidential interview, Mexico City, June 24, 1992 (translation by the author).

28. See Stephen, "Certifying the Future," for a useful case study of the implementation of the new legislation.

29. See DeWalt and Rees, *The End of Agrarian Reform*, pp. 22–26.

30. Ibid., p. 3.

31. Ibid., p. 57.

32. As cited in Neil Harvey, *Rebellion in Chiapas: Rural Reforms, Campesino Radicalism, and the Limits to Salinismo* (La Jolla: Center for U.S.-Mexican Studies, University of California, San Diego, 1994). This monograph provides extensive analysis of the uprising.

# 4

# Recent Electoral Reforms in Mexico: Prospects for a Real Multiparty Democracy

## *Jorge Alcocer V.*

Since 1978 Mexico has undertaken a series of four substantive reforms of its political and electoral system. As the federal elections of August 1994 approached, a fifth was being implemented, and the nation had in place a plethora of laws, institutions, procedures, sanctions, and technologies—many of recent vintage and quite a few just months old—all designed to level the electoral playing field between the ruling Institutional Revolutionary Party (PRI) and the other officially registered parties, and to preclude the ignominy attending the government's manipulation of the results of previous elections.[*]

If Mexico had a multiparty system only on paper in the past, today the scene is set for more vigorous political competition. This chapter will document the basic outlines of the electoral reforms of the 1978–1994 period and then offer some perspective on the necessary—but still missing—nexus between fully functioning, puissant political parties and an efficacious legislative branch. I will argue that the 1994 elections represent more than a test of the electoral reforms themselves. More importantly, they promise to be a turning point beyond which both the Mexican Congress and the parties must move to a sixth stage of internal reform if the nation is to become more than merely an "esoteric" democracy.

### The New Legal and Institutional Framework

The laws, rules, and procedures governing Mexico's electoral politics changed little between 1946, when the country's decentralized system was federalized with the creation of the Federal Electoral Commission, and

---

[*]*Note:* This chapter was written prior to the August 21, 1994, elections. To reflect the author's thoughts following the elections a postcript was added before the manuscript went to press.

57

1978, when the government officially registered three new minority parties. Enactment of a new Federal Electoral Code in 1986 kept the ball rolling, but it was the historic three stages of reform instituted during the administration of President Carlos Salinas de Gortari (1988–1994) that signaled a possible end to the decades-old system of state control of elections, electoral players, and electoral outcomes. In fact, all three of the most recent administrations (José López Portillo's, 1976–1982, Miguel de la Madrid's, 1982–1988, and Salinas's) have had to rely on continual evidence of attempted reform as a safety valve to channel the ever-growing public pressure on the electoral system. The reforms listed in Table 4.1 testify to the fluidity of the system over these years, but especially during the Salinas *sexenio*.

In December 1988, just after being sworn in to office, Salinas asked Secretary of the Interior Fernando Gutiérrez Barrios to call a meeting of the leadership of the political parties to discuss terms of new electoral legislation. That action was the inevitable result of bitter public controversy over the authenticity of the federal election results announced in July of that year. Widespread allegations—and much evidence—of fraud had sufficiently proven to the populace that the "official" results, favorable to the PRI in a highly contested election, had been extensively tampered with.

The political opposition was not able to produce sufficient evidence, however, that any other candidate, in particular, the dissident and former PRI member Cuauhtémoc Cárdenas Solórzano, had won instead. But it did manage to show that the vote for the PRI candidate had been fraudulently inflated. Salinas thus had taken office amidst the most vocal civic challenge any Mexican president had faced in the six decades since the ruling party was founded.

In his inaugural speech Salinas had declared:

> Faced with this new reality, my government will seek an opening in our democratic life. To this end, I suggest a new political agreement to strengthen our unity and allow for our differences. It has to be an agreement that improves electoral procedures, updates the party system, and modernizes the practices of the political actors, starting with the government itself.[1]

Based on this commitment, discussions began in January 1989 between the political parties and the government aimed at reforming the Mexican electoral system. The negotiations continued for more than a year and included two national forums for consultations with political scientists and other policy experts. In addition, each party, including the PRI, designated special commissioners, who spent many hours on the issues. Finally, in April 1990 Congress approved an amendment to Article 41 of the Constitution of 1917 that laid the basis for a new Federal Code for Electoral Institutions and Procedures (COFIPE), which in turn passed Congress in July 1990.

**Table 4.1   A Chronology of Recent Electoral Reforms in Mexico, 1978–1994**

| Stage | Year | Key Reforms |
|---|---|---|
| 1. | 1978 | Party system expanded from 4 officially recognized parties (PRI, PAN, PPS, and PARM) to 7 (adding PCM, PST, and PDM); proportional representation introduced in Chamber of Deputies: total number of deputies increased from 300 to 400, of which the original 300 remained "uninominal" (elected by majority vote within each of Mexico's 300 voting districts) and the new 100 seats were to be "plurinominal" (elected according to the percentage of votes cast for each party in each of five zones into which the country is divided for that purpose, with an equal number of representatives from each zone). |
| 2. | 1986–1988 | Federal Electoral Code enacted; Chamber of Deputies enlarged to 500, with 300 uninominal representatives and 200 plurinominal; Senate terms changed from concurrent with the presidential sexenio to half concurrent, half starting at midterm (concurrent terms reinstituted in 1993 reforms). |
| 3. | 1989–1990 | Constitutional amendments to electoral process; Federal Code for Electoral Institutions and Procedures (COFIPE) issued, establishing the independent Federal Electoral Institute (IFE); new electoral registry developed; tamperproof photo IDs issued to voters; sanctioning powers of Federal Electoral Tribunal broadened; "governability" clause enacted, guaranteeing majority of seats in Chamber of Deputies to ruling party. |
| 4. | 1992–1993 | Amendments to Constitution, COFIPE, and electoral law promoting pluralism in Congress (by doubling number of Senate seats from 64 to 128 and guaranteeing 25% of Senate seats to the leading minority party in each state, by preventing any party from holding more than 2/3 of Chamber of Deputies seats, and by repealing "governability" clause); establishing campaign-spending ceilings and prohibiting political contributions by government agencies and officials, the private sector, religious institutions, and foreign individuals and organizations; expanding rules promoting equal access to media coverage of political parties; establishing office for prosecuting electoral crimes and expanding sanctions on such crimes; creating double-blind random lottery to select 800,000 citizens to be trained and serve as polling officials. |
| 5. | 1994 | Multiparty agreements reached on accountability (external audit of voter registry, special prosecutor for electoral crimes, serial numbering of ballot stubs); Citizen Counselors on IFE General Council (proposed by parties not president, elected by 2/3 majority in Chamber of Deputies, and given voting majority on Council, while party representatives to Council lose right to vote on Council decisions); acceptance of international "visitors" during federal elections; new voting booth technologies; electoral registry (to be shared with parties monthly before elections); expanded programs for ensuring reliability of vote counts; expanded free media access to parties, monitoring of coverage by IFE, suspension of party-paid advertising and government promotion of PROCAMPO and PRONASOL programs 10 and 20 days, respectively, before federal elections; restrictions on government officials' political activity; replacement of over 400 electoral officials, including IFE Citizen Counselors, having perceived ties to a political party. |

This first electoral reform of the Salinas years met with opposition from the Party of the Democratic Revolution (PRD), which had been formed in May 1989 to bring together most of the independent forces that had supported Cárdenas's 1988 candidacy. PRD legislators on the whole voted against the constitutional amendment and the COFIPE.

Nevertheless, the importance of the reform can hardly be questioned since it gave rise to the most far-reaching changes in the electoral system since 1946. The old system of direct government control of the electoral process, exercised through the Secretariat of the Interior under the executive, was abandoned. Now elections were defined as a function of the state that would be exercised through a nonpartisan electoral entity, the Federal Electoral Institute (IFE), which would have independent legal status and funding and would comprise representatives of the executive and legislative branches, the political parties, and the citizenry. The role of the IFE would be to oversee federal elections (while counterpart institutes did so in the states and localities) and the multiparty Federal Electoral Tribunal in the latter's work in settling election disputes.

With the IFE the new code created a permanent body of executive-level civil servants charged with carrying out electoral activities under explicit principles of reliability, legality, impartiality, objectivity, and professionalism. By establishing a complex system of checks and balances to prevent any single party, formal or informal alliance of parties, or the government itself from controlling the country's highest electoral body, the code was designed to eliminate the main sources of the 1988 controversy.

The COFIPE also broadened and enhanced the powers of the Federal Electoral Tribunal, although it did not alter the congressional rules of *autocalificación,* by which each house served as the final judge of the election of its members (which allowed the ruling party to declare the election of its own candidates, whatever the ballot results were). Privileges and subsidies granted to the political parties were expanded, as was their involvement in various phases of the electoral process. One significant change, hardly noted by most political analysts, was to eliminate the multiple discretionary powers the electoral law had previously granted to the electoral authorities, which continually forced the Federal Electoral Commission and the state and district commissions, in effect, to make law in the process of interpreting it. Indeed, since 1990 the IFE's General Council (its highest decisionmaking body) and its counterparts in the states and localities have been dedicated more to overseeing enforcement of the law than to making or enforcing it themselves. That task is now delegated to the group of officials that fall under the General Direction of the IFE itself.

The 1990 changes governed the 1991 midterm elections, which covered the full Chamber of Deputies (elected every three years, with a prohibition on running again for the immediate succeeding term) and half of the Senate (elected for six-year terms, with the same prohibition). The

PRI's overwhelming victory in those elections revived the controversy over the law. To the PRD, whose congressmen had voted against the 1990 reform, the 1991 results demonstrated the wrongheadedness of the reform effort and showed that mechanisms precluding fair and legal elections were still in place. To the National Action Party (PAN), which constituted the second-largest party after the PRI, the 1991 results merely spoke to the need for further improvements. All told, then, from the perspective of the opposition, the first stage of the Salinas-sponsored reforms did not pass muster at the polls.

Originally intended to address three issues (party financing, campaign expenses, and the media), new reforms were developed in 1993. Drafted jointly by the PRI and the PAN (the PRD later joined the debate but offered no concrete suggestions), these changes resulted in new amendments to the Constitution and to almost two hundred articles of the COFIPE. Among the most noteworthy were suspending Congress's system of judging its own members' elections; converting the Electoral Tribunal in a judicial entity with full powers to decide on electoral disputes, including having the last word—the right to formulate a body of rules and precedents interpreting the law—on the legitimacy of a disputed election outcome; strictly regulating multiparty coalitions, to the point of rendering them impossible to form in practice; and granting the smaller parties the questionable privilege of maintaining their legal registration status—and thus the right to representation in the Chamber of Deputies—even if they did not obtain the required minimum of 1.5 percent of the national vote. (The Constitution requires that three hundred representatives out of a total of five hundred, or 60 percent, of the lower house be elected directly and the remaining two hundred be designated based on the proportion of votes in federal elections cast for each legally registered party.)

The most controversial of the 1993 changes also concerned the distribution of congressional seats. The 1990 constitutional amendment contained a clause on "governability," which guaranteed the party receiving the most votes in a congressional election the majority of the seats in the Chamber of Deputies. Whereas that clause virtually guaranteed the PRI a lockhold on the lower house, the 1993 reform, which abolished the governability clause, extended set-asides to both the majority party and the second leading party—to the detriment of the other parties.

To compensate at least in part for this problem, the new reform met what had been two long-standing PAN demands: restructuring the Senate, and indirect elections of the local government of the Federal District (Mexico City). The restructuring increased the number of senators from each of Mexico's thirty-one states from two to four and implemented a mixed election system; the majority party in each state would occupy three Senate seats and the fourth would go to the second leading party. (In the past voters elected all their senators directly.) The reform also suspended midterm elections for half of the upper house—a return to the rules in place before 1988, specifying that all Senate terms be concurrent with the presidential sexenio. Politicians and others from a variety of quarters, including within the PRI and the government, strongly questioned this decision, which will require a transition period extending to the year 2000 before all terms are concurrent.

The reform of Mexico City's electoral system expanded the powers of the Assembly of Representatives to the equivalent of a legislative body for the district and also created geographically defined administrative entities called Citizens' Councils that would report directly to the federal government. But it was new provisions on the seating of the district's governor that were controversial.

Since 1924 the local government of Mexico City, which encompasses the territory of the Federal District, has not been elected by the direct vote of its citizens. Under the constitutional system defining the district as "the seat of the Union's powers," the city's governor, called "regent" or "Head of the Department of the Federal District," is appointed directly by the president of Mexico. According to the 1993 reform, beginning in 1997 the president will choose the regent from among the federal or local legislators of the majority party in the Federal District's Assembly of Representatives. In effect, then, this will be an indirect "election" of a strange twist on parliamentary government, which is not surprising in a country with one of the strongest presidential traditions and practices.

The main outlines of the 1993 reforms represent, in my view and others', the principal expression of an unspoken alliance between the ruling party and the PAN, facilitating a political transition not to a multiparty system but to a bipartisan (PRI-PAN) system, particularly in the Congress and local governments. More comparable to the Spanish than, say, the U.S. or Italian systems, the intent here seems to be to allow for a two-way competition for the elective posts while marginalizing the PRD, despite its unquestionable public support.

Until December 1993 political developments seemed to confirm this view. From 1989 to 1993 the PAN had actually had three governors elected for the first time in modern Mexican history; it had the second-largest delegation in the Chamber of Deputies; and it governed more than 30 of the country's 115 major cities, including several state capitals. According to PAN figures, some 18 percent of Mexico's eighty-five million people live under PAN-dominated governments. The PRD, in contrast, has lost political power locally, although it remains the third leading electoral and parliamentary force nationally. It does not govern any major city and has not managed to win any governor's races.

Nonetheless, on January 1, 1994, the sudden outbreak of armed rebellion by the Zapatista National Liberation Army (EZLN) in the state of Chiapas completely transformed the apparently tranquil situation before this federal election year. Unlike earlier administrations facing civic unrest, the Salinas government was confronted not so much with an armed force whose roots, leaders' identities, and financing were (and continue to be) an enigma, but mainly strong national and international condemnation of the state's indiscriminate use of the army to repress the rebellion.

Although it is too soon to assess the full implications of the events in Chiapas, suffice it to note that one of the main demands of the EZLN had to do with the August 1994 federal elections. By making impartial and transparent elections one of its key demands, and urging the resignation of Carlos Salinas as president of Mexico, the EZLN reopened the issue of what legal and practical reforms were needed to foster a fair and lawful transfer of power in December 1994.

Amidst peace talks with the EZLN, on January 27, 1994, the new Secretary of the Interior, Jorge Carpizo, who by law serves as chairman of the IFE General Council, released a document, signed by eight of the nine presidential candidates and their party leaders, under the name "Agreement for Peace, Justice, and Democracy," also known as the "Accord for Political Civility."[2] In the accord the signers committed themselves to adopt by consensus and support a series of changes to guarantee the impartiality of the 1994 elections and, if appropriate, to propose further legal reforms to ensure that implementation of the agreements they reached would be feasible.

After a month of renewed negotiations in which the main actors were the three largest parties and the Secretary of the Interior, on February 28 the first agreements were made public and approved by the IFE General Council. These included an external audit of voter rolls; creation of an independent Technical Council made up of well-respected political scientists and specialists whose job would be to supervise and oversee the audit; ballots attached to a single stub printed with a serial number; new security provisions to guarantee secrecy in the voting booths; flexible rules to provide for the presence and involvement of national electoral observation groups; and a procedure to ensure random and impartial selection of the citizens who would serve as polling officials on election day.

None of these measures required legal reforms. Even so, the PRD's insistence on a new election reform as well as support for this demand by broad sectors of intellectuals and national public opinion, and on the part of the international community, led to a special congressional session in late March 1994 in which new constitutional amendments on electoral procedures were adopted.

That session led to important changes in the composition of Mexico's highest ranking electoral body, the IFE General Council; amendments to the Criminal Code to define electoral crimes and sanction them with exemplary severity; and amendments to several articles of the COFIPE designed to strengthen the impartiality of the electoral bodies at all levels and foster greater citizen participation in observation tasks. Mexico was also to receive electoral observers or "visitors" from abroad for the first time in its history.

The most significant change in the IFE General Council was to end the right of the political parties to vote in electoral bodies at all levels. The political parties will be represented on the electoral bodies on a parity basis, with one representative per party with voice but without vote. Representation of the executive and legislative branches continues unchanged: one commissioner for the executive and four for the legislature (two per chamber, one majority and one minority).

In addition, the requirements for magistrate counselors were changed, dropping the requirement that they be lawyers and henceforth calling them citizen counselors. Proposed by any of the nine registered parties and elected by a two-thirds majority in the Chamber of Deputies, the six citizen counselors now hold a majority of the eleven votes on the Council and are more likely to be persons respected for their independence and impartiality than those appointed in the past.

## The Party System

On paper, Mexico has had a multiparty electoral system since 1929. Never since have federal, state, or local elections been held in other than the manner and time periods prescribed by the Constitution and the electoral law. In practice, however, Mexico has been almost exclusively a one-party-dominant system closed to alternation in power, and for many decades the PRI has been inclined to repress its opponents at the extremes of the political spectrum.

The reform of 1978 expanded the spectrum of party options for the electorate by legally recognizing three new parties: the Mexican Communist Party (PCM), the Socialist Workers' Party (PST), and the Mexican Democratic Party (PDM). These parties joined the four other parties registered at the time (the PRI, the PAN, the Popular Socialist Party, or PPS, and the Authentic Party of the Mexican Revolution, or PARM), to form part of a political system of relative equilibrium that prevailed for ten years. For the "political opening" of 1978, like that of 1986, was nothing if not an example of the saying, "Change everything, so that everything may remain the same."

Indeed, official election results over those years reveal surprising stability of the system. It is true that the PRI, the official party, showed a slight downward trend over the long term, but it continued to come out as the unquestioned winner of all federal, state, and local elections from 1979 to 1985.

In 1988, however, the PRI came apart. The split in the party occasioned by the exit in 1987 of Cuauhtémoc Cárdenas Solórzano, son of the former Mexican president Lázaro Cárdenas (who enjoyed the greatest prestige and respect in the postrevolutionary period), and in that same year of Porfirio Muñoz Ledo, a former PRI party chairman and longtime public servant, shook the power structure. This split was a true schism in the PRI organization that was to signal the course of later events.

Cárdenas went on to win the backing of four of the eight parties legally registered in 1988—the PPS, the PARM, the Party of the Cardenista Front for National Reconstruction (PFCRN), and the Mexican Socialist Party (PMS)—thus generating a bipolar scenario, with the coalition led by Cárdenas, the National Democratic Front (FDN) versus the PRI. When the PRD was legally established in May 1989, the FDN was for all intents and purposes dissolved, as the other three parties in the coalition of 1987–1988 chose not to join. The PPS took refuge in its traditional ideology and conduct as the only party in Mexico that continues to consider itself Marxist-Leninist, while the PFCRN returned to its role as a satellite of the PRI specializing in dirty campaigns against Cárdenas and his backers. The PARM has undergone a series of internal crises that suggest it may dissolve soon.

The 1991 midterm elections were a major step toward the establishment of a system with three major parties (PRI, PAN, PRD), with the inevitable decline and dissolution of the subsystem of minor parties (PPS, PFCRN, PARM). Nonetheless, the PRD has not been able to turn its undeniable influence on public opinion into votes, thus engendering the new bipolar scenario noted earlier—two competitive parties and one radical shadow party. At the same time the government has maneuvered to artificially revive three parties that in 1991 did not receive the minimum number of votes required to retain their legal registration: the Work Party (PT), the Green Ecologist Party of Mexico (PVEM), and the Mexican Democratic Party (PDM). The first two tend to ciphon votes from the PRD, while the third appeals to a similar constituency as the PAN.

Thus, as the 1994 elections approached, Mexico had a formally multipartite system, with nine political parties and nine presidential candidates. Since the 1991 electoral rule changes were designed to impede presidential coalitions, the Mexican voters had to choose among all nine candidates. In reality, however, the competition was among three parties and three candidates: the PRI with Ernesto Zedillo Ponce de León, the PAN with Diego Fernández de Cevallos, and the PRD with Cuauhtémoc Cárdenas.

## Prospects and Predicaments

The assassination of the PRI's original presidential candidate, Luis Donaldo Colosio, on March 23, 1994—combined with the events in Chiapas—

did lend a large measure of uncertainty to the August 1994 elections. This round of federal elections will be a crucial test of how far we Mexicans have come along the path of change. I hope it will prove to be the first step toward a new stage in Mexican politics in which elections finally play the role they are supposed to have in all democratic societies: determining through the free vote of the citizens who is to govern.

## The Preelection Context

For fifty years Mexico's elections were a civic ceremony held to confirm the hegemony of a regime solidly grounded in the legitimacy conferred upon it by its leaders' role in the Revolution of 1910. Following the first of the recent electoral reforms, that of 1978, the situation began to change. Little by little the populace became more aware of the need for a new political system, particularly in the realms of electoral and party politics.

Many things have changed in Mexico since 1978, especially since 1988. Obviously, the economic system has undergone sweeping change, but less has been said, or said objectively, about Mexico's political evolution. Will the Mexican elections of August 21 be carried out in a free and fair manner? I am convinced that we have a better legal framework, improved electoral bodies, and at least some parties prepared to compete in the new environment. Most observers of the Mexican scene consider the current election campaign to be highly competitive. In contrast to the most recent past, the outcomes of the elections are not readily predictable.

The overwhelming hegemony of the PRI is a thing of the past. Other parties seriously aspire to emerge victorious in the presidential election, just as they hope to gain a larger share of the legislative seats up for grabs.

The most historic of the legal reforms since 1978 was adopted right in the midst of the campaign. I say this because the reforms instituted between March and May 1994 represent the first time that electoral change has resulted from and received the support of all three of the major parties. Moreover, the principal changes stemmed from opposition proposals. The electoral bodies are now under the control of citizens with no party affiliation. In the IFE General Council, the highest ranking electoral authority in Mexico, six of the eleven possible votes are held by citizen council members proposed by the parties but elected by a two-thirds majority in the Chamber of Deputies; the other five votes are four legislators (two from the PRI, one from the PRD, and one from the PAN) plus the council president, Secretary of the Interior Jorge Carpizo, who has no party affiliation and is widely respected for his public service. And the council president no longer holds a tiebreaker vote.

In the district and local entities of the IFE (Directive Councils) six of seven votes are held by citizen council members and only one by an officer of the professional electoral service. In each of the IFE entities the political parties shall have voice but not vote and shall be represented on a parity basis, with only one representative per party. This is what many of us have called "citizenization" (*ciudadanización*) of the electoral bodies. In addition, the parties undertook and have completed a review of the electoral officials at all levels. By consensus of the parties the IFE director general was reelected, while 247 members of the executive boards and 170 citizen council members were replaced because of a perceived link to a political party.

Thus, for the first time the government and the ruling party do not control the electoral authorities. This is no small matter. Moreover, practical measures have been agreed upon that are fundamental for guaranteeing free and fair elections. Many facilities and forms of support were provided for election observation by Mexicans, including a technical assistance mission from the United Nations. The IFE General Council laid down the rules for foreign visitors interested in observing Mexican elections; another UN technical mission was to analyze and render a report on the new electoral system; more than forty-four million citizens obtained their tamperproof voter registration card with photo. To date critics of the new voter registration process have yet to produce evidence of allegations of fraud.

On June 30, 1994, the results of the external audit of the voter rolls, supervised by an international business consulting firm, were made known. The most significant finding was that the accuracy and dependability of the voter rolls was placed at 96 percent, while only 4 percent of the registries showed any kind of inconsistency. The same day the parties received a copy on magnetic tape of all the voter rolls. Eleven social scientists of moral repute and prestige were in charge of overseeing the audit. The ballots had serial numbers; the indelible ink that was to be applied on the voters' thumbs before exiting the polling booth was in fact indelible; and polling officials were selected from among the persons registered in the voter rolls through a two-stage random lottery, as proposed by the PRD.

Free time for the parties and candidates on radio and television has been increased by 180 percent of what was available in 1991. In addition, the parties now have free access to 116 spots daily on all radio stations nationwide. Debates among the candidates are broadcast on the national radio and television networks on a noncommercial basis. Paid political advertising in these media will be suspended ten days prior to the elections, and the government agreed to suspend all advertising for its National Solidarity Program (PRONASOL) and its Program of Direct Support to the Countryside (PROCAMPO) twenty days before the elections.

Mexico is not the Greek agora, and it clearly will not be so on August 22. Inertia, special interests, and deep-rooted customs will continue to weigh down the pace of progress, but conditions today are certainly better than in the recent past for free and fair elections.

Electoral irregularities are still possible, but in contrast to the past it is now more feasible to detect them and above all to punish them to ensure that they do not cast a pall on the outcome. The amendments to the Criminal Code and the naming of a special prosecutor for electoral crimes are beginning to have a deterrent effect.

A nationwide poll taken by *Voz y Voto* in June 1994 showed that Mexican citizens were more interested than ever in the elections. Skepticism within broad sectors of the populace had not been completely allayed, but the poll suggested voter turnout would be high. The poll also indicated that in the presidential contest the PAN was gaining most quickly (26 percent), while the PRD was stagnant at its 1991 levels (9 percent).

From January to April 1994 the electoral context was dominated by ominous events and signs. Nonetheless, the reform and the agreements reached by the parties reveal a more hopeful sign: the parties are willing to settle their differences at the negotiating table to ensure that the elections are deserving of the credibility of both the Mexican people and the international community.

## The End of Showcase Multiparty Politics

For millions of Mexicans who came of age in the early 1970s, and for at least the two previous generations, the Mexican political system was like a sphinx sculpted in rock: immovable, impermeable, hardly worn by the years.

It was a sphinx with two faces, however, representing both the fusion and the confusion between a state—paternalistic, nationalistic, and in many cases repressive—and a party, founded in 1929, that was adaptable, amenable to the will and dictates of the president in office, and made up of well-defined sectors and alliances capable of taking in actors ranging from the radical left and guerrilla forces to the modern entrepreneurs who arose in the midst of the patronage and corruption of the Miguel Alemán Valdés administration (1946–1952).

Over these many years there were two functioning political parties, the PRI and the PAN. One was invincible; the other, a born loser. On the sidelines, like sardines alongside the shark, were two shadow parties, the PPS and the PARM. Both reflected more the state's will than a decision by citizens standing up to challenge the powers that be. Even farther off on the sidelines the PRM survived, isolated by the implacable mix of government repression and cooptation, as well as by its own history of unyielding sectarianism. Deprived of legal rights, it subsisted on the margins of electoral life and parliamentary representation.

I recall that in 1973, the first time I was old enough to vote, I did not, simply because it didn't make sense. The same thing happened in 1976 when the shark went it alone, with no sardines to devour in the sea of made-up votes. The PAN, internally divided, decided not to field a presidential candidate. The system encountered no crisis, the sphinx barely moved, but inside the belief flourished that this "Sovietization" of political competition had reached a limit. Despite the PRI Mexico was already a changing country, a changing society, with middle class and popular sectors increasingly critical of the reign of a single party over almost fifty years.

That "esoteric" democracy, as described by Giovanni Sartori,[3] that system of parties organized around a hegemonic will, with a leading party "surrounded by a periphery of secondary parties," was complemented and reinforced by an equally hegemonic configuration of the system of federal powers. The PRI was the center, with one satellite and two asteroids, shaping the federal powers—the executive, the legislature, the judiciary. But the Mexican political system is defined above all else by the president's central role. Authoritarian presidentialism subordinated and turned into its satellites the other two branches of government—indeed, all levels of government—in a republic that is federal in theory but fiercely centralized in practice.

The PRI has been and continues to be an instrument at the service of the president, which inevitably led the Mexican Congress, solidly dominated by the PRI for sixty years, to become a façade, an instrument at the service of the president in office, subjugated to the authoritarian presidentialism that by definition excludes any checks or balances, any room to maneuver.

PRI deputies and senators, still in the majority, know they owe their position not to votes, not to their party, but to the president, who approves the slates. It is that patronage that has made for the "*jibarización*" of Congress (borrowing from *jíbaro,* the disparaging Mexican term for a yokel or rube). Reinforcing the marginalization of the legislature is the antiparliamentary principle of no reelection set down in the Constitution. Self-evident though it may be, we should recall that without even a few career parliamentarians there can be no effective representative government.

And without real parties there can be no real parliament. The legislature is the natural and special forum for the development of political party leaders capable of designing projects and programs that will endure beyond the presidency in which they are proposed. A strong legislature is a sine qua non for a strong party system, and, obviously, in turn, a strong party system will bolster the legislature. Real representative government is also a condition for ensuring that alternation of power will not be destabilizing.

A superficial overview of the experiences of democratic countries is revealing of the fundamental nexus between parties and the legislature, in both parliamentary and presidential systems. Consider, for example, both the United Kingdom and the United States. The separation and balance of powers, federalism, and alternation in power all presuppose a body of practices and institutions, as well as laws, though practices are more important than institutions.

## "Todo por Servir se Acaba"

According to the anecdote, President Adolfo Ruiz Cortínez (1952–1958) used to say, "The chambers [of Congress] and the governors' offices belong to the president; the state assemblies belong to the governors; and the city halls belong to the people." The former president described with well-founded cynicism the struts that had upheld the PRI system of power for more than sixty years. Mexico has not been, not even from afar, a "different" democracy, in the words of T. J. Pempel;[4] it has been, in the best of worlds, merely an "esoteric" democracy. But *todo por servir se acaba*—all things that serve some purpose must come to an end.

The 1978 reform opened the door to new parties, and to make their presence meaningful it changed the make-up of the Chamber of Deputies, introducing proportional representation and increasing the number of deputies to four hundred, of which three hundred were to be "uninominal" (elected by majority vote within each of Mexico's three hundred voting districts) and the remaining one hundred were to be "plurinominal" (elected according to the percentage of votes cast for each party in each of five zones into which the country is divided for that purpose, with an equal number of representatives from each zone). In 1986 the number of deputies was increased again, to five hundred, maintaining the number of directly elected representatives at three hundred and increasing the number of proportional party representatives to two hundred. But this reform was not at all aimed at bringing about a change in the basic structure of the political system, namely, the central role of the president and the hegemony of his party. Reserving one hundred seats in the Chamber of Deputies for a weak opposition, whose presence in most cases did not reach beyond the streets of Mexico City, was a small cost if it worked to refurbish the façade and open a vent for pressures that had built up for too long. Moreover, the Senate was untouched as a forum set aside for the official party.

The remedy worked for ten years, but the sphinx did not emerge, as in the past, untouched. The system of power reached the point of exhaustion more from delegitimation of its economic project and regional rebelliousness than from electoral competition, which would follow on the heels of the delegitimation and rebelliousness rather than precede them. Up to 1978 the main idea was to impede the rise of new parties; beginning that year the pendulum swung back. In 1979 three new parties were registered (PCM, PST, and PDM); in 1982 two more (the Social Democratic Party, PSD, and the Workers' Revolutionary Party, PRT); in 1985 the moribund PARM had to be revived and yet another party was registered (the Mexican Workers' Party, PMT). In 1988 the pendulum swung back again, as the system was considered closed to the registration of new parties. In fact, the four-party (PARM, PPS, PFCRN, PMS) coalition formed to back Cuauhtémoc Cárdenas came as a surprise to many government political strategists.

Once past the summer 1988 crisis the PRI power structure returned to its old strategies—right alongside its reform efforts—with a greater incentive to do so than in the past, considering the registration of the PRD as the party of the belligerent Cardenista forces. For the 1991 election the government reregistered the PDM and PRT, which had lost their party registration in the previous election, and registered two additional parties, the PT and the PVEM. The effort came to naught, as the two revived parties and the two newborns failed to obtain the minimum number of votes required by law and so went into retirement. In 1993 the government adopted the strategy for the 1994 elections, to divide the opposition and impede a new coalition on the left in an effort to fragment the pro-Cárdenas vote.

Of the four dead parties three were revived in a wise equilibrium, with one for the left (PT), another for the right (PDM), and one more for whoever else might come on the scene (PVEM). I wonder whether this history can provide a basis for optimism for the prospects of democracy in Mexico, whether anyone can be pleased with the proliferation of small parties that reproduce and prolong the satellite system that we all knew and suffered from in the early 1970s. I think not.

The recent evolution of the legislative branch holds little more promise. The Chamber of Deputies became the main forum for debate among the parties, while in the Senate the only noises heard until 1988 were the flies interrupting the senators' sweet sleep. Yet no level of debate in the lower house could modify its key feature, its subordination to the executive. In 1986, however, when the new reform brought the number of deputies to five hundred, by increasing the number of proportional party representatives (the plurinominals) to two hundred, no one imagined what would come next.

From 1988 to 1991 the PRI experienced parliamentary terror for the first time in its history. Having only twelve more deputies than constituted a simple majority, and so unable to reform the Constitution by itself, the PRI had to negotiate and make concessions, learn to make alliances, and set in motion an incipient parliamentarianism that entailed sharing some responsibilities and accepting some opposition demands. Unfortunately the lessons did not go beyond the walls of the chamber, and the change did not loosen the president's control; quite the contrary it forced him to strengthen his iron hand over the PRI deputies. Nor did the opposition do much to give impetus to the change, spending its energy and time on squabbles and theatrics. Having the largest number of opposition-party deputies of any Mexican Congress in the century was still insufficient to generate a substantive change in practices or a new relationship among the branches of government.

And so the exhaustion of a paper party system, the continuing subjugation of the legislative branch, and the public's distrust of the electoral system, which has not yet turned around, all serve as a counterweight to the electoral reforms that otherwise might have promised an invigorated party system and a more representative democracy in Mexico by the turn of the century.

## An Ark or a Democracy?

Although Mexico's most recent presidents have largely succeeded in deploying electoral and political reforms as one means of stemming voter unrest, the next president will have no such luxury. The cycle of these reforms extending from 1978 to the 1994 election year has run its course. If after the most recent reform fair and credible elections do not take place, we shall have to bow in humble self-criticism and wait, with ark unbuilt, for the inevitable flood of party recriminations and civil instability.

But no level of fairness and credibility in the conduct of Mexico's electoral politics can any longer deflect attention from the conduct of the nation's *parliamentary* politics. Breaking the mutually reinforcing traditions of showcase multiparty politics and Congress's complete subservience to the president is the essential condition for the act of voting to have any meaning.

I believe the direction and pace of that next step toward a truer democracy will require a certain sequence: the party system must be reconfigured before Congress can be expected to function as a representative body. "Satellitization" has already effectively come to an end with the end of the state's ability to create and protect minority parties. One need not be an enemy of multiparty politics to propose a weeding out of the smallest and weakest of the parties so that the three current frontrunners can consolidate their messages, agendas, and constituencies.

Two of these three, the PRI and the PRD, continue to be enigmatic, for different reasons. The third, the PAN, appears more stable, more finished, and better prepared for the new electoral and political context.

Two hypotheses are usually offered regarding the old official party. One is optimistic, affirming the PRI's potential to become a real party, separate from the government, capable of independently acquiring and exercising power in the two houses of Congress. The other view, pessimistic, holds that the PRI is incapable of transforming itself, that its destiny lies in the contradictory poles of Mexican society, and that as long as it holds on to power—namely, the presidency—it will survive as is, but if it loses the presidency, it will dissolve.

The other enigma, the PRD, itself arose from a split in the PRI and has since been an amalgam of groups, ideologies, and tendencies. More than a party, it became a coalition of discontents, whose watchwords were nevertheless clear: opposing the PRI, and promising land in return for victory at the polls in 1994, which will always be an explosive mix. To date the PRD is the firmest paradigm of a challenging, almost testimonial group. Its influence on public opinion continues to be respectable, although that is almost entirely a function of the charisma of the party's leader and presidential candidate.

If Cárdenas were to win the presidency, a hypothesis worth considering, the PRD would not remain as we know it today. The party's coalition would necessarily become more inclusive, with room for those who would step over from the inevitable splits that would occur in the PRI and to a lesser extent in the PAN. A PRD victory would lend unprecedented importance to the legislative branch as well as local governments, which would be reorganized as salient factors in a new political equilibrium.

If Cárdenas does not win this, his second, bid for the presidency, on August 22 the PRD will face the question, Where do we go from here? One likely answer would be to continue down the beaten path: settle its accounts, and then bet on a third round. Another is possible, though: embracing a new project and perspective, which would first require consolidating the party internally so as then to rework its outward orientation. This latter tack might work, depending on national and international confidence in the election results. But win or lose, the PRD may have completed its cycle. It was born to back a single man, and to him its future is inexorably tied.

If I have given short shrift to the PAN in this discussion, it is because of what I noted above. This party has put forth a new program in recent years, a strategy for a nontraumatic political transition in which it would be a leading force, in or out of government. For the PAN the future is not posed in extreme terms, and the August elections are not the life-or-death matter they are for the PRI and the PRD. The PAN considers itself prepared to govern, although it may be better prepared to co-govern.

Regarding Congress, I will reiterate my hypothesis on the line of causality: if the party system changes, the legislature will change. I do not deny other possibilities, borne out in the experiences of other nations, such as new majorities giving rise to unstable situations of co-governance, or reforms from above if euthanasia of Mexico's authoritarian presidentialism is imaginable. But these possibilities are quite remote. In any event, congressional reform must perforce include a change in the numerical composition of the body. And as the fifty-fourth session of the Chamber of Deputies demonstrated in spades, a good measure of intelligence and pragmatism on all sides will be required.

I conclude with an observation and a hope. Although the prospects for a more representative democracy in Mexico are not yet strong, and its risks are great, we should not underestimate the importance of what the parties themselves have shown over the past few months. Unlike its predecessors this last stage of electoral reform for the most part did not go through Congress but instead was the result of genuine dialogue and consensus among the parties. Its immediate result may be a democratic election. The hope is that its longer term consequence will be to encourage the parties to strengthen themselves, so that they can then turn their sights to Congress, the locus in which Mexico must begin to express the plural mosaic of its diversity with mutual respect and tolerance.

## Postcript

The elections of August 21, 1994, did not produce a dramatic change in the balance of power among the parties, although voter turnout was the highest in Mexico's history, with over 35.5 million voters, or nearly 80 percent of those registered, casting a ballot. Based on preliminary results (before the Federal Electoral Commission performed its duties), the PRI was able to maintain its hold on a majority of the presidential vote, at 48 percent. The PAN regained second place (which it had lost to Cárdenas in 1988), and for the first time in its history, it received more than a fifth of the vote, with 27 percent. The PRD, on the other hand, consolidated its standing with 17 percent, receiving almost the same number of votes as it had in 1988 (6 million). Far behind in fourth place was the PT, with only 3 percent. Thus, the contest was not as close as had been anticipated, but the PRI did not obtain an absolute majority.

In the Chamber of Deputies, thanks to the constitutional regulations on the distribution of plurinominal seats, the PRI will have 300 representatives of the total 500, while in the Senate the party will have an overwhelming majority, with 95 of the 128 seats.

The PRI has held on to the presidency in what most Mexican and foreign analysts consider to have been the cleanest election in the nation's history. In the weeks following the elections the two opposition parties have adopted divergent views. The PAN has denounced multiple electoral irregularities but recognizes that the overall results and the results for each party would not be substantially different if the results they consider fraudulent are corrected. More specifically, party officials accept the fact that the PRI won the presidency, but they dispute spaces in the two federal chambers and in some states (for example, the mayoralty of Monterrey, the capital of the strategically situated state of Nuevo León, which shares borders with Texas, has since been adjudicated by the magistrates of the electoral tribunal to the PAN candidate).

The PRD has not moved from its line of complete dissatisfaction with the election results. Its denouncements refer to a "discommunal fraud" in which ten million citizens were impeded from voting and another ten million votes were falsified in favor of Ernesto Zedillo. The truth is that neither Cárdenas nor other PRD officials have been able to support their accusations with evidence, which would be necessary for the PRD to petition for nullifying the elections and holding new ones.

Beyond these reactions, what is significant is that there has not been any popular mobilization in support of the accusations of fraud, and in the entire country it is openly accepted that the PRI's candidate will be the next president of Mexico. Ernesto Zedillo Ponce de León will therefore take office without having to shoulder the ghost that haunted Carlos Salinas during his six years in office—the ghost called fraud.

## Notes

1. Presidencia de la República, Dirección General de Comunicación Social, "El Gobierno Mexicano," no. 1 (Mexico City: Presidency of the Republic, December 1988), p. 31.

2. The Popular Socialist Party (PPS) did not sign.

3. Giovanni Sartori, *Parties and Party Systems: A Framework for Analysis* (Cambridge: Cambridge University Press, 1976), p. 283.

4. T. J. Pempel, ed., *Uncommon Democracies: The One-Party Dominant Regimes* (Ithaca, N.Y.: Cornell University Press, 1990).

# = 5 =

# Entrepreneurial Interests and Political Action in Mexico: Facing the Demands of Economic Modernization

## *Matilde Luna*

The economic and institutional reforms promoted by the Mexican government since the mid-1980s have had a significant impact on the business world and on relations between the government and the private sector. Traditionally, Mexican business has had economic but not political power, but the new national emphasis on achieving a free-market, open economy linked, most closely, with the North American market, has mobilized business leaders throughout Mexico to seek greater influence in national politics. Recent public airing of business's concerns can be viewed as a likely prelude to future negotiations over the nature of further, much-needed microeconomic reforms and national industrial policies.

The process of modernizing the Mexican economy has unfolded through a mutual interest on the part of the government and various social sectors, especially entrepreneurs, to move from the postrevolutionary social order governed by the state to an order governed by market forces, in which competition—both economic and political—has become a fundamental value.[1]

Consequently, public policy discourse in recent years often accorded the private sector the key role in the development process. Although the state has come to play a new interventionist role in this process, the form and functions of that role are very different from past patterns, with the state transforming itself from a proprietor and regulator to a facilitator of development. More specifically, the state now views its role as setting the direction and framework for efficient private sector performance.

Two sets of policy changes in particular have served to redefine the role of the private sector itself in development. First has been the opening of the Mexican economy to free trade, symbolically marked by Mexico's entry into the General Agreement on Tariffs and Trade (GATT) in 1985 and by its signing of the North American Free Trade Agreement (NAFTA) in 1993. Consonant with principles of free trade are priorities to abandon market protectionism and production subsidies, promote exports, and open the country to foreign investment. Second is the broad array of institutional reforms promulgated by the administration of Carlos Salinas de Gortari (1988–1994), which includes several measures certain to alter the basic rules and outlines of economic activity in Mexico, namely:

- Reducing the size of the public sector and curtailing government spending
- Accelerating the privatization of public enterprises, most notably the banks
- Deregulating many aspects of industries and markets
- Redirecting the role and functions of the state, as noted above, from an interventionist to a facilitative stance toward business

These reforms have also included major political-administrative changes, such as eliminating the powerful Secretariat for Programming and Budget, as part of the strategy to accord greater weight to market forces, and granting autonomy to the Bank of Mexico. Along with other fiscal and financial reforms, these have tended to restore to the private sector the power it traditionally held before the nationalization of the banking system in 1982, albeit in new forms.

In the light of this changing framework of economic activity and political action by the business class in Mexico, this chapter will first define the traditional role business has played in Mexican politics and then identify recent ideological divisions within the business community, the emergence of a new political discourse by the private sector, and the role it has played in public policy formulation. To conclude, I identify the challenges facing both business and the government in fashioning new rules, structures, and roles to achieve the broader macroeconomic program of market reform. Throughout, the discussion is necessarily exploratory, as Mexican society on the whole is undergoing rapid and large-scale transformations.

## Background: The Corporatist Tradition, 1940–1981

Relations between the state and business from the 1940s to the 1980s have commonly been characterized as following a "corporatist" model, that is, a highly elaborated balance of power among the key actors in the economic and political life of the nation: government, business, and labor. While workers have long had ready access to political power in Mexico because of the union bureaucracy's status as a key member of the Institutional Revolutionary Party (PRI), business executives were excluded from politics by law, as explained below. For its part the government performed its role as arbiter between labor and business based on the political and economic power it derived from the presidentialist regime and its interventionist powers.

The legal basis for the private sector's role in the political system is contained in Articles 73 and 123 of the Mexican Constitution of 1917. Article 73 grants the right of workers and employers "to join together in defense of their respective interests," while Article 123 calls for "balance among all the factors of production" and "harmonization" of their rights by the state.

The Law of Chambers of Commerce and Industry of 1936, still in force today, established compulsory affiliation of business owners with their corresponding commerce or industry chambers and defined these organizations as "organs of consultation for state," subject to government regulation. The same law prohibited business leaders and business associations from participating in party politics. Over the years the private sector has tacitly accepted this law, although not without engaging in complex forms of informal lobbying of the government.

Formal exclusion of the private sector as a political actor in Mexico is grounded in the popular, grassroots ideology of the Mexican Revolution, which has informed all the governments in power since 1917. Most notable in this regard is the PRI's consistent exclusion of the private sector from party membership.

The founding of the Business Coordinating Council (*Consejo Coordinador Empresarial,* or CCE) in 1975 brought together for the first time the main industrywide associations as well as other national private sector associations. The CCE represented an important change in the structure of private sector interest representation in two respects: first, it sought to represent all of the business class nationwide under one organization, and second, it arose voluntarily, independent of the government (as opposed to the legally mandated membership in chambers of commerce and industry). Although the CCE originated from the business movement that opposed the "statist" reform program of president Luis Echeverría Alvarez (1970–1976), during the *sexenio* of José López Portillo (1976–1982)—until before the nationalization of the banking system—the council limited its activities to negotiating certain aspects of economic policy that favored the private sector.

Given the legal proscriptions on political activity by the private sector, the one sphere in which substantive interactions between government and business was allowed was in the core set of financial institutions—the Secretariat of the Treasury and Public Credit, the now-defunct Secretariat for Programming and Budget, the Bank of Mexico, and the private financial sector—that together (as the principal sources of capital and credit for Mexican businesses) guided the course of economic development.

## Politicization of the Business Community, 1982–1987

The government's unilateral decision to nationalize the banking system in September 1982 was therefore a key element in altering relations between business and government, since it, in effect, dismantled the traditional structures for guiding economic development. As could be expected, two issues were particularly sensitive to business leaders: the more philosophical issue of the expansion of state intervention into the operations of the private sector, and the more practical problem of the government's having broken the rule of obligatory consultation.

As a result, the private sector became increasingly vocal and active in the political life of Mexico beginning in 1982. Business associations became hotbeds of debate over political ideologies and strategies and by the late 1980s had shifted from a characteristically *reactive* stance toward the government to a new *propositional* and in some cases even *oppositional* stance.

Two main ideological currents evolved within the business community over the 1980s that would come to prominence in national debates by the time of the 1988 presidential election: technocratic (or pragmatic) liberalism, and conservative liberalism. A third, less commonly voiced ideology revolved around calls for greater government protectionism of the Mexican market. Table 5.1 identifies the leading proponents of each position within the CCE.

While proponents in both of the first two camps have sought to weaken the power of the state and free up market forces, and both share a desire for further political-administrative reforms favoring business, the technocratic liberals have emphasized the primacy of free-market, productivity, and efficiency considerations over what they characterize as more distributive, populist, and political criteria for determining public policies on the economy. Not surprisingly, since their agenda has echoed that of the De la Madrid (1982–1988) and Salinas administrations, the technocratic liberals have exhibited a greater willingness to negotiate directly with government officials and consider themselves to have played a decisive role in decisionmaking on public issues in recent years—in effect, fashioning a bipartisan arrangement between business and the state. They applaud the concurrent waning of labor's economic and political influence over these same years (see Chapter 2).

The principal proponents of technocratic liberalism, as shown in the table, are large-scale capital and the financial and export sectors, largely based in Mexico City, whose industry associations tend to be highly centralized.

The conservative liberals, by contrast, have a more confrontational stance toward the government, raising more sweeping demands based on the hypothesis of a close relationship between market predominance,

Table 5.1   Ideological Factions and Principal Members of the Business Coordinating Council (CCE)

| Characteristic | Technocratic liberalism | Conservative liberalism | Protectionism |
|---|---|---|---|
| Principle sectors | Financial, export | Services | Manufacturing |
| Size of businesses in member organizations | Large | Large and small to mid-sized | Small to mid-sized |
| Structure of member organizations | Centralized | Decentralized | Decentralized |
| Most prominent member organizations | Mexican Council of Business Executives (CMHN) Mexican Association of Brokerage Houses (AMCB) Mexican Association of Insurance Institutions (AMIS) Mexican Association of Banks Confederation of Chambers of Industry (Concamin)[a] | Employers' Federation of the Mexican Republic (Coparmex) Confederation of National Chambers of Commerce, Services, and Tourism (Concanaco) National Agricultural Council (CNA) | National Chamber of Manufacturing Industries (Canacintra) |

*Source:* Matilde Luna and Ricardo Tirado, "El Consejo Coordinador Empresarial: Una radiografía," *Cuadernos del Proyecto Organizaciones Empresariales en México,* no. 1 (Mexico City: Institute for Social Research, National Autonomous University of Mexico, 1992).

*Notes:* The CCE has 8 affiliated organizations and some 900,000 indirect affiliates.

a. As explained in this chapter, Concamin holds an ambivalent position—both technocratic liberal and protectionist—given that Canacintra (a protectionist organization) is formally part of Concamin.

liberal democracy, and an ethic of upholding private initiative, the family, religion, and the teaching of "transcendent values"—in short, calling for a profound transformation of civil society and Mexican culture itself. The conservatives have also tended to exercise political power more directly, by establishing alliances with the National Action Party (PAN) and the hierarchy of the Catholic Church. These activist tendencies have led, at least in part, to what is a novel demand to emanate from the business sector—to democratize the political system—and to further calls for a wide-ranging debate to legitimate political action by business.

The conservative liberal current is backed by a broad mix of large, mid-sized, and small employers ranging from manufacturers to service firms, and it enjoys strong regional support. The main employer associations supporting the conservative agenda include Mexico's only employers' union, the Employers' Federation of the Republic of Mexico

(Coparmex) as well as the Confederation of National Chambers of Commerce (Concanaco); these tend to function as relatively decentralized organizations.[2]

Within the CCE the technocratic liberal current has predominated, despite the relatively small number of its adherents. Promoting the technocratic approach are four associations (the elite Mexican Council of Business Executives, the Mexican Association of Brokerage Houses, the Mexican Association of Insurance Institutions, and the Mexican Association of Banks), which account for only 0.016 percent of the indirect affiliates of the CCE yet hold 50 percent of the votes.

The protectionist current, represented by the National Chamber of Manufacturing Industries (Canacintra), has played a marginal role in the debate within and outside the CCE. Canacintra enjoys relative political autonomy with respect to the Confederation of Chambers of Industry (Concamin), although formally it belongs to the confederation (which is why it is included at the same level as all the other associations). Largely because Canacintra is one of Concamin's largest affiliates, the confederation has adopted an ambivalent stance toward the issues, but it also includes some of the most important businesses in terms of their economic power.

From 1982 to 1987 the opposing viewpoints represented by these three ideological currents played themselves out in a very complex manner. Nonetheless, by the time the 1988 presidential election approached, the conservative liberal tendency had become ascendant, reaching a high point in the PAN candidacy of Manuel J. Clouthier. A well-known business leader, Clouthier was a former director of several regional business associations and also of such first-tier organizations as Coparmex and the CCE.

## Toward a Participatory Strategy, 1988–1994

The results of the 1988 election led to a shift in strategy by both the technocratic and the conservative liberals. The former began to be more active politically and publicly, while the latter shifted the nature of their discourse, notably attenuating their belligerence toward the government. In general, both groups moved from a propositional posture promoting principles of business organization and values for the nation's economic, social, and political systems to a more active involvement in public policy decisionmaking. This transition was facilitated by the reforms undertaken by the new Salinas administration.

Not only had the conservatives' candidate, Clouthier, lost his bid for the presidency, but the left-leaning Party of the Democratic Revolution (PRD) made an unexpectedly strong showing. Coupled with the depth of the economic crisis and the breadth and direction of the changes on Salinas' horizon, these events forced the conservatives to reconsider the more radical aspects of their preelection agenda.

More specifically, the emergence of the PRD led the most radical current of the private sector, which had backed the PAN, to let up in its criticism of the PRI. Clouthier's premature death in October 1989 also seemed to have contributed to the low profile of the conservative liberals, as it was his charismatic leadership that had mobilized business executives to become involved in party activities and election campaigns.

While the business associations pulled back politically,[3] individual entrepreneurs legitimated their political action. This was the result of two parallel processes. On the one hand, they held a direct public confrontation to construct themselves as valid political actors. On the other, they promoted an image of good subjects in any sphere as an indirect generalization of the idea that they were key economic agents. Since then they have participated actively in public life, occupying administrative posts and elective office as candidates of both the PRI and the PAN.[4]

The depth of the economic crisis facing Mexico since 1982 contributed significantly to a certain internal unity in the business community and its leaders' willingness to seek policies for addressing the crisis together with the government. This interest was expressed, for example, in the tripartite economic pacts that began in 1987 with the participation of the government, the private sector, and the "social sector."[5]

Tensions were also eased by the Salinas administration's proposed reforms, which included significant constitutional amendments on issues that had concerned the radical conservatives, such as education, the churches, and land tenure (as described in other chapters in this volume). Several of the specific reforms opened up areas that had been the exclusive domain of the state, such as education, to the organized participation of employers.[6]

Within the framework of this process of political distension, it was the major economic groups that played a leading role in promoting the structural change in the Mexican economy. This helps to explain the currently ascending leadership of the technocratic liberal tendency.

But it was not just individual entrepreneurs who were becoming political actors in Mexico. In the second half of the 1980s the CCE itself came to be directed by prominent business executives, giving rise to a high degree of concentration of both economic and political power in this important structure for interest representation. Unlike earlier CCE leaders, Claudio X. González (1985–1987), Agustín F. Legorreta (1987–1989), and Rolando Vega (1989–1991) were director-shareholders of large conglomerates tied to the export sector and the refurbished financial sector, and their experience in the elite business organizations and degrees from prestigious Mexican and foreign universities lent them greater credibility than their predecessors.[7]

While the conservative liberals have been deemphasizing their participation in the PAN, many of the CCE leaders and other business executives affiliated with the select Mexican Council of Business Owners
(CMHN) have become more closely associated with the PRI and more
involved in committees and employer associations linked to the PRI.[8]

## Forces Polarizing Entrepreneurs

The reorganization and opening of the Mexican economy have had a substantial effect on the interests of private sector firms. Company and industry interests in next steps for the nation's economic agenda vary widely,
depending on whether the firms in question produce for the domestic or international market; their geographic location, such as in the border regions
of the north or regions whose principal products face strong international
competition; the extent of their access to financial resources, for example,
through their links with the new banking groups formed since the repriva-
tization of the banks in 1991; their technological capabilities; the extent of
their integration in productive chains; their market share; and their involvement in high-technology sectors.

The size of the enterprise is a more critical factor today than in the
past. Salinas's new economic development policies have heightened
the economic power of large enterprises and led to the creation of others
geared primarily to the financial markets and international competition.
The new policy most notable in this regard is the privatization of state-
owned financial and nonfinancial enterprises, such as Teléfonos de México, the Cananea Mining Co., Aeronaves de México, Fomento Azucarero,
Banamex, Bancomer, and Serfin.

Although the president has recognized the importance of small enterprises, especially in generating new jobs, he has been criticized for his
lack of attention to small business. His explicit program through the end of
his term continued to emphasize that encouragement was needed for large-
scale companies to create the conditions necessary for Mexico to compete
in the major international markets.[9]

According to the 1988 census, small businesses and microenterprises
made up 99.5 percent of all Mexican firms but accounted for only 64.4
percent of the labor force and only 49.8 percent of the incomes measured.
In contrast, large establishments made up only 0.18 percent of all firms yet
employed 24.7 percent of the labor force and generated 37.3 percent of
incomes.[10]

By the early 1990s the private conglomerates were clearly growing
much stronger, in some cases taking on monopolistic dimensions. The large-
scale companies are characterized by their concentration of activities in only
a few sectors, in a limited number of conglomerates, and in geographically

concentrated locations. According to the 1990 census, of the ninety-eight largest conglomerates registered in Mexico six alone accounted for 40 percent of total assets (86.1 percent if Petróleos Mexicanos, or PEMEX, is included), and 50 percent of sales were concentrated in the ten leading conglomerates and in nine sectors (excluding PEMEX once again). As for geographic concentration, 59.8 percent of sales, 70.1 percent of assets, and 68.6 percent of employment were in the Federal District (metropolitan Mexico City), while the percentages for the industrialized state of Nuevo León were 23.7 percent, 16.7 percent, and 12.5 percent, respectively.[11]

The growing importance of large companies in the national economy is perhaps best illustrated by their sales as a percentage of the gross domestic product, which rose from 20.0 percent in 1987 to 31.1 percent in 1992.[12] The number of "super rich" entrepreneurs, according to *Forbes* magazine, jumped from two to twenty-four from 1991 to 1994.[13]

In the manufacturing sector only 1.3 percent of the firms accounted for 71.8 percent of aggregate value in 1990, while at the other extreme, the microenterprises, which accounted for 86.9 percent of all manufacturing enterprises, provided only 4.7 percent of aggregate value.[14]

From a broader perspective, it has been noted that government strategy in the privatizations sought to reallocate the property of the large public companies mainly among the major national private sector oligopolies, but also to some conglomerates that had been medium-scale and have more recently become giants—giving rise to new and very powerful economic actors. These are large conglomerates that in addition to having a dominant weight in the domestic market have become increasingly transnational in scope, and have sought to establish strategic alliances with foreign capital, with which they share a leading role in Mexican exports. And in privatizing the financial enterprises, the government reproduced the traditional duopolistic domination of the financial market by Banamex and Bancomer.[15]

It should be noted that in the process of disincorporation, forms of "corporatist negotiations," or what has been called "high-tech political clientelism,"[16] have dominated more than market forces. These negotiations have entailed government allocation of state-owned companies to large private conglomerates through reciprocal commitments, concessions, and personal favors at the highest level.

Polarization in the organized efforts of entrepreneurs had its first significant political expression in an unprecedented conflict over leadership of the CCE in 1989–1990. The clash of interests resulted in the election of an interim president (Rolando Vega) for six months. His post was finally ratified after several months of intense debate among the various business associations grouped in the two major camps (the technocratic and conservative liberal interest groups identified above), as well as changes in procedures for electing CCE leaders. The procedural changes partly made up for the marginal role that small and medium-sized as well as provincial firms had in designating the leadership of the CCE. Again, these smaller and less influential enterprises were primarily represented by the conservative Coparmex and Concanaco and garnered additional support from the National Agricultural Council.[17]

The difference between these more recent conflicts and those of the 1982–1987 period lies precisely in the marginalization of the small, mid-sized, and provincial businesses. Earlier the conflicts had been primarily ideological; now they were over more fundamental matters of economic power. During the course of the NAFTA negotiations in the early 1990s, associations were created or reenergized to represent these sectors, while the historical representative of these sectors—Canacintra and other associations of the smaller firms (such as ANIT, the National Association of Manufacturing Industries) and regional business associations (mainly from Monterrey) challenged the leaders of the Coordinating Body of Foreign Trade Business Associations (COECE), which was created in June 1990 to formally represent the entire Mexican private sector but whose direction was from the start controlled by the large enterprises.

Time and again in the framework of the negotiations the leaders of the associations of smaller firms pointed out that they had not been taken into account and that NAFTA would benefit only the large consortia. They demanded information and procedures for obtaining credit from the financial institutions so that it would not be directed solely to export activities.[18]

If we bear in mind that the CCE has been the central force in the articulation of organized action by business, since the mid-1980s the small and mid-sized entrepreneurs have asserted their interests through three main channels: first, within the CCE, through the chambers to which they belong by law, particularly Canacintra, and through organizations such as the Confederation of National Chambers of Commerce, Services, and Tourism (Concanaco) and the Employers' Federation of the Mexican Republic (Coparmex); second, outside of the CCE and opposed to it, through recently created dissident organizations, namely ANIT and the National Federation of Microindustries (Conamin); and third, outside of the CCE but without opposing its general direction, namely through the Association of Mexican Entrepreneurs (Mimexa) and the credit unions supported by the government.[19]

Despite all the forces leaving rifts in the Mexican business community—including both ideological differences and severe differences in economic power—several trends in the past few years may actually strengthen its unity. The prospect of an integrated North American market is demanding greater cohesion and was a principal motivation for the 1990 creation of the COECE, which draws on the existing institutional infrastructure, with the CCE at the vertex, to bring together the country's most important business organizations as well as associations explicitly linked to foreign trade that had formerly been dispersed. In fact, the explicit mission of the COECE is to establish a broad-based business-government alliance to mitigate Mexico's economic disadvantages with respect to its neighbors to the north.

In effect, then, the COECE is an even broader umbrella group than the CCE, with a broader mission. And its formation has lent greater power to the major groups in the structure for interest representation.

Several other forces point to the possibility of greater cohesión in the business community in the future:

- Mobilizing economic activity around NAFTA as a principal means to end the nation's more than decade-long economic crisis
- Recent changes in the by-laws of the CCE, which have indirectly opened it up to new interests by enabling affiliated organizations, based on seniority, to propose a slate for the association's leadership; and changes in the COECE that require bringing smaller and formerly underrepresented industries into the trade negotiations—industries such as textiles and footwear, which grew in prominence because of concerns raised in the context of the negotiations among Mexico, the United States, and Canada
- Penalizing the expression of autonomous positions by the member organizations of the COECE through a confidentiality agreement that evoked highly corporatist features. Despite numerous violations, the penalties have been an important factor in disciplining the members
- A tacit agreement on a division of functions between the government and the conglomerates that have exercised leadership of the COECE, which suggested that the marginalized entrepreneurs would survive, and which was concretized in March 1991 with the government program for modernization of small and medium businesses and microindustries ("Programa para la modernización de la micro, pequeña y mediana industria, 1991–1994"). In addition, the collective action of this sector was channeled through the credit, purchasing, and marketing unions that, beginning in 1992, were fostered by Nacional Financiera, the federal agency in charge of providing credit to small and medium-sized businesses
- The rapid growth, instability, and heterogeneity of the microenterprise sector, which prevents the sector from creating an organization that might counterbalance the economic power of the major conglomerates[20]

## Problems and Prospects for State-Business Relations

Mexico is entering the 1990s with an open economy and relative macroeconomic stability.[21] Although that stability is a necessary condition for

further economic development and international competitiveness, it is not
sufficient; the economy still faces major constraints to achieving a sustained cycle of investment, growth, and job creation. Indeed, for the last
thirteen years industrialization has been stagnant.[22]

Of particular concern is microeconomic reform—that is, efficiency at
the level of the firm or plant—which has come too little and late. The new
conditions being imposed by the globalization of the world's economies
are demanding a strengthened organization culture oriented toward labor-
management cooperation and high productivity and efficiency. The prime
symbol of this new business culture is the innovative entrepreneur who in-
troduces new technologies and new forms of organization for labor, sensitive to the need to increase the standard of living of workers as a condition
for development and interested in education and training as necessary conditions for increasing the productivity and quality of their workers' economic performance.

In recent years both the government and entrepreneurs in general have
coalesced in recognizing microeconomic reform as a priority for moving
to a new stage of development. As Germán Cárcoba, the president of the
CCE, stated, "The macroeconomic masterpiece needs to be made into the
masterpiece for cultural change in society, which in turn supports the masterpiece of total transformation of microeconomics of the firm."[23] Two demands the business sector is making of the government are germane here:
to further educational reform and to effect substantive changes in labor
legislation. For the government the central concern in achieving economic
recovery is the continuing problem of high rates of unemployment.

But though they may agree on basic goals, the problem lies in the details. A harsh debate prevails between the state and business over who
should promote the reforms, and how. While government officials and
even President Salinas himself emphasized that microeconomic reform
was mainly up to the entrepreneurs,[24] a new business current represented
by Coparmex, Concanaco, and Canacintra warned that microeconomic efficiency depends not only on the internal organization of each productive
unit and on macroeconomic stability, but also on an effective competitive
economic environment, pointing to the need for a well-articulated and effective industrial policy.

Most recently, business criticism has targeted the newly privatized
banking sector and the Secretariat of Treasury and Public Credit as responsible for the continuing lack of capital and absence of tax incentives
for production, and the Secretariat of Commerce and Industrial Development as failing to establish any plan for industrial modernization.

Business demands on the government to adopt an industrial policy are
well summarized in the document "Proposals from the Private Sector for
the 1994–2000 Sexenio," published by Coparmex, Concanaco, and Canacintra in early March 1994.[25] Expressing serious concern over the status of

small and medium-sized businesses and microenterprises, the briefing calls for a far-reaching industrial policy, one not constrained by generalities but targeted to the needs and characteristics of each main sector of the economy. This demand recognizes three very basic conditions that prevail in Mexican industry: the coexistence of modern businesses with traditional ones whose modernization requires very specific actions; uneven advances in manufacturing technologies; and imbalanced development across regions. Further proposals for the industrial policy include solid financial support; modernization of infrastructure; further deregulation, particularly at the state and municipal levels; and retaining and expanding the newly created or reinvigorated structures of state-business policy negotiation and coordination.

The debate, though no doubt fed by the impending presidential election of 1994, focuses on two long-standing issues of national policy: the monopoly of interest representation in the private sector by the business elites, and the continually shifting role of the state in the economy.

As to the monopolistic influence of the business elites, there is an underlying differentiation or polarization in the private sector based on industries—such as manufacturers versus bankers—as well as on firm size, which in turn is related in part to the marginalization of regional interests. It is no coincidence that a new alliance has taken shape among associations with such diverse ideologies as Coparmex and Concanaco, which have pursued the conservative liberal agenda, and Canacintra, the traditional representative of the protectionist agenda. All three associations share a common base of smaller firms, and all three have a decentralized structure. Together the alliance members have a chance of countering the political influence seized in recent years by the large conglomerates.

These concerns are not unrelated to the question of the type of state that the new economy needs. Representatives of provincial industries have taken a much more belligerent stance toward the government than the national associations, pointing to the banks and the three levels of government—federal, state, and municipal—as the parties responsible for stagnant production.[26] They have demanded that the government come forth with a "clear and definitive position" on the continuing conflicts between manufacturers and bankers.[27] The underlying desire does not appear to be for renewed protectionism but for the creation of viable conditions for fair market competition and equal opportunities for investment and credit.

The Salinas administration, for its part, had dismantled the established industrial policy (in the form of selected support for industry), opened the economy to foreign competition, and eliminated regulatory controls, but it also introduced incentives to promote quality and fostered innovation through mechanisms for quality control and certification. Likewise, federal laws and regulations on property rights began to come into line with international standards and agreements. For example, new norms were formulated to improve the image of brand products and to reduce transaction costs derived from changing or unclear rules of measurement and practices. As a result, the National Metrology Center and the National Institute of Industrial Property were created.[28]

Moreover, in the early 1990s the government introduced several programs—promulgated through Nacional Financiera, the National Council for Science and Technology, and National Bank of International Trade (Bancomext)—that were specially tailored to microenterprise and small and mid-sized firms, such as the Programa Impulso; programs to coordinate the business activities of Mexico's export firms; and several funds and mechanisms to provide incentives for technological modernization, training, and linkages between academia and industry.[29] To round out the picture, in 1993 the Antimonopoly Law and the Federal Law on Economic Competition were passed, and the Commission on Competition was created. Overall expenditures on research and development in Mexico are still, however, low (0.6 percent of the gross domestic product), and most of it is government-financed. Private business's share of R&D spending is very low (only about 1 percent) by international standards.[30]

As explained in Chapter 7, the Salinas administration also sponsored major reforms of the educational system, including an extension of the duration of compulsory education to nine years and administrative decentralization of basic education services.

In light of the precarious conditions of Mexican industry overall, and considering the current debate, this package of measures has nonetheless been insufficient. The problem is related at least in part to the strategies for formulating public policy, to the existing structure of interest representation, and to the nature of the business associations.

In a context of major societal changes such as those unfolding in Mexico, the success of the nation's economic policy will depend on how and whether the marginalized entrepreneurs and other social sectors are effectively reintegrated into a broad and flexible structure of interest representation. Still lacking is a scheme for negotiating and coordinating the making of federal policy—one that while decentralizing the process, also facilitates coordination among a variety of sectors and policy areas, particularly in the case of such issues as environmental protection.

The business associations themselves also must change, to open up representation beyond the privileged elites of large firms and to create flexible, expeditious organizational structures and procedures for representing the interests of the many and turning them into long-term demands. Greater coordination of private sector interests—the original objective of the CCE—would in turn propel greater coordination of business activities in such fundamental areas as investment and scientific and technological research.

Toward these ends two aspects of state-business relations will have to be reconsidered: the stipulation in the Laws of Chambers that each firm must affiliate with its respective local and industry chamber; and the monopolistic practice of interest representation in the federations of commerce and industry governed by those laws, as well as the monopolistic practices of other private-sector associations such as Coparmex and the associations of bankers, stock brokers, and insurance institutions. Throughout the past decade there has been debate on reforming the Laws of Chambers, but no satisfactory agreement has been reached. Some big business sectors such as petrochemicals have sought repeal of the laws, while others, like the leaders of Concanaco, do not consider it necessary to modify them.[31] In March 1994 the Secretary of Commerce and Industrial Development proposed, without any reform of the law, modernization of the business associations, with the intent that these would in turn promote the transformation of businesses. From his point of view, business associations would have to be more propositional in order for businesses to reach high levels of competitiveness and productivity.

From a macrosocial perspective the changes that have occurred in Mexico's economy, politics, and society in recent years have significantly shifted the balance of economic and political power noted at the outset. While the business sector has notably enhanced its economic power and legitimated its role as a political actor, workers and their unions have lost economic and political power, as the old forms of state interventionism have dissolved. Moreover, the practice of politics in Mexico has become more complex, not only because the parties and electoral politics have come alive with challengers to the PRI, but also because new actors and new problems associated with the process of economic globalization have emerged. Unfortunately, however, no stable scheme of political relations has yet come forth to replace this balance with new formulas.

To date the transition from the state-driven model of the economy to the market-driven model has not been complete, for the government or for the business sector. The challenge is to come up with a more comprehensive industrial strategy to bolster international competitiveness and consolidate an industrial base with high productivity and quality products. Such a strategy may evolve with changes in the international arena (particularly in the United States) in favor of an active industrial policy to shape national industrial structures to meet the demands of globalization (as exemplified in the policies of Japan and Germany). The strategy needed will require a comprehensive reformulation of the state's role in related areas such as education and scientific and technological development, as well as a new vision of entrepreneurs, both national and foreign, that goes beyond a zero-sum conception of power.

The transformations under way in Mexico obviously have generated and will continue to generate new economic actors and new differences among sectors, as well as new forms of identity and of interest representation. It should also be recognized that as part of a long-term strategy, and particularly in periods of change, the most effective and efficient political technique is creating consensus on the problems so as to reach agreement on solutions.

## Notes

1. This chapter will not discuss the complex relationships between the economy and politics that play out in processes of modernization; rather, the focus will be the impact of economic liberalization on the political structures and behavior of business leaders. For a more extensive analysis of the first point, see Riordan Roett, ed., *Political and Economic Liberalization in Mexico* (Boulder, Colo.: Lynne Rienner Publishers, 1993).

2. For a more detailed analysis of the emergence of these political tendencies among entrepreneurs and their behavior from 1982 to 1987, see Matilde Luna, *Los empresarios y el cambio político* (Mexico City: Era/Institute for Social Research, National Autonomous University of Mexico, 1992).

3. Ricardo Tirado and Matilde Luna, "El estado y los empresarios: De la activación al repliegue político," in *El nuevo estado mexicano, vol. III, Estado, actores y movimientos sociales,* ed. J. Alonso, A. Aziz, and J. Tamayo (Mexico City: Nueva Imagen, 1992), pp. 13–32.

4. An extensive account of this phenomenon can be found in José Ignacio Rodríguez Reyna, "La 'privatización' de la política," *Expansión* 25, no. 619 (July 7, 1993): 54–75, and, by the same publication's writing staff, "Los empresarios-legisladores (1991–1994)," 76–79.

5. The "social sector" is defined as the group of collective organizations (cooperatives, unions, etc.) as a whole, integrated for the most part by workers and peasants. It should be noted that the pacts' main objective has been to control inflation, principally by setting salary caps. See Edmundo Jacobo, Matilde Luna, and Ricardo Tirado, "Empresarios, pacto político y coyuntura actual," *Revista Estudios Políticos* 8, no. 1 (January–March 1989): 4–15.

6. On basic education, see Eusebio Hidalgo Flores, "Modernización educativa: El proyecto empresarial," (undergraduate thesis, Faculty of Political and Social Sciences, Autonomous National University of Mexico, 1992). And on higher education, see Matilde Luna, "El sector privado y las políticas de ciencia y tecnología" (paper presented at the Seminar on Technology and Cultural Processes, Center for Technological Innovation, Autonomous National University of Mexico, Mexico City, January 1994).

7. A comparative study of the elite leadership of the CCE can be found in Matilde Luna and Ricardo Tirado, "El Consejo Coordinador Empresarial: Una radiografía," *Cuadernos del Proyecto Organizaciones Empresariales en México,* no. 1 (Mexico City: Institute for Social Research, National Autonomous University of Mexico, 1992), pp. 48–57.

8. See Matilde Luna and Ricardo Tirado, "Los empresarios en el escenario del cambio," *Revista Mexicana de Sociología* 60, no. 2 (April–June 1993): 260. Along these same lines is the much-debated meeting in mid-1993 of thirty prominent business leaders with PRI officials, who asked that their businesses contribute seventy-five million "new pesos" (the peso was revalued in 1993 from approximately three thousand to the dollar to just over three to the dollar and is now called the new [nuevos] peso[s]) to the PRI presidential campaign.

9. Presidency of the Republic, *El Gobierno Mexicano,* no. 57 (August 1993), p. 31.

10. Celso Garrido, "Los grupos privados nacionales en México: Evolución entre 1988 y 1993," mimeo (Azcapotzalco, Mexico: Autonomous Metropolitan University, Azcapotzalco, Mexico, 1993).

11. See Matilde Luna, "La estructura de representación empresarial en México: La década de los noventa y los cambios en las estrategias corporativas," in *Los empresarios mexicanos, ayer y hoy,* ed. Cristina Puga and Ricardo Tirado (Mexico City: Ediciones El Caballito, 1992), pp. 273–276.

12. Garrido, "Los groups privados," pp. 18–22.

13. Rossana Fuentes Berain, "Latinoamérica, incubadora de millonarios," *Forbes,* cited in *El Financiero,* July 5, 1994, p. 11.

14. Enrique De La Garza Toledo, "Restructuración y polarización industrial en México," *El Cotidiano,* no. 50 (September–October 1992): 143, 147.

15. Garrido, "Los grupos privados."

16. The first description is from the analysis by Enrique Quintana, "Las negociaciones corporativas y la política neoliberal," in *Relaciones corporativas en un período de transición,* ed. Matilde Luna and Ricardo Pozas (Mexico City: Institute for Social Research, National Autonomous University of Mexico, 1992), pp. 181–188. The second is from the academic director of the Center for Research on Free Enterprise (CISLE), cited in Luna, *Los empresarios,* p. 277.

17. For a more detailed discussion of this conflict, see Luna and Tirado, "El Consejo Coordinador Empresarial."

18. For a more detailed discussion of the behavior of the associations during negotiations of NAFTA among Mexico, the United States, and Canada, see Matilde Luna, "Las asociaciones empresariales mexicanas y la apertura externa" (paper presented at the Latin American Studies Association, 17th International Congress, Los Angeles, California, September 24–27, 1992).

19. See Cristina Puga, "Empresarios medianos, pequeños y micros," *Cuadernos del Proyecto Organizaciones Empresariales en México,* no. 3 (Mexico City: Institute for Social Research, National Autonomous University of Mexico, 1992).

20. On this point see ibid.

21. A useful report on economic opening and macroeconomic stability can be found in Organization for Economic Cooperation and Development, *Mexico* (Paris: Economic Studies of the OECD, 1992).

22. See "Reporte global sobre industrialización y desarrollo" of the United Nations Industrial Development Organization, a summary of which is presented in *El Financiero,* March 16, 1994, p. 3A.

23. Presidency of the Republic, *El Gobierno Mexicano,* no. 55 (June 1993), p. 114.

24. This debate can be followed in the national press beginning in mid-1993. The specific reference from President Salinas is from Presidency of the Republic, *El Gobierno Mexicano,* no. 57 (August 1993), p. 31.

25. Concanaco, Coparmex, and Canacintra, "Propuestas del sector privado para el sexenio 1994–2000," internal document for discussion (not dated). Reference to this document has been made in various publications, including: Norberto López and Alberto Navarrete, "Una nueva era de civilidad democrática demanda la IP [Iniciativa Privada]," *Excélsior,* March 4, 1994, pp. 1, 10; Concanaco-Servytur, "Propuestas del sector empresarial para el sexenio 1994–2000," *Revista Decisión* 16, no. 185 (May 1994): 3–40; and, "Propuestas del sector privado para el sexenio 1994–2000," *Revista Transformación* 38, no. 4 (April 1994): 49–50.

26. Julieta Medina, "Denuncian terrorismo fiscal: Demandan a Colosio apoyar a industria," *Reforma,* March 2, 1994, p. 1A.

27. Claudia Olguín/Finsat, "No se encuentra aún el parámetro para medir la productividad industrial," *El Financiero,* October 18, 1993, p. 3A.

28. For a detailed report on this process, see Organization for Economic Cooperation and Development, *Mexico,* pp. 146–170.

29. See Rosalba Casas, "La modernización de la ciencia y la tecnología y la política biotecnológica en México" (paper presented at the International Symposium on Science and Technology, National Autonomous University of Mexico/Autonomous Metropolitan University, Mexico City, October 1992); and Luna, "El sector privado."

30. Data from Organization for Economic Cooperation and Development, *Mexico,* p. 168.

31. For a discussion of the debate on the Law of Chambers and its possible consequences, see Luna and Tirado, "Los empresarios."

# 6

# The 1992 Reforms of Mexican Law on Religion: Prospects of Changing State-Church Relations

## *Roberto J. Blancarte*

The armed rebellion in the southern state of Chiapas that began on January 1, 1994, whatever its ultimate outcome, has shaken the foundations of the Mexican political system. The uprising has also affected, if only indirectly, relations between the Mexican state and the country's social and political organizations, as well as their opinion of the nation's sociopolitical development and the role that they can or should play in it. Among the institutions most sensitive to these events have been Mexico's churches, which have been at the center of national attention because Chiapas is the state with the largest number of Protestants in Mexico and also because the Catholic church in the Diocese of San Cristóbal de las Casas, Chiapas, has been at the center of the conflict. Indeed, the diocese is the standard-bearer in the defense and organization of the indigenous peoples of Chiapas.

Although these events and trends might lead us to explain the recent changes in relations between the state and the churches by reference to Chiapas, it is necessary to examine these relations in the period immediately prior to the Chiapas rebellion and to situate them in a broader historical context. The indigenous uprising in Chiapas is neither the sole nor the most important factor that has affected state-church relations; in fact, other sociopolitical trends in Mexico over the preceding months and years arguably had much to do with setting the stage for the events surrounding the Diocese of San Cristóbal de las Casas.

One earlier event that may be just as illustrative and even causative of recent changes in relations between the state and the Catholic church, and that can be viewed as an immediate, if indirect, antecedent to the Chiapas rebellion, was the assassination of Cardinal Juan Jesús Posadas Ocampo on May 24, 1993. On that day Cardinal Posadas, archbishop of Guadalajara and one of the three most powerful figures in the Mexican Catholic church, was taken by his driver to the Guadalajara airport. He was on his way to pick up one of the other most important Catholics in the country, Monsignor Girolamo Prigione, the papal nuncio, who was arriving from Mexico City to spend a few hours inaugurating and blessing local businesses.[1] Posadas's luxury car, a white Grand Marquis, slowly rolled into the airport parking area at about 3:45 P.M. As it pulled in front of the terminal, two armed men suddenly appeared, took positions in front of the car, one just to the left, the other just to the right, and opened fire. More than a dozen bullets lodged in the Cardinal's body; he was killed instantly.

The assassination of Cardinal Posadas shook the Mexican conscience. But it also raised serious questions in the eyes of many Catholics in Mexico and elsewhere about the new ties between the Mexican state and the Catholic church established just a few months earlier. In September 1992 formal diplomatic relations had been established between Mexico and the Vatican for the first time, with President Carlos Salinas de Gortari announcing that the new relationship represented "the culmination of a long process of national reconciliation"—the essential aspect of which was reform of the legal framework governing the public actions of organized religion in Mexico.[2]

Reactions to the Cardinal's death indicated that many in the ecclesiastic hierarchy and the Catholic church generally disagreed with the way the reforms had been carried out and with their results. At the extreme some clergy members held that Cardinal Posadas's death was actually caused by the new relations between the Mexican state and the Catholic church; they assumed that his assassination was a consequence of the heightened political exposure of the Catholic prelates.

The Mexican populace seemed to be of two minds about the reforms. The first seemed to operate on the assumption that the new legal framework governing religious expression was more sensitive to the needs of both individual believers and religious groups, which, in turn, would lead to greater religious freedom. The second tended to find expression in the fear of privileged relations between high-level religious and political leaders, which might subject the church to the whims of the political authorities and, in turn, result in undue state control and manipulation of the faithful. Under this second scenario religious leaders might become tempted to be more involved in elite politics and more exposed to the risks inherent in power struggles. And it was this hypothesis that was at the root of suspicions that Cardinal Posadas's assassination was attributable to the new linkages between church and state.

The real motivations behind the archbishop's assassination are still not known. For the purposes of this chapter, however, the event and its repercussions serve to illustrate the sensitive nature of current relations between the state and the churches, particularly the Catholic church, in the wake of the institutional reforms of 1991 and 1992. To provide a broader context for understanding the reforms—their scope and their likely sociopolitical ramifications—I will first enumerate the nature of the reforms and then analyze the various reactions to them in several key sectors of Mexican society. The last section of the chapter reviews events from September 1992 through early 1994 and compares them with previous trends to assess the extent and import of the institutional reforms.

## Background to the Reforms

Beyond what any individuals may have been seeking, particularly President Salinas, who no doubt contributed to the institutional reforms on religion, in the late 1980s a series of national and international factors, both short-term and historical, converged to make the changes possible. Of special importance was the change in relations among the state, the church, and society, set in motion by a strategy initiated by the Catholic hierarchy, at least as far back as the 1950s, aimed at recouping the prestige and influence that it had lost in the years following the Mexican Revolution.[3]

The reforms instituted in July 1992 governing religious associations and public worship overturned the legal framework that had been in force since 1917 but not the liberal reforms of the second half of the nineteenth century. The so-called Laws of Reform of 1859 that established freedom of religion, separation of church and state, and the expropriation of church property were clearly liberal and, in the context of the political conflicts of the day, anticlerical. Nonetheless, the 1917 Constitution, in addition to being influenced by a form of social radicalism, was drafted mainly as a document of the victors against the groups and institutions that the revolutionaries considered their enemies. Among those enemies were the militant Catholics who had participated in the National Catholic Party and, by extension, the Catholic clergy in general. Tacit approval by party members of the assassination of President Francisco I. Madero in 1913 and of the dictatorship of General Victoriano Huerta (1913–1914) had convinced the revolutionaries that it was necessary to proscribe *any* political participation on the part of the churches or their members.

The history of relations between the state and the Catholic church since 1917 is one of continual confrontation between the respective social agendas of these two institutions, as well as a search on the part of the church to recover its lost legal legitimacy and thus a series of rights for itself as an institution and for its members. This confrontation found expression at times through a suppressed struggle between social organizations or social institutions, at times in open warfare, but most of the time through a doctrinal battle against the ideology of the revolutionary regime.

Events unfolded accordingly. The war of the *cristeros* (1926–1929)[4] was followed by a period of religious persecution, until an implicit agreement of understanding was reached in the late 1930s known as the *modus vivendi*. This accommodation between the parties, in place throughout the 1940s, essentially represented the church's abandoning social issues as the appropriate purview of the state, in exchange for greater tolerance by the state of the church's other activities, particularly in parochial education. But by the early 1950s the Catholic hierarchy began to recognize that the modus vivendi would not enable it to reestablish its own social agenda, and so it began to question the accommodation and to demand restitution of its rights. Thirty years would elapse, however, before social conditions would allow for a new legal framework for all religious associations in Mexico.[5]

Once those conditions existed in the late 1980s, it must be recognized that the legal reforms on religion, from the time they were first proposed, had a general framework of principles but not a specific content. Soon after President Salinas announced in his inaugural speech his plans to modernize relations between the state and "the Church," Secretary of the Interior Fernando Gutiérrez Barrios suggested there could be a public dialogue to examine the situation. The secretary stated that considering that "the Church exists," the fundamental premises of the dialogue should be separation between church and state, secular education in the public schools, and freedom of religion.[6] Yet it was still to take three years for completion of the formal proposed amendment. In his Third State of the Union Address, presented on November 1, 1991, President Salinas finally set out to promote a new legal status for the churches under the same three principles.[7]

Evidently those principles were sufficiently general to allow for any type of reform. After all, there are many ways to construe the separation of church and state, ranging from total separation to participation of the state in some ecclesiastic matters, be it a confessional tax or involvement in the designation of bishops. Likewise, freedom of religion can also mean different things. In fact, Article 24 of the Constitution of 1917 already guaranteed freedom of religion. So it was from December 1988 to November 1991, when public debate and consultations took place between the government and the churches, that the ultimate nature of the reforms was decided.[8]

In his Third State of the Union Address Salinas expounded somewhat on his idea as to what direction legal reform on religion should take. By that time most of the main aspects of the reform had been drafted by his advisers. The president stated:

> Let us recall that in Mexico the current legal status of the churches derived from political and economic considerations found in history, and not from doctrinal disputes on religious beliefs; therefore the solution should recognize what should endure and what should change. Experience teaches that the Mexican people do not want the clergy to participate in politics, or to accumulate material goods, but neither do the people of Mexico wish to live under pretenses or in a mistaken complicity. It is not a question of returning to situations of privilege, but of reconciling

the definitive secularization of society with effective freedom of religion, which is one of the most important human rights.[9]

The debate from 1988 to 1991 gradually illuminated two points that were not clear at the start: first, the fact, until then hardly acknowledged, of the secular nature of Mexican society; and second, and as a consequence of the first, the fact that most Mexican Catholics neither shared nor followed the church hierarchy's views on social and political issues. Thus it was possible for Catholics, who account for approximately 80 percent of the population, to embrace simultaneously both a deep-rooted anticlericalism and a profound religiosity. And thus it was possible for the president to insist that "the Mexican people do not want the clergy to participate in politics, or to accumulate material goods." As will be shown below, however, achieving the reforms would prove to be a much more complex challenge than one might think.

By the end of the debate, the government's discourse had changed almost imperceptibly from references to "the Church," clearly meaning the Catholic church, to "the churches," taking into account the growing heterogeneity of religion in Mexico. Although at first the change seemed to be merely a matter of rhetoric, later it came to reveal a hitherto little-recognized reality that the new law would reflect: a great many minority faiths had taken root and acquired a new social status in Mexico. For example, as of early 1994 the General Office on Religious Affairs of the Secretariat of the Interior had registered more than 1,500 religious associations, more than three-fourths of which were Protestant and only one-fifth Catholic. Of course the number of associations does not reflect the number of believers affiliated with each religion, but conservative calculations suggest that 10 to 15 percent of Mexicans are Evangelical, Protestant, or members of other non-Catholic congregations. This fact, in itself, confirms the growing importance of the minority religious associations, as well as their unquestionable role in Mexican society.

## The Legislation of 1992

Ultimately, Salinas's formal justification for updating the legal framework on ecclesiastic actions was the need to promote "congruence between what the law mandates and the everyday behavior of citizens, taking one more step in the direction of internal harmony in the context of modernization."[10] Many of the concerns raised in the debates over reform found wording in the new laws of 1992, but identifying who would benefit from them is harder to delineate.

In general terms the most important change occasioned by the new legislation was formal recognition of the right to religious association and therefore to the freedom that the faithful have to be organized and to express their faith collectively. From 1917 to 1992 the Mexican state did not recognize the legal status of "religious groupings called churches." This means that the state dealt only with individual believers and granted no legal rights to religious associations or their members per se. The January 1992 amendment to Article 130 of the Constitution contains a legal innovation in the concept of "religious associations," which could now win legal recognition once registered with the Secretariat of the Interior.

The 1917 Constitution had guaranteed freedom of religion in Article 24, but with certain important constraints, namely:

> All men are free to profess the religious belief of their preference and to practice the respective ceremonies, devotions, or rites *in the temples or in their private homes,* so long as these do not constitute an offense or violation penalized by law.[11] [Emphasis added.]

The same article affirmed that "All religious acts with public rites shall be celebrated necessarily in the temples, which shall always be under the vigilance of the authorities."

Thus, on the one hand the Constitution granted freedom of religion while, on the other, it limited public religious ceremonies to religious buildings and homes, thereby prohibiting any public form of religious expression. This is another example of the tendency in the Constitution to consider religious matters as corresponding essentially to the individual. In its place the new Article 24 of the Constitution has struck the requirement that religious rites be performed only in churches or private homes and has added a paragraph to the effect that Congress cannot pass laws that establish or prohibit any religion. Finally, Article 24 does indicate that public religious ceremonies shall normally be held in the churches and that those celebrated outside of them shall be subject to regulation. The law setting forth these regulations, passed in July 1992, once again established that public religious ceremonies (outside of churches) are to be reserved for special occasions and lays out a series of requirements for holding such events. It nonetheless exempted pilgrimages, transit between private homes for religious purposes, and activities held in homes to which the public does not have free access.[12]

Regarding education the January 1992 amendment to Article 3 of the Constitution did away with the absolute prohibition on the involvement of religious organizations in primary and secondary schools, teacher-training institutes, and schools for workers and peasants. This made it possible for the many religious schools that had been operating illegally, most of them Catholic, to emerge from their underground existence. Nevertheless, the article also establishes that public education will be secular "and therefore will be completely independent of any religious doctrine." The Catholic hierarchy has since criticized this provision.

Another provision repealed in the Constitution and left for final determination to the new enacting legislation of 1992 has to do with real property owned by churches. Article 27 simply forbade them from acquiring, owning, or administering real estate or capital left to them, in addition to considering all churches as property of the nation. The amendment did away with this prohibition, but limited churches to owning "property indispensable for their purposes, within the requirements and limitations established by the regulatory law." Obviously the definition of just what property is indispensable for religious purposes is hard to define. This inherent ambiguity, as well as the margin of discretion the new law grants to the Secretariat of the Interior to decide on these matters, has been one of the points most hotly debated and challenged by the churches.

Finally, in addition to granting legal status to churches and religious groups, the amendments to Article 130 of the Constitution gave clergy members the right to vote and did away with several limitations on their freedom of expression in speech and in publications, such as the prohibition on criticizing the country's fundamental laws and commenting on national politics. Nonetheless, the new Article 130 retains some restrictions on the actions of religious groups and their clergy. For example, it still prohibits clergy from running for or holding public office and from joining any political campaign for political purposes or proselytizing on behalf of any political party candidate. Nor can the clergy voice opposition to the country's laws or institutions in public religious ceremonies or activities or in religious publications, or attack the nation's symbols in any way. Moreover, the political restrictions extend to all of the faithful, as there is a strict prohibition on "the formation of any kind of political grouping whose title includes any word or indication whatsoever that it has ties to any religious faith." At least in name, therefore, there can be no Christian democratic or social Christian party in Mexico. Article 130 also prohibits political meetings from being held in churches.

Contrary to the expectations of some Catholic prelates, the reforms instituted on religion are markedly liberal. Not only does Article 130 adopt as its guiding principle the historic separation between the state and the churches; in addition, Article 3 of the new regulatory law establishes that the Mexican state is secular and will exercise its authority over all religious expression, individual and collective, "only in relation to observance of the laws, maintenance of public order and morality, and safeguarding of the rights of third parties."

By registering the religious associations and the consequent acceptance of the law that this presupposes, the Mexican state thereby establishes its supremacy over religious groupings. It thus imposes a liberal and secular conception of religious matters, yet it is a conception that would not be fully accepted by all.

## The Catholic Hierarchy Responds

Members of the Catholic hierarchy have exhibited divergent views of the new laws, although they seemed to be in consensus that the legislation represented an improvement over the past. Even though some prelates actively sought to influence the drafting of certain sections, it was clear that the final document was not going to meet exactly the demands of the Catholic bishops.[13] In fact, there was some talk, without justification in my view, of "Salinista bishops" standing in opposition to others who wanted to maintain greater autonomy vis-à-vis the political authorities.

Since passage of the new laws, however, it has indeed become clear that not all the bishops were in agreement as to what position to adopt in this regard, that is, whether to accept the legislation, question it, or demand that it be changed in the short or medium term. As might be expected, the differences stated generally reproduced the duality of positions expressed during the earlier debate over the direction of institutional change. On the one hand were those (the majority) who believed the legislative reforms represented an opportunity to improve relations between church and state and, as a result, to further the Catholic church's role in society. On the other hand were those who disagreed with the new law, either considering it insufficient in scope or believing their acceptance would countenance a restriction of ecclesiastic freedom in some cases, since, in their view, the Secretariat of the Interior had excessive powers. One could perceive a fear underlying the latter position that the church might stand to lose its critical capacity, or phrased in theological terms, its "prophetic" role of denouncing social injustice and corruption.

In the end, after several days during which the nation's Catholic bishops held their plenary, the Conference of Mexican Bishops (CEM) issued a joint declaration on the new law on August 13, 1992. The majority of the bishops supported critical acceptance of the new law, or acceptance with reservations. The document affirmed that the new law opened a way to end church-state hostility and was "a firm step to overcome the forced simulation and to begin to live in a fundamentally just legal order, though one that could be improved upon."[14] The bishops recognized that the new framework represented an improvement:

> Henceforth the expression of religion is not legally circumscribed to the private sphere of individuals; rather the law guarantees its associative and public nature. It is a notable advance that within a society oriented to civilized plurality, it is possible to carry out the service mission that the Catholic community must exercise for a future of reconciliation in our homeland. With the clarity and certainty that is provided by the possibility of legal recognition of the Church, we can find better ways to carry out our mission in conditions of congruence and cooperation.[15]

The bishops pointed out, however, that the law on religious associations had its limitations and ambiguities, which could be attributed to "the imperfection of all human undertakings" and the lack of experience in addressing these issues. They noted, for example, that "the right to religious freedom in education is one of the human rights not yet fully recognized, rights the nonrecognition of which clearly puts our country behind in the international context."[16] The bishops also complained that the legislation included certain measures and expressions that denoted distrust and suspicion, "as if the Church, in particular the hierarchy, were hunting for wealth or seeking political power or social prestige." Yet the Catholic prelates expressed their "firm confidence" that these limitations and ambiguities would soon be overcome.[17] Finally, perhaps as a concession to the bishops who had questioned the significance of the new relations with the state, the CEM document recognized that modernization of state-church relations in Mexico was but one aspect of their pastoral mission. They thus recommended, among other things, that the spirit of dialogue should not remain at the level of representatives of the church and the civilian authorities, but that it should extend to all members of the political and ecclesiastic community.

## Reactions from Other Quarters

Other sectors of Mexican society had their own reservations about the reforms. Of particular note were the reactions from politicians; other, non-Catholic churches; jurists; and the more critical, progressive wing of the Catholic church.

Mexico's main political parties focused their criticisms on the fear that the churches, especially the Catholic church, would be tempted to get involved in politics. Professional politicians perceived a dual danger: the temptation to "clericalize" or "confessionalize" politics, and the risk that the religious hierarchies might become politicized and thus unduly subjected to political authorities. In fact, all the political parties in Mexico, from left to right, agree on this concern. In so doing they mirror the anticlericalism of the Mexican populace, which ultimately ignores the impossibility of keeping the Catholic hierarchy from participating in national politics—not in party politics, but in the political process that ultimately defines the country's direction.[18]

Echoing a concern of the bishops' conference, leaders of some of the minority churches denounced the dangers inherent in granting "excessive powers" to the Secretariat of the Interior, in particular the Secretariat's excessive discretion in ruling on some church activities, such as determining which of the properties that religious associations would like to own or administer are indispensable. The minority churches also struggled throughout the drafting of the legislation and afterward to keep one church—the Catholic church—from receiving any sort of preferential treatment, as some bishops and the nuncio in Mexico City had demanded.[19]

Quite a few jurists also attacked the constitutional amendments and their enacting legislation on the basis of arguments favoring freedom of religion and human rights. They criticized the new Article 130, for example, for continuing to limit some of the political rights of clergy members, such as their ability to run for or hold public office and to oppose the country's laws and institutions. Some jurists were also critical of other new restrictions in the law, such as those prohibiting the churches from owning or managing mass electronic media companies, from acquiring concessions to exploit radio or television stations, and from providing religious education in the public schools.[20]

Finally, the harshest criticisms not only of the new legal framework but also of the type of state-church relationship it was likely to generate came from the more progressive wings of the Catholic church. In their view, "The ambiguity of the written law allows the government to subject the Churches in their drive for liberation as it pleases." This position even questioned the need for the legal reforms:

> It is better to live in law than without law in equal conditions. But it is also better to live clandestinely with evangelical freedom than in legality subjected to a constituted authority that does not tolerate anything that goes beyond its limits and that threatens with its questioning.
> In Mexico this constituted authority is made up of the political authority, the power elites, and the official theology of a power ecclesiology. Not the state, nor the elites, nor a current of the official churches likes a church that causes discomfort with its yearning for justice and liberty, with its longing for respect of all human rights, with its speaking out in the face of all power, ecclesiastic and state, as power is no more than a simple Caesar and never an absolute owner as if it were God.[21]

This "liberation theology"[22] perspective thus rejected not only the theoretical conception of the law contained in Article 130, "because of its absolutism," but also a vision of the church based on the search for earthly power.

## Recent Events as They Illustrate New Relations

As of this writing it is not yet two years since the reforms of the law on religion passed. Nonetheless, recent events in Mexico reveal tensions the law has not been able to contain—in fact, tensions the reforms may have escalated. We will look first at the assassination of the archbishop of

Guadalajara and then turn to other events, particularly in the church's relations with the military.

### The Case of Cardinal Posadas

The long-standing dispute between the "church of power" and the "prophetic church,"[23] somewhat latent after the new laws were passed, resurged with the sudden and brutal death of Cardinal Posadas and ultimately affected relations between the Catholic church and the state. This does not mean that the archbishop of Guadalajara was identified with the more progressive sectors of the Church. To the contrary, some of his positions fell within the most traditional and common tendencies found among the bishops. Nonetheless, his assassination, committed just months after the new relationship between the state and the Catholic church was established, led many members of the clergy to claim—in my view, without justification—that the cardinal's death had somehow resulted from the new relationship. That belief, in turn, tended to fuel the position of those who were advocating a more liberating or prophetic church, and a church that enjoyed even greater autonomy from state intervention.

But beyond the progressives' agenda, the assassination of the archbishop provoked tensions between certain bishops and the federal government, and also within the bishops' conference. The official version of the event—that the incident was part of a confrontation between drug-trafficking gangs and that the cardinal had been mistaken for one of the drug kingpins—did not satisfy all the Catholic prelates. Indeed, in the first weeks after the assassination the Catholic bishops, through the president of the CEM, unanimously demanded a "clear and credible" explanation of the case.[24] Some bishops openly refuted the official version of the murder. For example, bishop of León Rafael García mentioned that the proposal made by the governor of Jalisco to hold a referendum on the death penalty was "a government concoction to hide the true causes of Mr. Posadas's death."[25] Carlos Quintero Arce, bishop of Hermosillo, held that the government version "is full of contradictions, includes incoherent data, and is not convincing."[26] Others, more cautious, such as the bishop of Chilpancingo-Chilapa, Efrén Ramos Salazar, expressed trust in the authorities but also stated that the church would not be satisfied so long as the police investigations lacked "coherence and certainty."[27]

Over time two main groups of opinion formed regarding the cardinal's death. On the one hand were leaders among the bishops, such as archbishop of Monterrey and president of the CEM, Adolfo Suárez Rivera, and secretary-general of the CEM and auxiliary bishop of Guadalajara, Ramón Godínez Flores, who, along with papal nuncio Girolamo Prigione and other bishops close to them including the bishop of Cuernavaca, Luis Reynoso, expressed satisfaction with the way the investigations were conducted, and especially with the version and official hypothesis provided by the Office of the Attorney General. This position was somehow endorsed by Pope John Paul II when, during his third visit to Mexico in August 1993, he said that Posadas's assassination would not affect relations between Mexico and the Vatican.[28]

On the other hand were many other bishops who continued to express doubts about the investigations and about possible motives for the murder. For example, Adolfo Hernández Hurtado, Javier Navarro, and José Guadalupe Martín, three of the auxiliary bishops of the Archdiocese of Guadalajara, worried that "the assassination of the cardinal could have had other motives that would affect not only the church, but the very stability of the country."[29] The abbey of the Basilica of Guadalupe stated that "Mexican society is not convinced that the events in which Cardinal Juan Jesús Posadas Ocampo lost his life were accidental or circumstantial."[30] Doubts regarding the investigations of the attorney general's office and the official hypotheses regarding the cardinal's death were even shared by some sectors of the Curia in Rome. Vatican Radio, for example, expressed perplexity at the conclusions of the investigative commission and voiced doubts on unclarified aspects of the case.[31] Even Cardinal Roger Etchegaray, an important figure in the government of the Holy See, stated during the pope's visit to Mexico that "doubts still remain, and questions persist" regarding the murder of Posadas.[32]

In short, the Mexican government became plagued by a terrible crisis of credibility, one for which there was no solution despite the efforts of the attorney general to offer swift, satisfactory results. As the bishop administrator of the Diocese of Guadalajara, Guadalupe Martín Rábago, was to state, "As in every assassination, no one is happy with the explanation. It is thought that 'something more' is behind it. We want it to be investigated further, as this official explanation is looked upon with doubt."[33]

The repercussions of the assassination of Cardinal Posadas revealed the complexity of relations between the state and the Catholic church, with some leaders accepting the government's actions and others more than skeptical. This division reflected much of the same divisions as those expressed in the debate preceding passage of the institutional reforms on religion. Clearly some bishops and many Catholic lay leaders displayed a certain distrust toward the new law out of fear that the church would be brought under the sway of or subjugated by the political authorities. Nonetheless, at the same time the top-ranking Catholic prelates, including the nuncio, were to a certain extent led to adopt more conciliatory postures toward the government's actions and thus were more cautious in their condemnation of attitudes that perhaps in other circumstances they would not have hesitated to disapprove. In adopting this position, they revealed the limits that the new laws imposed on the Catholic leadership by leading it to act under the ethic of political responsibility more than under the ethic of religious conviction.[34]

## Drug Traffickers, Soldiers, and Priests

The death of Cardinal Posadas brought more than an unresolved investigation and renewed fears of closer state-church relations. It also shocked some of the Catholic clergy into a more committed struggle against social injustice and the moral corruption of the political system.

Just two months after Posadas's death an important conflict arose between the Catholic hierarchy and the military sparked by a document prepared by the Social Pastoral Commission (CEPS) of the bishops' conference entitled *Pastoral Message on Violence and Peace.* In that document the CEPS, which is the CEM commission that handles social issues, held that "a large number of public officials and members of the military had been bought by or had become associated with" drug-trafficking money. The direct reference to the military provoked an angry response from the Secretariat of National Defense, which demanded a clarification. Ultimately the Secretariat of the Interior had to mediate in the dispute, and the CEPS equivocated by adding the phrase "in several parts of the continent," meaning in Latin America, not necessarily Mexico in particular.[35]

The meeting in which the wording was changed included Secretary of Defense General Antonio Riviello Bazán, Secretary of the Interior Patrocinio González Garrido, papal nuncio Prigione, and president of the CEM, Suárez Rivera, thereby bolstering the thesis that the top-ranking bishops were more willing to yield on certain principles because of the new state-church relationship. Archbishop Suárez Rivera nonetheless hastened to declare that although the CEPS document had not included any doctrinal errors, it did have "imprecisions" that needed to be "contextualized."[36] The secretary-general of the CEM, Monsignor Godínez, affirmed that the new legal framework greatly facilitated a rapprochement with the government and military authorities to clear up all "the misunderstandings." Questioned as to the danger that under the new legal framework the church might come to be more controlled by the government, Monsignor Godínez answered, "It may be, but we will try to be adult enough to try to live our freedom."[37]

This kind of dispute between Catholic leaders and government and even military officials was in fact nothing new. The best-known case in this regard, though not the only one in Mexico, is that of the Diocese of San Cristóbal de las Casas, Chiapas, led for more than thirty years by Bishop Samuel Ruiz.

The particular social and political situation of that diocese—situated along the border with Guatemala, where an indigenous majority has historically suffered exploitation at the hands of a few local caciques—has provoked constant friction and continual explosive events, the latest being the armed uprising of January 1994. Bishop Ruiz's status as one of the few defenders of the rights of indigenous people living in the region has made him a suspicious character in the eyes of many local officials and caciques, who are interested in maintaining the status quo.

The situation was particularly tense in the late 1970s when guerrilla movements were growing in Central America, heating up frictions along the Mexican-Guatemalan border. Pressure from local power groups increased even more in recent years as the social situation in Chiapas grew increasingly explosive. One example is Joel Padrón, the parish priest of Simojovel, Chiapas, who was jailed in September 1991. When he won his release two months later (with the help of national and international media), the leader of the local ranchers' union (Unión Ganadera) requested that the priest be changed "because the ones from San Cristóbal are all the same; they're guerrillas and they get involved in politics."[38] The ranchers and principal merchants in the area constantly accused Bishop Ruiz of provoking destabilization of the region. A year after the parish priest was released, several slogans began appearing on the walls in San Cristóbal alluding to Bishop Ruiz that read, "The red bishop with his guerrilla priests should leave" and "Death to the Human Rights Center."[39] That same Fray Bartolomé de las Casas Human Rights Center, directed by Bishop Ruiz, was at the forefront of another dispute with the army in April 1993, when the center defended a group of Tzotzil Indians accused of killing two officers.[40]

Situations such as these, which have recurred time and again in recent years, led the Bishop of San Cristóbal to state on one occasion:

> If stability means stealing from the Indians, killing them with impunity, despoiling them; and [if] destabilizing means that through the gospel the Indians realize that they should unite, and based on their analyses they organize and defend their rights—then yes, the diocese destabilizes.[41]

Evidently Bishop Ruiz was voicing his support for a "prophetic church" more than for a "church of power."

The Diocese of San Cristóbal has not been the only one to denounce widespread extreme poverty, political corruption, and mounting social injustice. In late 1992 seven bishops from the state of Veracruz denounced the facts that in Mexico the real exercise of democracy "is far from ideal," that the growing impoverishment of the people "is reaching intolerable extremes," that the lack of work and unemployment is "alarming," and even that the North American Free Trade Agreement could lead to a consumerist lifestyle and the danger that "a more just and dignified social organization" could become difficult or hindered.[42] Many such messages have been issued by Mexico's Catholic bishops in recent times, by both high-level bishops and bishops of smaller dioceses. The key point of these criticisms is the neoliberal system and the unrestrained market economy that appears to be expanding its influence in Mexico. Does this mean that in reality the division between two churches, one prophetic and the other power-seeking, is in fact only ephemeral? Or might there be different pastoral strategies or positions but also a certain doctrinal unity?

## Conclusions

With the institutional reform on religious groups and public worship finally in place, many Mexicans thought that a time of tranquility in state-church relations was also finally at hand. The new legal framework seemed to have created a group of Catholic bishops who were grateful to the regime and above all more willing to accept the social order imposed by it. Reality, however, has proven to be much more complex than these simplistic assumptions. Any analysis of the nature and essential characteristics of the new relationship between the state and the churches in Mexico must first clarify what aspect of the relationship is in question. Only then is it possible to assess whether the positions of the parties in question are close or distant.

For example, it could be said that there is a much improved relationship between the ruling political sectors and the religious leaders, as there are now formal channels of communication between them. Nonetheless, this does not mean that ideological and doctrinal differences have disappeared between the Mexican state, liberal if no longer revolutionary, and the Catholic church, once again largely antiliberal.[43]

Nor does it mean that all the bishops and other Catholic leaders share the same view on the role the church should play in Mexican society. We have seen that at least in the Catholic church there is a seemingly permanent tension between two types of ecclesiastic projects: that of a church of power, interested in capitalizing on political opportunities to advance its social agenda, and that of a prophetic church, more committed to an integrated vision (that is, religious, but also social and political) of the liberation of the faithful.

Throughout this chapter I have not meant to imply that there are actually two churches or only two groups within the Mexican Catholic church, the traditionalists and the progressives. Rather, the church hierarchy and the faithful are engaged in an ongoing, tense debate over different ideas of what it means to be Catholic, as well as different theological attitudes and conceptions as to the role the Catholic church should play in today's world, especially in Mexico. Chiapas shows that the situation is not static and that motivating forces and therefore social agendas within the church can change quickly. As recently as late 1993 the conception of a more prophetic church, one linked to an agenda demanding liberation of the poor, was under attack, but the armed uprising of the Mayans of the Lacandón Jungle on January 1, 1994, reversed that situation. The seriousness of the circumstances and above all the shout of desperation of those who had taken up arms led the bishops as a whole to change their attitude and unconditionally back the bishop of San Cristóbal, whose pastoral positions just weeks earlier had been called into question by the nuncio to the point that there was talk he might be removed or resign from the diocese.[44] Although the assassination of PRI candidate Luis Donaldo Colosio hardened the Mexican morale and generated a growing conservatism in Mexican society as a whole, the position of the bishop of San Cristóbal had become significantly consolidated.

Therefore, contrary to what many expected, the trend in the Catholic church in the wake of the institutional reforms has not been subjugation by the political authorities, but rather the bolstering of a more critical stance toward Mexico's political, social, and economic systems. It should be recognized that there are doctrinal reasons to explain the growing opposition of Catholic leaders to the neoliberal project, which to date has fostered only greater marginality, poverty, and social polarization.[45] The hierarchy's rapprochement with the state stemming from the reform itself may have temporarily constrained a critical stance toward the government, but the assassination of Cardinal Posadas, ongoing confrontation with the military, and above all the armed uprising in Chiapas are likely to continue to be important catalysts driving greater expression and dissemination of that stance in the future.

## Notes

1. It is customary in Mexico to have a priest or church representative bless a business at the time of its inauguration.

2. "Hoy se vive una nueva época de tolerancia y libertad," *La Jornada,* September 22, 1992, p. 3.

3. For more on the historical and sociopolitical roots of the reforms, see Roberto J. Blancarte, "La reforma a los artículos anticlericales de la Constitución: Decisiones coyunturales y razones históricas," in *Relaciones del Estado con las Iglesias* (Mexico City: Editorial Porrúa-National Autonomous University of Mexico, 1992), pp. 33–40; and Roberto J. Blancarte, "Recent Changes in Church-State Relations in Mexico: An Historical Approach," *Journal of Church and State* 35, no. 4 (Autumn 1993): 781–805.

4. The *Cristiada* or war of the cristeros took place between 1926 and 1929, as a direct consequence of the closing of all churches as ordered by the Catholic hierarchy and as a product of growing tensions between the church and the state following the promulgation of the revolutionary Constitution of 1917, which had a clear anticlerical tone. The mostly rural war, openly "antirevolutionary," took place for the most part in the Bajío region (midwestern Mexico), a part of the

country where clerical Catholicism was deeply rooted. For further information on this topic, see the classic three-volume work by Jean Meyer, *La Cristiada*, 5th ed. (Mexico City: Siglo XXI, 1977).

5. For a detailed history of state-church relations during this period, see Roberto J. Blancarte, *Historia de la Iglesia Católica en México (1929–1982)* (Mexico City: Fondo de Cultura Económica, 1992).

6. "El gobierno aceptaría un debate sobre la relación Iglesia-Estado: Gutiérrez Barrios," *La Jornada,* December 8, 1988, p. 3.

7. Carlos Salinas de Gortari, *Third State of the Union Address,* November 1, 1991.

8. On this debate, see Roberto J. Blancarte, *El poder. Salinismo e Iglesia Católica: Una nueva convivencia?* (Mexico City: Grijalbo, 1991). See also Roberto J. Blancarte, "Religion and Constitutional Change in Mexico, 1988–1992," in *Social Compass: International Review of the Sociology of Religion* 40, no. 4 (December 1993): 555–569.

9. Salinas de Gortari, *Third State of the Union Address,* November 1, 1991.

10. Ibid.

11. The following discussion is based on the comparative texts of Articles 3, 24, 27, and 130 of the Constitution prior to the 1992 reforms and the same articles as amended. The amended articles appear in annex XI of the book *Una ley para la libertad religiosa,* ed. Armando Méndez Gutiérrez (Mexico City: Fundación Mexicana Cambio XXI-Editorial Diana, 1992).

12. Secretariat of the Interior, "Ley de Asociaciones Religiosas y Culto Público," published in the *Diario Oficial,* July 15, 1992, p. 11.

13. The Catholic church in Mexico has 78 ecclesiastic districts and 109 bishops, 94 of whom are members of the Conference of Mexican Bishops (CEM), the other 15 being bishops emeritus or retired bishops.

14. Conference of Mexican Bishops, 52nd Plenary Assembly, "Declaración de los obispos mexicanos sobre la nueva 'Ley de Asociaciones Religiosas y Culto Público'" (August 13, 1992), p. 2.

15. Ibid., p. 2.

16. Ibid., p. 3.

17. Ibid., p. 3.

18. Innumerable statements have been made along these lines. Likewise, some examples of party positions in this regard can be found in the above-noted book *Una ley para la libertad religiosa.*

19. One of the churches that worked the hardest and the most publicly to prevent any such differential treatment was the Methodist Church of Mexico.

20. See, for example, Raúl González Schmal, "Prospectivas, tareas jurídicas: Evolución de los criterios y las líneas jurídicas de acción, tanto de las Iglesias como del Estado," in *México frente al nuevo siglo,* ed. Fundación Konrad Adenauer (Mexico City: Fundación Konrad Adenauer, 1993), pp. 152–158.

21. Jesús Vergara Aceves, S. J., "Análisis teológico de la evangelización en el nuevo marco jurídico de las Iglesias y de las relaciones con el Vaticano," in *México frente al nuevo siglo* (Mexico City: Fundación Konrad Adenauer, 1993), p. 139.

22. So-called liberation theology is in reality composed of many liberation theologies. It is a movement to explain the faith, rooted in the results of the Second Vatican Council and of the Second General Conference of Latin American Bishops, which took place in Medellín, Colombia, in 1968. The complexity of this theological movement makes it practically impossible to give it one sole definition. Some simply affirm that liberation theology is that which is created by a believing and oppressed community. According to this definition, the believing communities

of Latin America saw that the biggest historical and current events have been marked by their domination by external forces. Therefore, they argue that theology should have the opposite purpose: that of "liberation." This means that liberation theologies are theoretical elaborations that rise from the practice of liberation itself of the oppressed classes and communities. See Luis G. del Valle, "Teología de la Liberación en México," in *Las ideas sociales del catolicismo en México,* ed. Roberto J. Blancarte (Mexico City: Fondo de Cultura Económica, forthcoming).

23. The "prophetic church" is commonly used to define that part of the Catholic church that is committed to the religious, social, political, and economic causes of the people, in other words, that seeks to lead the people to complete liberation. "Liberation theology" is part of this prophetic church but not its only component. Indeed, the prophetic church includes other currents less radical than liberation theology but equally committed to grassroots causes. It may also include some of the more traditional bishops, depending on their reading of Christian social doctrine.

24. "Explicación 'clara y creíble' en el caso Posadas exigió Suárez Rivera," *La Jornada,* May 28, 1993, p. 3.

25. Ibid., p. 6.

26. "No es convincente la versión oficial sobre la muerte de Posadas Ocampo," *La Jornada,* June 1, 1993, p. 3.

27. "Las investigaciones no son claras: Clero," *Excélsior,* May 31, 1993, p. 4.

28. "La muerte de Posadas no afectará las relaciones con México: Wojtyla," *La Jornada,* August 10, 1993, p. 3.

29. "Pudo haber tenido otros móviles el asesinato del cardenal Posadas," *La Jornada,* June 4, 1993, p. 8.

30. "Demanda el pueblo esclarecer la muerte de Posadas. Se reconoce la labor oficial: Guillermo Schulemburg," *Excélsior,* July 10, 1993, p. 4.

31. "No satisfacen al Vaticano las conclusiones del homicidio del Cardenal Posadas Ocampo," *Excélsior,* July 5, 1993, p. 38.

32. "Etchegaray: Persisten dudas sobre el crimen de Posadas," *La Jornada,* August 11, 1993, p. 7.

33. "Traer un obispo de fuera es un error," *Excélsior,* August 26, 1993, p. 29.

34. I refer here to the classic distinction that Max Weber makes in *Politik als Beruf, Wissenschaft als Beruf* between an ethics of responsibility and an ethics of conviction. See Max Weber, *El político y el científico* (Madrid: Alianza, 1989), p. 231.

35. "La Comisión de Pastoral de marcha atrás en sus críticas a militares," *La Jornada,* June 30, 1993, p. 5.

36. "Reunión privada entre autoridades de la Defensa y la Iglesia Católica: Secretaría de Gobernación," *Excélsior,* July 1, 1993, p. 4.

37. "El asunto de los militares quedó cerrado, señala la Iglesia Católica," *La Jornada,* July 2, 1993, p. 5.

38. "La Junta de Festejos, causa del pleito entre católicos de Simojovel," *La Jornada,* September 24, 1991, p. 11.

39. "Pintas en contra del obispo Samuel Ruiz en San Cristóbal," *La Jornada,* November 7, 1992, p. 21.

40. Armando Guzmán and Rodrigo Vera, "Militares y sacerdotes se enfrentan por el caso de los dos oficiales asesinados e incinerados en Chiapas," *Proceso,* no. 858, April 12, 1993, pp. 6–9.

41. "Distanciamiento pero no aversión al gobernador: Samuel Ruiz," *La Jornada,* June 29, 1992, p. 8.

42. This "Christmas message" by the bishops of the pastoral region of the Gulf was reproduced in *La Jornada,* December 30, 1992, pp. 1, 6.

43. Particularly in the wake of the collapse of communism in the former Soviet regime and Eastern Europe.

44. This matter was discussed in the national press in the first weeks of November 1993. See in particular *La Jornada* and *Proceso.*

45. On the doctrinal positions of the Catholic hierarchy in Mexico, including their roots and characteristics, see Blancarte, *Historia de la Iglesia Católica.*

# PART 2

## Public Policy Reforms and Challenges

# 7

# The Politics of Educational Reform in Mexico: Ambivalence Toward Change

## Guillermo Trejo

Educational reform represents one of the major social policy initiatives of the presidential *sexenio* of Carlos Salinas de Gortari. It serves as an interesting case study simply because reforming education has entailed an intricate bargaining process, involving the largest federal bureaucracy in Mexico, the Secretariat of Public Education (SEP), and the largest labor union in Latin America, the National Union of Education Workers (SNTE).[1] Education also stands out as the only social policy arena in which the Salinas administration has undertaken comprehensive institutional change. Hence, the educational experience illustrates the complexities likely to constrain any future efforts to reform other social policies.

This chapter examines the politics and basic parameters of the Salinas educational reform and concentrates its analysis on the state's capacity to change the rules and incentives that have historically motivated and constrained participants in the education system.[2] The chapter opens with a review of the traditional institutional arrangement that prevailed over the past fifty years. A second section details the nature of the Salinas reforms, including the National Agreement for the Modernization of Basic Education (ANMEB) and the institutional changes introduced both in the Constitution of 1917 and in the Federal Law of Education. This section also devotes special attention to the bargaining process over the reform and to the politics of implementation. A third section evaluates the scope and limits of the reform and its potential political consequences for state-society relations.

The ANMEB and the other changes in education law, passed in July 1993, represent the boldest attempt to alter the institutional arrangement that has governed the educational process in Mexico in over half a century. In essence, the reforms are designed to alter fundamental rights in the educational policymaking process and, in turn, the structure and distribution of power throughout the broader system. With the agreement the Salinas administration has succeeded in bringing an autonomous state back into the educational sector, which is now capable of undertaking reform from above.

Nevertheless, the state has not been equally capable of implementing reform. Two constraints are paramount. First, some of the major reform initiatives are subject to structural constraints that result from past policy choices. This is particularly clear in the decentralization endeavor: the process of power delegation to state governments has been designed in a rather incremental and selective fashion, primarily because the traditional educational arrangement served as a disincentive to the creation of strong and coherent educational bureaucracies at the state level. The ongoing process of institutional change will therefore continue to be incremental and will be shaped by historical structural constraints. And second, despite the state's *dirigisme* of the reform process, the educational reform will be, in the end, the result of the dynamics of the power struggle between state and societal actors that the reforms themselves have instigated at the regional and local levels.

## The Traditional Institutional Arrangement

Before the 1992–1993 reform, educational policymaking in Mexico was conducted through the institutional arrangement that had emerged in the 1940s with the creation of the national teachers' union (SNTE). SNTE was conceived as a state initiative to bring fractious and ideologically fragmented local unions under a national umbrella organization within the Institutional Revolutionary Party (PRI), with the dual purpose of channeling conflict through a corporatist organization while facilitating educational policymaking for the state. As a result SNTE was designed to closely resemble the highly centralized and pyramidal organization of the Secretariat of Public Education (SEP), which had been in existence in the executive branch since 1921.[3]

### The Politics of Power Accommodation, 1940–1970

Article 3 of the Constitution of 1917 and the Organic Law of Public Education of 1941 (later transformed into the Federal Law of Education in 1973), together with an array of informal rules, constituted the institutional framework that determined SEP's and SNTE's rights within the policymaking process. Those definitions of rights largely shaped the power structure of the educational sector and thus configured the educational decisionmaking process. According to law federal, state, and municipal governments were coresponsible for public education. In practice, however, the federal law defined as SEP prerogative almost every aspect of educational decisionmaking, from the design and planning of educational services to their provision and evaluation. Moreover, from the outset parents were alienated from the educational process, since parents' associations were prohibited by law from participation in pedagogical and labor matters.

At least until the early 1970s educational policymaking was the result of continual negotiations and accommodation between government and union officials at the federal, state, and local levels. In the federal sphere SNTE leaders quietly won important positions within the educational bureaucracy itself, including SEP general directorates in charge of the provision of educational services. In this way the union was able to monopolize a host of academic and operational decisions at the state and local levels, such as the recruitment of teachers, siting of schools, appointments of principals and area supervisors, and general guidelines for teachers' promotion.[4] For its part the educational bureaucracy retained rights over most top education positions in the executive branch.

Until the early 1970s the paramount aim of educational policy in Mexico was universal primary education, in other words, a quantitative goal. As has been well argued elsewhere, that goal was designed to reinforce the hegemony of the Mexican state.[5] Likewise, the merely quantitative goal also served as a means for the union to enhance its own size, resources, and power. In fact, even in the local school every teacher had to adapt attitudes, strategies, and activities to mobilizing toward this goal. And all were successful in reinforcing and extending the power structures, but the results for educating the populace were devastating, as we will see.

### Alternating Accommodations and Power Struggles, 1970–1992

Power sharing and accommodation, albeit in different degrees, formed the strategy followed by most educational authorities and union leaders until the early 1970s. The administration of Luis Echeverría Alvarez (1970–1976), however, inaugurated a long period, which still endures today, characterized by cycles of power struggles, formal and informal bargaining, and further accommodations between SEP officials and union leaders. Two powerful new groups within each organization sparked the struggles during those years: a group of reformers in SEP brought together with the creation of the Subsecretariat of Planning and Educational Coordination in 1971,[6] and a group called the Revolutionary Vanguard, which became the hegemonic force in SNTE under the union presidency of Carlos Jonguitud Barrios in 1972.

For the new SEP officials the primary goal of reform was administrative and educational efficiency. Deconcentration and later decentralization[7] were the principal means to that end. But the principal goal of the decentralization agenda was, again, political. SEP reformists embraced deconcentration, and later decentralization, to regain the islands of power SNTE had conquered in the administration. Not surprisingly, then, until

1992 the SNTE leadership always opposed the decentralization agenda, arguing that it carried the seeds of a potential fragmentation of the national union. Decentralization thus became a magic concept for some, and an anathema for others. Almost two decades of stop-and-go decentralization attempts followed, but as will be discussed shortly, most were fruitless. Both the union's bargaining power and the regime's dependence on SNTE's capacity for massive electoral mobilization repeatedly compelled a variety of state actors to rein in the decentralization venture.

The rise of the Vanguard opened a new chapter in the life of the union. As the number of teachers rose yearly in the sixties and seventies, both the central bureaucracy and the union expanded dramatically. By the late 1970s SNTE had grown into the largest national union in the country and thus into the most powerful single union within the sectorial organization of the PRI. Traditionally, SNTE's loyalty to the regime had been partially recompensed not only with bureaucratic positions in SEP, but also with political niches in state legislatures and municipal governments. The expansion of the union, and the fortification of the Vanguard's bargaining power, allowed SNTE to reap political positions at the national level and to further penetrate regional and local governments, including a state governorship, seats in the Senate and the Chamber of Deputies, as well as a host of municipal presidencies and seats in state legislatures during the late 1970s and 1980s.

The history of educational decentralization in Mexico is one of ambivalence and ambiguity. The first step in the long road of attempts traces back the Echeverría administration when the emerging "technocrats" in SEP formed nine Regional Offices of Decentralized Administrative Services. Most of those offices remained under strict control of the central bureaucracy, however, and practically no power was delegated to regional authorities. By the end of the Echeverría administration, the offices' activities had become meaningless. The second attempt was a policy of deconcentration inaugurated by Fernando Solana, secretary of education in the sexenio of José López Portillo (1976–1982). Solana created General Delegations of SEP in each of Mexico's thirty-one states. Each delegation was headed by a representative of the Secretary of Education and had the task of coordinating educational policy in the state. Although the regional offices were generally kept from the policymaking process, SEP regional delegates initially replaced the union's delegates as intermediaries between state and federal authorities. SNTE managed to survive, however, and even to grow stronger in the process, mainly because of the emergence, in the late 1970s, of a vocal dissident movement within SNTE known as the National Coordinator of Education Workers (CNTE). In the wake of the 1982 presidential election, and before the consolidation of CNTE, the state elite restrained the deconcentration strategy and offered PRI candidacies and bureaucratic positions to SNTE's leadership in order to avoid electoral difficulties.

The third and most ambitious decentralization initiative was announced in the inaugural address of President Miguel de la Madrid Hurtado in December 1982. The president's original goal was to transfer the
responsibility and revenues for basic educational services to state governments. The SEP General Delegations created by the previous administration changed names twice, eventually to General Directorates of Coordinated Services of Public Education. Their designated tasks were to be
expanded to include coordinating and unifying federal and state activities,
hand-in-hand with the newly created State Councils of Public Education.
The final result, however, would resemble past failures: SEP ultimately
bypassed the state governments, agencies, and councils; and SNTE, em-
powered by the electoral crises of the mid-1980s, captured a large number
of the SEP Directorates.[8]

### Power Structures in the Schools

The macroinstitutional arrangement defined at the apex of Mexico's educational pyramid provided every actor in the hierarchy with a clear set of
incentives, including patronage for jobs and promotions and posts in the
legislative and executive branches of all levels of government, from national to municipal. At the micro level, in the schools' domain, the formal
and informal rules have been a major contributing factor in determining
the schools' academic and power structures and, consequently, the performance of inspectors, principals, teachers, and students.

Under the traditional arrangement practically every primary school in
Mexico was headed by a principal appointed by the teachers' union. The
principal, in turn, was subject to the vigilance of an area inspector, who
also was a SNTE appointee. The fate of school teachers rested in the hands
of the inspector and the principal, for they defined and implemented the
hiring and promotion policies; the annual evaluation of the teacher was
typically drafted by the principal and signed by the supervisor and the
school's union representative.[9] Hence, the structure of power along the
educational hierarchy turned interactions in the school into patron-client
relations.

A pristine manifestation of this phenomenon lies in the functioning of
the school itself. To fulfill the academic and administrative goals of the
school, every principal was assisted by two organizations: the Scholastic
Technical Council (the council, hereafter), and the Working Commission.
The council, as the academic organ of the school, had as its goal to support
the principal in implementing the academic programs designed by SEP, as
well as to evaluate the school's academic performance. The commission, a
nonacademic organ, addressed such issues as the search for alternative funding, the organization of the annual *kermis,* or festival, and other administrative issues.[10] Given that every actor's performance had been traditionally

judged according to the fulfillment of the quantitative goals, most teachers rationally strove to participate in the commission rather than the council, even at the cost of sacrificing teaching hours. Clearly, teachers had little incentives for academic updating or investing time in academic matters related to the council. It is no surprise that, according to a study conducted in the early 1980s, primary school teachers devoted less than 50 percent of the time children spent at school to academic activities, spending the majority of their school hours on administrative tasks.[11]

As a result, in terms of the educational process schools turned into credential factories: teachers hardly taught, and students seldom learned. The overall results, however, never unmasked this profile of the educational system, for evaluation was left in the hands of school teachers and inspectors. Since quantity was the paramount goal, teachers systematically overinflated grades. This has been dramatically proven by official and privately conducted standardized exams in recent years.[12]

## The "Educational Disaster"

The institutional framework that governs the production of education in Mexico, the organization of schools, and the incentives principals and teachers have traditionally faced has had a direct effect on students' performance.[13] Educational outcomes in Mexico can be succinctly summarized with a few revealing figures. In the 1990–1991 school year 14.6 million students—over 90 percent of children of primary school age—were officially enrolled in primary school in Mexico. But in that same year only half of the children who had entered school six years earlier completed it, and according to standardized exams, only 16 percent of those who finished primary school met the minimal academic requirements of that scholastic cycle.[14] Moreover, educational outcomes varied dramatically across the country. The most developed states, such as Baja California Norte, Nuevo León, and the Federal District (Mexico City), displayed much higher average grades and school completion rates than poor, rural states such as Chiapas, Guerrero, Campeche, and Oaxaca.

All told, the system has proven to be highly inefficient and unequal. The political implications of the "educational disaster" are enormous, for education has historically been one of the cardinal elements of the rhetoric of the postrevolutionary regime. In fact, in the absence of clean and credible elections, education, together with other social "revolutionary achievements" such as land reform and workers' constitutional labor rights, has been historically invoked as one of the primary sources of the regime's legitimacy. Hence, the educational disaster is a potentially explosive issue for the Mexican regime, simply because it contributes to the image triggered by the economic crisis of the mid-eighties: a Leviathan without clothes.

## Educational Reform Under the Salinas Administration

The educational reforms of the Salinas administration can be divided into two stages, according to the level of uncertainty the state elite was facing at the time. In the morning of the administration, confronted with a high level of electoral uncertainty and political insecurity, the Salinista elite reduced the nation's educational goals to dismantling the Vanguard's power base in SNTE. As the sexenio unfolded, and uncertainty diminished as a result of the administration's early political maneuvers, Salinas managed to bring an autonomous state back in, capable of initiating the pending educational reform.

### Initial, Tentative Reforms, 1988–1991

The first stage of the Salinas reforms was constrained by the "electoral earthquake" of July 1988. In the 1988 presidential elections two very threatening factors for the regime converged. On the one hand, the ballot boxes echoed the growing discontent of the middle class and the urban poor with the social costs of the economic crisis and the adjustment process. On the other, the election turned into a plebiscite on the electoral rules and the corporatist system of interest representation, which the regime lost.[15] The political insecurity triggered by the electoral crisis strongly influenced the state leadership's priorities, and that, in turn, shaped the goals of educational policy in the early years of the Salinas term.

During the first days of the administration the priority of the executive branch was simply to secure its place in office. Very early on Salinas attempted to separate the presidency from the corporatist pillars of the PRI. The rationale then seemed transparent. Not only did they embody the organizations in crisis; most of them had opposed Salinas's candidacy. Accordingly, by appointing Manuel Bartlett, former secretary of the interior during the De la Madrid administration, as secretary of education, Salinas sent a clear message. With a hard-liner at the helm of SEP, the key aim of educational policy would be to dismantle the Vanguard's power base in SNTE by confronting Jonguitud directly. The rationale for this goal was twofold: first, to recapture the state's power over educational decision-making from the national union, and second, to gain control over conflict resolution in the education system, because SNTE was no longer effectively absorbing teachers' dissent. It is critical to note, as well, that the Vanguard and Jonguitud were viewed as part of the old guard of the PRI, which continued to oppose the cornerstone of the Salinas agenda, namely, economic reform.

Continuous public demonstrations by the dissident CNTE during the first months of 1989 cleared the path for Jonguitud's ouster. The dissidents' demands included substantial wage increases, after six consecutive years of real wage loses,[16] and union democratization. After three months of intense mobilizations of CNTE, Salinas succeeded in provoking Jonguitud's resignation. He was replaced by Elba Esther Gordillo. With strong presidential support Gordillo grew out of her initial weakness in the post by introducing an agenda that included an ambitious plan of union reconstruction and the elaboration of a union program of educational reform. In January 1990, at the First Extraordinary National Congress of SNTE in Tepic, Nayarit, Gordillo presented her project of Frente Amplio (Wide Front). The purpose of the project was to open institutional channels to absorb the dissidents within SNTE, to provide the sectionals with some formal autonomy, and to break the umbilical cord linking SNTE with the PRI. More fundamentally, the program was intended to reestablish legitimacy for the SNTE leadership. Without a power base to support her agenda, however, Gordillo's program did not materialize in Tepic.

Thus, within the first six months of the administration Bartlett had accomplished the objective that had arguably made him the right man for SEP. But from that point on, and until his removal in January 1992, the Salinas educational project did not advance in any substantial manner. Bartlett was not aloof, however. Under his control SEP elaborated a project to draft regional programs for the modernization of basic education. According to this project every state government would elaborate a regional program of education that would unite federal and regional bureaucracies in the provision of educational services.[17] The underlying purpose of the project was to recover SEP's lead in a host of states in which SNTE had taken control of the regional educational bureaucracies by the end of the De la Madrid term. Bartlett was successful in this endeavor, and the federal government ended up drafting most of the programs. By mid-1991 Bartlett's team had prepared an ambitious plan for educational decentralization and a pilot program for the reform of primary school programs and curricula, as well as textbooks. Those materials were put to the test in the 1991–1992 school year.[18]

Although the Bartlett reform package was congruent with the Salinas educational policy aims, it never saw light. Undoubtedly, the uncertainty of the first months in office kept Salinas from carrying out deep reforms. Beyond the administration's timing, however, perhaps the most important factor that kept Salinas from allowing Bartlett to take his reforms out of the oven was the stalemate to which the secretary had driven SEP's relationship with SNTE. The reform package envisioned by Bartlett entailed a complex bargaining process with the union. By all accounts Bartlett was not up to the task; the virtues that had gained him SEP's office had become his Achilles' heel. In the eyes of the Salinista elite his policy style would have put the decentralization process in jeopardy. Amidst other important ministerial changes, and particularly with the fusion of the Secretariat for Programming and Budget with the Secretariat of Finance and Public Credit, Bartlett was forced to resign in January 1992.

## Fundamental Reforms, 1992–1993

In the second stage of Salinas's educational reforms, the administration overcame the political crisis and insecurity of its early days and therefore could risk more comprehensive change. The second stage took off in January 1992 when Ernesto Zedillo Ponce de León, then Secretary of Programming and Budget, was appointed to replace Bartlett at SEP. Within a few months Zedillo announced the long-awaited educational reform: the National Agreement for the Modernization of Basic Education. The ANMEB was translated into amendments of Articles 3 and 31 of the Constitution and into the General Law of Education in the spring and summer of 1993, respectively.[19]

By any account this set of reforms is the most far-reaching educational initiative since the creation of the teachers' union in the early 1940s. The core idea behind the reform was to change the institutional arrangement that has traditionally governed the educational process, in other words, to redefine the property rights in the educational policymaking process.

The roots of the 1992–1993 reforms are many. The most important ones are of an economic, political, and policy nature.[20] In the official rhetoric education has been systematically portrayed as a necessary condition for economic modernization. In every official document, in the National Development Plan, in the presidential exposition of motives for reform of Articles 3 and 31 of the Constitution and the General Law of Education, Salinas emphasized, again and again, the role of education and human capital development in determining Mexico's competitiveness in world markets and, hence, the long-term growth of its economy. Is there any solid foundation for this apparent educational fervor? Both theory and practice provide sound bases for a strong concern with education. In years past the most influential neoclassical models of economic growth have demonstrated that human capital is the single most important determinant of sustained growth in the long run.[21] Additionally, the experience of most Southeast Asian countries suggests that a low-cost labor force is only a short-lived comparative advantage. There sustained growth has relied heavily on large investments in human capital.[22] Hence, the change in relative prices induced by Mexico's process of marketization and insertion in world markets gave a strong incentive for institutional reform of education.[23]

Beyond the economic argument lies a clear political rationale. To consolidate his place in office, Salinas pursued a double track: He proceeded to break down the leadership of union groups that were a latent threat to his project, while concurrently building a coalition of support for reform.[24]

By dismantling the Vanguard's power, Salinas managed to recover the state's leadership at the federal level. But to establish the state's lead over educational policymaking at the regional level, there seemed to be only one option: to transfer, finally, educational decisionmaking to the state governments, thereby destroying the union's state-level islands of power in the General Directorates of Coordinated Services of Public Education. In the end a long-term perspective prevailed. As the Salinas project will eventually result in further decentralization of economic and political life, state bureaucracies that are strong, autonomous, and highly coherent will increasingly become a sine qua non for the implementation of reform at the regional and local levels. Since education represents the largest public sector enterprise in the country, its decentralization seemed to be the natural starting point.

Reforming education was viewed as politically desirable for two other reasons. The first, as mentioned earlier, was that education has historically been an ideological pillar of the postrevolutionary regime. Since the "educational disaster" further threatened the legitimacy of the regime, reforming education represented an essential element of the overall Salinista project of "reforming the revolution." The second reason was that the academic curricula and programs, as well as the textbooks, had been designed by previous administrations, based on a radically different ideological orientation. Indeed, the social sciences textbooks, particularly for the sixth grade, reflected the "Third World" Echeverrista rhetoric of the early 1970s, in which nationalism, anti-imperialism, and populism predominate. (For instance, in the sixth grade text the section dealing with the Chinese Cultural Revolution objects to the main political aspects of the Mao regime but leaves unquestioned its other socioeconomic and organizational facets.) Beyond any strongly avowed concern for historical objectivity, the main problem for the Salinas administration was that the content of the books was ideologically antagonistic to the Salinista discourse. History had to be rewritten for the "children of the Salinismo," the NAFTA generation.

Notwithstanding the importance of education, one of the most puzzling questions about the educational reform is why did Salinas's social reforms begin with education and not with other social policies such as health or housing? Certainly part of the answer has to do with the relative size and, hence, importance of the educational sector. But the other side of the coin is of a policy nature. Decentralization in education, albeit largely constrained, had already been an articulated state policy for more than a decade. That accumulated precedent did not exist in other policy areas, except for some decentralization attempts in the health sector under De la Madrid.

## The Design of the ANMEB and the Politics of Implementation

The National Agreement for the Modernization of Basic Education consists of three basic policy goals. The first one is the "reorganization of the educational system," including two main objectives, to decentralize the administrative and financial management of preschool, primary, secondary, and teacher education to state governments and to create school-based, municipal, and state councils to involve teachers and now parents and students in an organization for "social accountability" for each school's performance. The second policy goal is the "renovation of educational materials and contents" through the Emerging Program of Educational Content and Material Reformulation. Briefly, this program aims at the complete redesign of curricula and programs for basic education, as well as the national textbooks. Lastly, the third goal is the "revaluation of the teaching function." Two programs stem from this target: the Emerging Program of Educational Updating, which will train teachers to use the new curricula and materials, and the Magisterial Career, which arose from an old union demand to establish mechanisms for horizontal promotion of school teachers according to their experience and merit.[25]

A cluster of questions immediately comes to the fore. How was the agreement designed? Did the state conceive the reform autonomously? Has the state been capable of implementing reform? What role has the teachers' union played in the process? Although Zedillo frequently consulted the general secretary of SNTE throughout the elaboration of the ANMEB, the state remained, in essence, relatively autonomous in designing the final reform package. The role the union played in the design of the agreement was confined to adapting its structure and discourse to the imminent changes. In February 1992 the union celebrated its Second Extraordinary National Congress. For Gordillo the purpose of the congress was to realize her agenda of Tepic, which was still pending. The two most important statutory changes achieved in the congress involved (1) the delegation of resources and collective bargaining rights, as well as decisionmaking power, from SNTE's National Council to the sectionals, to negotiate labor relations with state governments, and (2) a prohibition against any union member holding a SNTE appointment to head a political party or, by the same token, occupying a popularly elected position. Despite a final retreat by some of the dissident CNTE delegates to the congress, the meeting overall served to revitalize SNTE in the wake of the approaching reform, as a moderate CNTE group was partially reabsorbed into SNTE, and Gordillo's leadership was strengthened. The partial recuperation of teachers' real wages during the years since Salinas's election, albeit insufficient, also contributed to fortifying Gordillo's position.[26]

Before delving into the implementation process a puzzling question still awaits an answer: Why did SNTE agree to a decentralization process it had historically opposed? In theory, no sectional of the union, except for those strong ones that had opposed the national leadership of Gordillo and that faced weak state governments, had the incentive to comply with the decentralization process. Arguably, the reason no sectional launched a strong opposition to the decentralization initiative was because, despite

their regional force, they simply lacked the political resources and lever-
age to challenge a decision made at the apex of SNTE. As discussed earlier, since its inception the corporatist nature of SNTE reserved little independent power and autonomy to the sectionals. It was not until the
Second Extraordinary National Congress in 1992, faced with the imminent
decentralization, that the sectionals gained some formal independence
from SNTE's General Secretariat. But this does not solve the puzzle entirely. Why, then, did the national leadership not oppose the decentralization process until the end? In spite of the extensive housecleaning Gordillo
had undertaken since 1989, and despite the changing trends that were securing her leadership, she remained in a relatively weak position vis-à-vis
the reinvigorated SEP, headed by a secretary who had full presidential
support. Gordillo had but two choices: to oppose the impending reforms
from a position of relative weakness, or to jump on the wave of reform and
try to shape the final outcome. Gordillo chose the second strategy. As we
will see, the statutory changes in SNTE, and Gordillo's choice to participate in the ANMEB, have in fact allowed the union to influence the nature
of the reform during its implementation stage.

The instrumentation of the agreement set in motion an intense bargaining process between the state and a variety of actors in the broader society. The reorganization of the educational system began with a series of
accords on implementation signed by federal and state governments. Yet
the formal completion of the process, as well as the definition of the terms
under which social participation would take place, had to await changes
in the General Law of Education in July 1993. Meanwhile, the emerging
programs for the reformulation of educational curricula and materials and
the programs to revaluate the teaching function started immediately. I will
first address these two sets of programs and leave the substance of the
General Law for the final part of this section.

The reform of educational curricula and materials has been only partially undertaken because of a battle over the gist of the history textbooks.
In August 1992 the educational authorities imparted new courses to the national faculty through satellite television broadcasts.[27] The courses were
not as fruitful as the authorities had expected, because new textbooks had
not yet been distributed to all areas, and teachers remained skeptical about
teaching the new courses with old materials. The only textbook that was
available for the 1992–1993 school year was the highly contested history
book for the fifth and sixth grades. During the summer of 1992 a group of
prestigious historians elaborated those texts. Thousands of books were
printed for the 1992–1993 school year. Yet as the books were being distributed, the teachers' union, together with a variety of state and social actors (including the military, most opposition parties, influential journalists,
intellectuals, and academics), disputed the historical accuracy and objectivity of the books. As the academic year started, a joint commission of

SEP officials and SNTE representatives was created to discuss the content of the history books. As a result of the negotiations Zedillo was forced to cancel distribution of the new books. A second version was elaborated a few months later through a national competition. The awarded version, however, was not published either; at the last minute SEP found it pedagogically inappropriate.[28] A third version is now being developed.

Regarding the reevaluation of the teaching function, the Program of Academic Updating was structured once the initial program had been terminated in August 1992. This was an important task designed to help meet the second goal of the reevaluation: the Program of the Magisterial Career. In January 1993 a joint commission of SEP authorities and union representatives announced the main guidelines of the Magisterial Career. It is to be a five-tiered career ladder for teachers' promotion, based on the following criteria: experience, academic credentials, participation in the Program of Academic Updating, professional skills and knowledge, and performance. State government authorities, under guidelines from the federal government, are now responsible for evaluating professional skills and knowledge. For its part the Scholastic Technical Council (STC) of each school and the newly created State Commissions of Evaluation are to evaluate teacher performance. Teachers, principals, and inspectors can participate in the program.[29] In the end SEP managed to convince the union to accept the evaluation of teachers' skills and knowledge. In exchange, however, SNTE won an important participative role in the assessment of teacher's performance, through the STCs and the state commissions.[30] According to official figures 200,000 teachers—nearly half of the primary school faculty in the country—were evaluated in March 1993. More exams are planned in the near future, since by mid-1993 three-quarters of the national faculty had already registered into the Magisterial Career.[31]

Finally, the reorganization of the educational system was only roughly delineated in the ANMEB. The nature and the scope of the changes therefore required the formal transformation, and the clear definition, of property rights in the policymaking process. In early summer 1993 SEP presented an initiative for a new Federal Law of Education, which was approved by the Chamber of Deputies in July. The final institutional outcome largely resembles the decentralization project previously presented in the ANMEB. Only the chapter on social participation suffered some important changes that resulted from concessions SEP made to SNTE, namely, prohibiting parental participation in pedagogical and labor matters. The final outcome on this subject was eventually modified by opposition parties in the legislature.

As portrayed in the first part of this chapter, decentralization has consistently been an anathema in the union's agenda. Fearful of any resulting fragmentation, SNTE has always intensely opposed the concept. Nonetheless, after almost a decade of fruitless attempts by earlier administrations,

Salinas's finally institutionalized the process. The 1993 General Law of Education (LGE) defines a new structure of rights in the educational system. According to the new law the federal government has the right to determine the academic curricula and programs; to elaborate the national textbooks; to regulate the national system of teachers' education, updating, and training; and to regulate social participation in education in general. Furthermore, SEP has the obligation to evaluate the national educational system and to design, together with state governments, compensatory programs for the most backward regions in the country. For their part state governments have the right to manage educational expenditures and the administration and provision of preschool, basic, indigenous, and teacher education.

The LGE opens the possibility that the regional and federal authorities will reach agreements on issues of coordination and requires that they get together systematically to exchange opinions and formulate recommendations to develop the decentralization process. In the original LGE initiative SEP suggested the creation of a National Council of Educational Authorities (CNAE), formed by the secretary of public education and the regional and local educational authorities. The purpose was to create an institutional mechanism that would provide SEP with the regulatory capacities to suggest policies and coordinate federal and state governments.[32] During the legislative deliberations, however, the opposition parties managed to prevent SEP from retaining large regulatory capacities and thus impeded the creation of the CNAE.

Nevertheless, there was still the possibility that the secretariat would be the de facto conductor of the decentralization process. In fact, a few important organizational changes within SEP itself and in most regional bureaucracies will allow the federal agency to determine the pace and terms of the decentralization. To initiate the delegation of educational services, twenty-six out of the thirty-one state governments in the country created administrative bodies charged with "receiving and operating" the educational services delegated by the secretariat. These parallel bureaucracies had the role of conducting the federal delegation of power through an institutional channel different from the established ones, which were still dominated by SNTE. Similarly, SEP undertook a bureaucratic reorganization to adapt the agency itself to its new tasks. In this organizational reform the executive created an organ for coordination between the federation and the states, the Coordination of SEP Representatives in the States (CRSE). According to SEP documents the CRSE will promote, support, and verify the execution of the federal and state governments' accords resulting from the ANMEB.

As called for in the General Law and reflected in the organizational changes in SEP and the regional educational bureaucracies, the decentralization process has been designed, and will be carried out, as an incremental process. This is not the result of technical wisdom but rather of the difficulties involved in the political management of the reform. The regional organisms created by state governments to carry out the delegation process, and the CRSE, will function as the organizational channels through which SEP will negotiate the pace of decentralization with each state governor. In fact, the process is not only incremental but discretionary too, depending on the corporate coherence of the state bureaucracy and on the relative strength of the respective sectional of SNTE. Since most states do not have a coherent educational bureaucracy to carry out the reform, full decentralization will take years to come. Further, because not all leaders of the sectionals will comply with the reform and most have strong organizational capacities, the central bureaucracy will be very cautious in leaving the educational process in the hands of all the governors.

Probably one of the most important innovations of the LGE is its chapter on educational equality. For the first time in Mexican educational history, the state is formally obliged by the Federal Law of Education to design compensatory programs to assure equal educational opportunities across the country. In the 1992–1993 academic year the state provided a variety of scholarships to more than a million students through six compensatory programs. According to official accounts the majority of the resources were funneled to the least-developed regions in the country, including the states of Chiapas, Oaxaca, and Guerrero. A final assessment of the capacity of those programs to reach the poorest Mexicans still awaits further disaggregated empirical research.

The chapter of the General Law on social participation delineates the scope and limits of different social actors' involvement in the educational process. The law still bans parents' associations from participating in "pedagogical and labor" aspects of the school. Yet new channels of participation were opened. According to the General Law school, municipal, state, and federal authorities are all obliged to stimulate creation of Councils of Social Participation (CSP) at their respective level of the educational system. Each CSP is composed of parents and parental associations, teachers and union members, and educational authorities. The task of the CPSs is to foster collaboration between parents and the school, the school and the municipality, and so on up to the federal authorities. As noted earlier, in the SEP-SNTE negotiations leading to the first draft of the General Law presented to Congress, the union retained its long-standing claim to independence from parental influence: no parental association, or any CSP, was to be allowed to intervene in pedagogical issues. Indeed, in the executive's initiative the school remained as the teachers' "greenhouse." The union's reservations on the subject stem from a deeply rooted union concern that opening the school to parents would be tantamount to opening the door to the Catholic church and to the conservative National Action Party (PAN).[33] But in the later legislative negotiations leading to the approval of the General Law, the opposition parties managed to change the wording of the restriction, allowing for the CPSs' right to "express an opinion" on pedagogical issues.

## Political Consequences and Prospects for Further Reform

The 1992 educational reform and its ongoing implementation so far display a half-full, half-empty glass. On the one hand, the state has been capable of undertaking such a Herculean task as having the faculty nationwide undergo standardized examinations. On the other, it has failed to elaborate a new history textbook, and most significantly, it has been compelled to pursue a rather incremental decentralization process. The fate of educational decentralization is uncertain, insofar as the regional bureaucracies remain relatively weak and the local sectionals of the union are well organized and quite likely to take over the reform at the local level. At the bottom line the educational decentralization offers an interesting example of how past policy choices can constrain present alternatives. Indeed, under the Salinas administration the state might have been capable of instigating a historic educational reform. As it has tried to further the decentralization process, however, it has encountered a bottleneck in the regional balance of power engendered by the very institutional arrangement that the reforms were designed to change.

How far do the reforms go in changing the traditional institutional arrangement and the resulting balance of power that, to a large extent, have caused the "educational disaster"? How conducive is the new arrangement to better educational results than the current ones? In the final analysis do the changes set the stage for further reforms, namely, more autonomous schools with greater parental involvement? In principle, the programs derived from the ANMEB, the constitutional reforms, and the LGE call for an institutional arrangement that will increase the system's overall efficiency and that, through compensatory programs, will result in a more equitable provision of educational opportunities. Below the surface, however, the educational outcomes are still highly uncertain. By reorganizing the structure of the system and redefining property rights in the policymaking process, the reforms *have* changed the educational balance of power. Yet the new distribution of power is not at all clear, for the balance will differ from one region to another and will be determined by the organizational power and the different strategies educational and social actors will follow. In short, the reform has opened a Pandora's box.

Although SEP has formally delegated a great deal of decisionmaking power to the state governments, it has, paradoxically, revitalized its own power. The decentralization process has compelled the agency to reorganize. In so doing, SEP has crippled the functional branches of the bureaucracy devoted to operationalizing the system—the very islands of power SNTE had held in the past. Further, the General Law reserves large regulatory capacities for SEP, which will allow the agency to shape the decentralization process, especially in those states with little bureaucratic coherence and educational management expertise.

Yet power delegation invigorates state governments. The regional educational authorities have been not only strengthened by that delegation of power but also indirectly fortified by the disappearance of some of the power niches SNTE had gained by taking over the ambivalent decentralization policy pursued in the past. The road toward a strong and coherent regional bureaucracy is still long and contingent. In the meantime, the reform will be in jeopardy in those states in which neither the bureaucracy, nor civil society, can outweigh the regional power of the union sectionals that originally opposed the reform.

Uncertainty about the future is nowhere more acute than within SNTE. Upon rising to power, Gordillo introduced an agenda of union reform that allowed her to remain at the forefront of the General Secretariat of SNTE and to fortify the union before the reform process began. As already argued, these developments did allow the teachers' union to shape the implementation of the reform. But the very changes that are currently being implemented will have a dramatic effect on the union itself. However mild the short-term impact has been on the unity of SNTE, the medium-term effect will determine the very viability of the national union. The fate of SNTE will be determined in part by the balance of power at the regional and local levels. In principle, all the sectionals have an incentive to safeguard a national union that could continue to serve as support in negotiations with regional authorities. This will be particularly the case for those sectionals that face relatively strong state governments. Ultimately, however, the future of the union will depend both on the sectionals' needs and strategic choices and on SNTE's flexibility in adapting to new circumstances. Here is where the corporatist structure of the union, and the remaining informal links with the PRI, will come to a crossroads.

For their part the fifty-five sectionals of the union have experienced impacts with opposite effects. On the one hand, those that had taken over the decentralization efforts of De la Madrid lost, at least in principle, a share of power in the branch of the federal bureaucracy in each state. On the other, after the statutory reforms of the union's Second Extraordinary Congress, the sectionals are now more autonomous to negotiate with state authorities. Moreover, SNTE managed in large part to safeguard the union's hegemony over the functioning of the school. Although teachers have complied with the standard examinations, the Program of the Magisterial Career remains to some extent in union hands. True, inspectors and principals no longer hold the final word on teachers' promotion. Yet, as heads of the Scholastic Technical Councils, principals still have unchecked power, and therefore large incentives to carry on with traditional patron-client relations in the schools. Their main source of power is that their personal assessment of teachers' performance still has an important, albeit not determinant, weight in the teachers' pursuit of the Magisterial Career.

The Program of the Magisterial Career has nevertheless created a somewhat different set of incentives for teachers at their workplace. In fact, their participation in the program is potentially the key to the success or failure of the reform. Only by strong participation in the program will the teachers be able to take control of the Scholastic Technical Councils and thereby diminish the likelihood that patron-client relations will prevail in the schools. In so doing, teachers can break the authoritarian structure of Mexican schools and expand the horizon for the establishment of autonomous educational institutions. As a result, SNTE itself would be driven toward democratization.

Finally, parents still remain as the outcasts of the educational process. Although parents now have the right to express their opinion in the process through the Councils for Social Participation, their true involvement in academic affairs will ultimately be subject to teachers' willingness to open the classroom door. Insofar as parents are not systematically involved in the educational process of their children, not only will valuable information be lost, but the Mexican school system will remain unaccountable at its roots. If that happens, the scholastic achievement of Mexican students will remain unsatisfactory.

## Conclusion

The 1992–1993 reform of the Mexican educational system outlines a new institutional framework that, in principle, allows for significant improvements in the performance of the educational system. Whether the new framework will prove more efficient and equitable than the traditional one, however, remains to be seen. The true scope of the reform awaits its further implementation.

Undoubtedly, one of the most important changes included in the reform is that, in the future, the fate of the educational system will increasingly depend on state and social actors at the regional and local levels. Although SEP retains substantial regulatory capacities under the new set of institutional rules, its ability to shape the implementation of the reform will decline as a new, decentralized institutional equilibrium is reached. Nevertheless, that process itself will be constrained by the weakness of Mexico's regional and local bureaucracies, which for decades have stood in the shadows of the strong, centralized, presidentialist system fostered by the nation's postrevolutionary policies. Their weakness is likely to be the main obstacle to further educational reforms.

The success of the reform's implementation will ultimately depend, therefore, on regional and local actors and on the outcomes of their bargaining over the implementation process. Should the current reform initiatives succeed, more and more teachers and parents are likely to try to gain control over their schools. And, in turn, if the teachers and parents are able to harvest the fruits of the reform at the school level, the authoritarian nature of Mexican schools will be close to an end.

Greater participation in defining the academic goals of the school—by teachers and parents, as well as principals and students—certainly will not be a frictionless process. In fact, in the years to come we can expect to witness a fierce struggle among state and social actors over control of Mexico's schools. At stake in the struggle is nothing less than Mexico's future.

## Notes

1. SNTE comprises 1,400,000 members. Gilberto Guevara Niebla, "El malestar educativo," *Nexos,* no. 170 (February 1992): 25.

2. I am grateful for the helpful comments and suggestions made by Sergio Aguayo, Anne Bax, Roberto Blancarte, Alain de Remes, Matilde Luna, and Riordan Roett. The usual disclaimers apply.

3. From its inception SNTE was constituted by "sectionals," the regional representatives of the national union. According to the statutes of SNTE, however, the sectionals have very little autonomy. See Susan Street, "El SNTE y la política educativa, 1979–1990," *Revista Mexicana de Sociología* 2 (April–June 1992): 62–64.

4. For a detailed account of power accommodation between the "normalists" and "technocrats" within SEP, see Noel McGinn and Susan Street, "The Political Rationality of Resource Allocation in Mexican Public Education," *Comparative Education Review* (June 1982): 182–189.

5. See Daniel Morales-Gomez and Carlos A. Torres, *The State, Corporatist Politics, and Educational Policy-Making in Mexico* (New York: Praeger, 1990). It is important to point out the difficulties involved in arguing that the Mexican educational policy of these years had a clear economic objective. The fact that the import substitution industrialization strategy seldom requires technological change, innovation, and hence large investments in human capital is largely reflected in the purely quantitative educational policy goals of different administrations. In a similar vein McGinn and Street have concluded that the educational process in Mexico has been more a process of political capital formation than one of human capital generation. Noel McGinn and Susan Street, "Has Mexican Education Generated Human or Political Capital?" *Comparative Education Review* 20, no. 3 (1984): 323–336.

6. McGinn and Street, "The Political Rationality," p. 187.

7. *Deconcentration* refers to the delegation of decisionmaking power within one organization, whereas *decentralization* refers to the delegation of power to a different organization. See Development Research Center (CIDAC), *Educación para una economía competitiva: Hacia una estrategia de reforma* (Mexico City: Diana, 1992), pp. 88–110.

8. For a more detailed analysis of the history of the decentralization policies, see ibid.; Isaías Alvarez García, "La descentralización," in *La catástrofe silenciosa,*

ed. Gilberto Guevara Niebla (Mexico City: Fondo de Cultura Económica, 1992); McGinn and Street, "The Political Rationality"; and Francisco Miranda López, "Descentralización educativa y modernización del estado," in *Revista Mexicana de Sociología* 2 (April–June 1992): 19–44.

9. See Street, "El SNTE"; and Justa Ezpeleta, "El Consejo Técnico: Eficacia pedagógica y estructura de poder en la escuela primaria mexicana," in *Revista Latinoamericana de Estudios Educativos* 20, no. 4 (Mexico City: Center for Educational Studies, 1991): 13–33.

10. For a description of the councils and commissions, see Ezpeleta, ibid., pp. 13–33.

11. Elsie Rockwell et al., "El uso del tiempo de clase y los libros de texto en primaria," quoted in José Angel Pescador, "Innovaciones para mejorar la calidad de la educación básica en México," *Perfiles Educativos* 19 (1983): 28–42.

12. During the De la Madrid administration SEP created a directorate in charge of evaluating the educational process. SEP has conducted standardized exams since 1985, but they have included only a handful of states. The results of these exams strongly contradict the "official" average passing grade. See CIDAC, "Educación."

13. The latest studies on students' performance have led to a growing consensus that the institutional arrangement that shapes school organization and the organization of the school itself are among the most relevant variables in explaining students' academic achievement. For a detailed study of the factors explaining student performance in Mexico, see CIDAC, "Educación."

14. Data from a survey conducted by *Nexos*. See Gilberto Guevara Niebla, "México: Un país de reprobados?" *Nexos* 162 (June 1991): 33–44. For an account of the results of different standardized exams, see CIDAC, "Educación."

15. On the 1988 elections, see Juan Molinar, *El tiempo de la legitimidad* (Mexico City: Cal y Arena, 1990), pp. 217–243.

16. Teachers' real wages fell by more than 40 percent between 1982 and 1987. See René González Cantú and Roberto Villaseñor, in *La catástrofe silenciosa,* ed. Gilberto Guevara Niebla (Mexico City: Fondo de Cultura Económica, 1992), p. 197.

17. Miranda López, "Descentralización educativa."

18. Ibid.

19. The following discussion will concentrate on the General Law. For our purposes here suffice it to say that the reform of Article 3 made secondary education compulsory and prepared the way for the decentralization process, while the reform of Article 31 made it a constitutional obligation that parents send their children to secondary school. See Secretariat of Public Education, *Artículo 3 Constitucional y Ley General de Educación* (Mexico City: SEP, 1993).

20. Ornelas identifies a multiplicity of factors behind the decentralization, including efficiency, power, and international competitiveness. See Carlos Ornelas, "The Decentralization of Education in Mexico," *Prospects* 18, no. 1 (1988).

21. See, in particular, Robert Lucas, Jr., "On the Mechanics of Economic Development," *Journal of Monetary Economics* 22 (1988).

22. For the Southeast Asian experience, see Robert Wade, *Governing the Market* (Cambridge: Cambridge University Press, 1992).

23. The argument of a causal link between changes in relative prices and institutional change is forcefully made by Douglass North, *Institutions, Institutional Change and Economic Performance* (Cambridge: Cambridge University Press, 1990).

24. To a large extent the National Solidarity Program (PRONASOL) embodies the second track.

25. Secretariat of Public Education, *Acuerdo Nacional para la Modernización de la Educación Básica* (Mexico City: SEP, 1992).

26. According to SEP figures, accumulated real wage increases during the Salinas administration reached 70 percent by the end of the 1992–1993 school year. Secretariat of Public Education, *Informe de Labores* (Mexico City: SEP, 1993).

27. Ibid.

28. SEP officials argued that the authors had not included the 250 corrections the secretariat had made to the semifinal draft.

29. SEP, *Informe de Labores;* and Secretariat of Public Education, "El modelo de la federalización educativa en México: Impacto en la organización y funcionamiento de los gobiernos federales y estatales," *Documento de Trabajo* (Mexico City: SEP, 1993), pp. 1–8.

30. Pablo Latapí, "Evaluar Maestros" in *Proceso,* no. 847 January 25, 1993, 37–38.

31. SEP, *Informe de Labores.*

32. For the initiative, see Secretariat of Public Education, "Iniciativa de Ley General de Educación," *El Nacional,* July 16, 1993.

33. The historical roots of this perception should be traced back to the parental mobilization of the 1930s, which was in response to the Cardenista project of "socialist education." See Soledad Loaeza, *Clases medias y política en México* (Mexico City: Colegio de México, 1988), pp. 65–118.

# 8

# Designing Social Policy for Mexico's Liberalized Economy: From Social Services and Infrastructure to Job Creation

## Wayne A. Cornelius

With the virtual completion of the great wave of economic adjustment and restructuring that swept through Mexico and many other Third World countries during the 1980s and early 1990s, scholars have begun to ask increasingly tough questions about the social concomitants of this phenomenon. How can the ruling coalition reshape its social bases to support a sustained, market-driven, internationalist development strategy? Will the restructured economy have the capacity to generate enough jobs in a country in which the potential labor force is still growing by 3 percent or more each year? Can new compensatory policies be devised that are both consistent with the fiscal constraints of the new macroeconomic model and able to cushion the social costs of economic restructuring and prevent mass explosions of discontent? If the long-entrenched corporatist structures and patron-client networks of Mexico's regime are inadequate as tools for implementing such policies and actually obstruct their implementation in many parts of the country, what can replace them? This chapter will argue that the medium-to long-term sustainability of Mexico's new economic structures and policies mix will depend fundamentally on finding innovative, fiscally responsible, and politically unconstrained answers to these questions.

### Threats to Sustainability

This is an especially appropriate moment to examine the social implications of economic restructuring in Mexico. Even though the process may still be far from complete in some sectors, further deepening of economic liberalization no longer seems socially tolerable or politically prudent in the short to medium term. As Mexican economist Rogelio Ramírez de la O has observed, the peasant insurrection in Chiapas that began January 1, 1994, "has buried the long-held notion that in Mexico you can operate without anesthesia."[1]

139

Not just to win future elections convincingly, but to maintain social peace, the government must now move more aggressively than it has in recent years to ease the pain that economic liberalization and internationalization have inflicted on millions of Mexicans. What is required is stepped-up spending on social programs and on productive projects that will create jobs more quickly in the most impoverished parts of the country, even if doing so necessitates a return to modest levels of deficit spending.[2] Perceiving a need to shift priorities, Ernesto Zedillo Ponce de León, presidential candidate of the ruling Institutional Revolutionary Party (PRI) in 1994 and one of the principal architects of neoliberal economic reforms during the presidency of Carlos Salinas de Gortari (1988–1994), pledged during the campaign that his government would emphasize such goals as raising rates of economic growth and job creation, boosting labor force productivity (which will require major new investments in public education and vocational training), improving health services, and increasing the flow of credit to small and medium-sized businesses.[3]

Since the start of 1994 clear danger signals have indicated that the economic reforms of the 1985–1993 period remain vulnerable to mounting social problems that, if unchecked, could cause an unraveling of the broad coalition that has thus far supported radical economic restructuring in Mexico. Most conspicuously, the new development model has yet to demonstrate that it is capable of generating rates of economic growth that even begin to approximate the average of 6 percent annually achieved during earlier periods of Mexican development. The high point of economic growth during the Salinas *sexenio* occurred in 1990, when the gross domestic product grew by 4.5 percent; subsequently, the growth rate has plummeted, to 0.4 percent in 1993—far below the rate of population growth (officially, 1.8 percent in 1994).[4]

High inflation has a disproportionately severe impact on low-income wage earners, especially in an economy in which most workers do not receive automatic cost-of-living increases. Thus it could be argued that during the Salinas sexenio, reducing inflation was the government's most successful policy for cushioning the impacts of economic restructuring on the average Mexican. Since 1987, inflation declined steadily, from 159.2 percent in that year to roughly a tenth of that in 1991, reaching single-digit levels in 1993–1994 for the first time in more than two decades.[5]

In the absence of a rate of employment creation that keeps pace with labor force growth, however, the sharp drop in inflation has been inadequate to reduce poverty and income inequality during a period of massive economic restructuring and opening of the Mexican economy to foreign competition. Only about 1.5 million new jobs were created, and some 500,000 jobs were lost because of business closures and downsizing from 1988 to 1993—a period when 800,000 to 900,000 new job seekers were entering the labor force each year.

Since the debt crisis hit with full force in 1982, the majority of new job seekers as well as workers laid off by employers in the formal economy have been absorbed into the informal or underground economy (consisting mostly of petty commerce and services), which according to some estimates now accounts for as much as a quarter to a third of the jobs held by economically active Mexicans.[6] As economist Nora Lustig has pointed out, in a country offering no unemployment insurance benefits, wage earners forced out of formal-sector employment by economic restructuring have had little alternative but to accept much lower paying work in the informal sector. "To be unemployed is a luxury that most Mexicans cannot afford."[7]

Net job creation continues to be anemic, despite a heavy influx of foreign capital, partly because well over half of the foreign funds are still being invested in stocks and other financial instruments rather than job-creating, direct investment projects. And the industrial reconversion process must continue if Mexican businesses are to withstand the greatly intensified competition from foreign imports that the North American Free Trade Agreement (NAFTA) and unilateral trade liberalization measures have brought, raising the likelihood of further significant job losses in the remainder of this decade.

Not surprisingly, economic restructuring has brought no progress in reducing the degree of income inequality in Mexico. On the contrary, large new concentrations of wealth have emerged, partly as a result of the sale of the country's banks and other large public enterprises to consortia of private investors. *Fortune* magazine's annual list of the world's richest persons in 1994 was replete with Mexican billionaires, whose assets had been acquired largely during the period of intense economic restructuring. A 1994 study by the Economic Research Institute of Mexico's National Autonomous University (UNAM) found that the sweeping privatization policy pursued by the De la Madrid (1982–1988) and Salinas governments had resulted in 50 percent of the country's assets being held by just five conglomerates.[8] The internationalization of the economy has created other types of inequalities. For example, workers employed in foreign-linked companies have seen their real wages rise in recent years as much as 30 percent, while the wages of workers in domestically owned firms (such as textile and apparel producers) have dropped as much as 15 percent.

Extreme inequalities in income and on most indicators of social well-being persist among states and regions, and between urban and rural areas. Since 1984 poverty has become more concentrated than ever in rural Mexico, which today contains at least 70 percent of the population classified as living in extreme poverty. In 1990 the percentage of persons with incomes lower than two minimum-wage salaries ranged from 40 percent in Baja California Norte to 80 percent in Chiapas.[9] A composite index of socioeconomic marginality shows the Federal District (Mexico City) and the northern border states as being the most privileged, and the southern states (especially Chiapas, Oaxaca, and Guerrero) as the most impoverished (see Table 8.1). This pattern of spatial inequalities has remained essentially unchanged for many years, although the gap between rich and poor regions seems to have widened over the past decade.[10]

At the family level, national surveys conducted by the National Institute of Statistics, Geography, and Information (INEGI), the government's statistical research agency, reveal that the degree of income inequality increased by 10 percent between 1984 and 1989, before leveling off during the years 1989–1992.[11] In the 1994 presidential campaign the growing inequality of wealth distribution in a "reformed" economy became an object of severe criticism not only by the Cardenista left but also by the conservative National Action Party (PAN). In an effort to curb abuses by large private enterprises that have benefited from its free-market economic policies, the government in 1994 began to levy substantial fines on such companies for monopolistic practices of various sorts.[12]

Government officials and scholars have been engaged in a sharp dispute over the magnitude and direction of changes in mass poverty levels during Mexico's most intense period of economic liberalization, 1989–1993. A controversial national survey conducted jointly by the United Nations Economic Commission on Latin America and the Caribbean (CEPAL) and INEGI found that the number of Mexicans living in extreme poverty (as measured by their capacity to purchase a minimum "market basket" of basic foodstuffs) fell from 14.9 million (18.8 percent of the national population) in 1989 to 13.6 million (16.1 percent of the population) in 1992. Overall this survey found 37.2 million Mexicans (43.8 percent of the population) living at or below the official poverty line.[13] The apparent reduction in extreme poverty, which was viewed with skepticism by independent Mexican researchers, has been touted by President Salinas's former chief of staff José Córdoba as evidence that "the social safety net provided by the government offered some shelter to poor households" from the ravages of economic crisis and restructuring, and that "a gradual improvement has already taken place with the economic recovery and the advent of the Solidarity program [described below] in the early 1990s."[14]

The CEPAL-INEGI findings also show, however, that the *absolute number* of Mexicans living in extreme poverty was higher in 1992 than in 1984, when the figure was 11.0 million (15.4 percent of the population at the time). Moreover, the 1989–1992 overall drop in extreme poverty masks a trend in the opposite direction in the country's rural areas, where more than two-thirds of "extremely poor" Mexicans reside. Whereas the number of "extremely poor" urban dwellers fell from 6.5 million in 1989 to 4.8 million in 1992, according to the CEPAL-INEGI study, the number of "extremely poor" rural dwellers *increased* from 8.4 million to 8.8 million.[15] A 1984 survey by INEGI had found 6.7 million rural dwellers

**Table 8.1    A Ranking of Mexico's States by Level of Poverty and Underdevelopment in 1990**

| *Least Developed* | *Developed* |
|---|---|
| 1. Chiapas | 20. Morelos |
| 2. Oaxaca | 21. Estado de México |
| 3. Guerrero | 22. Tamaulipas |
| 4. Hidalgo | 23. Colima |
| 5. Veracruz | 24. Jalisco |
| 6. Puebla | 25. Sonora |
|  | 26. Chihuahua |
| *Underdeveloped* | 27. Aguascalientes |
|  | 28. Baja California Sur |
| 7. San Luis Potosí | 29. Coahuila |
| 8. Zacatecas |  |
| 9. Tabasco | *Most Developed* |
| 10. Campeche |  |
| 11. Yucatán | 30. Baja California Norte |
| 12. Michoacán | 31. Nuevo León |
| 13. Guanajuato | 32. Distrito Federal (Mexico City) |
| 14. Querétaro |  |
| *Somewhat Developed* |  |
| 15. Durango |  |
| 16. Tlaxcala |  |
| 17. Nayarit |  |
| 18. Sinaloa |  |
| 19. Quintana Roo |  |

*Source: GEA Asociados*, based on data from the National Population Council (CONAPO). Derived from "Pobreza en México," *Este País*, July 1994, p. 54, table 1.
*Note:* Numerical rankings are based on a summary index of indicators of poverty and underdevelopment, including the availability of basic services (potable water, sewage systems, electricity), the quality of housing construction, and education and income levels.

living in extreme poverty. Noting this disturbing trend, Jonathan Fox cautions that

> while national economic growth is likely to have significant spillover effects within urban areas, reaching at least some of those near the poverty line, there is no reason at all to assume that [aggregate] economic growth will reduce extreme poverty in rural areas . . . unless the Mexican government pursues an antipoverty strategy that is much more targeted to employment creation and basic service provision in rural areas.[16]

## Social Policies in the Salinas Years

After falling sharply in the austerity budgets of the De la Madrid administration (from 7.6 percent of GDP in 1981–1982 to 5.6 percent in 1987–1988),[17] aggregate spending on social programs rebounded under Salinas.

From 1988 to 1993 social spending increased by more than 85 percent in real terms. By 1994 such expenditures represented 10 percent of GDP (higher than at any point in Mexican history) and 54 percent of the discretionary federal government budget, as compared to only 32 percent in 1988.[18] After the Chiapas rebellion began in 1994, the government authorized a further boost in social spending, including a (U.S.) $900 million package of social service and infrastructure investments for the state of Chiapas alone.

As has been characteristic of Mexican social policy during most of the postrevolutionary period, social spending in the era of intensified economic restructuring has been selectively targeted.[19] Across-the-board subsidies to consumers and guaranteed support prices for all agricultural producers gave way to more focused programs like National Solidarity (PRONASOL), the Salinas administration's principal antipoverty initiative, and PROCAMPO, a transitional, direct-subsidy program for very small-scale agricultural producers, including those who do not produce enough to commercialize (and thus had never benefited from government price supports for agricultural commodities). PROCAMPO was announced in the fall of 1993 as a program scheduled to operate over the following fifteen years; all government crop price supports are to be eliminated within three years.

During PRONASOL's first five years of operation (1989–1993) the Mexican government invested about (U.S.) $12 billion in the program, which quickly became the Salinas administration's most important signature program, as well as one of the factors most responsible for the PRI's impressive recovery at the polls in the 1991 midterm elections.[20] While National Solidarity encompasses a very large and diverse set of subprograms, its emphasis has been on providing basic social services and "urban" infrastructure (electricity, potable water, health care, refurbished public schools, paved streets and feeder roads, regularized land titles, environmental clean-up projects, and so forth) to residents of low-income urban neighborhoods and rural communities, ostensibly in response to the articulation of specific needs by groups of beneficiaries organized into local *Comités de Solidaridad.* Although government reports showed Solidarity projects being undertaken in more than 95 percent of the country's 2,378 municipalities by 1993, field studies found little uniformity in the program's impacts.[21] Moreover, opposition party leaders frequently complained that PRONASOL funding levels per state or locality were being determined by partisan political criteria; that is, the program's resources seemed targeted to areas of demonstrated opposition strength.

The available evidence does not support the conclusion that the poorest segments of Mexican society were consistently the foremost beneficiaries of Solidarity program expenditures during the first five years of the Salinas presidency. On a per capita basis Mexico's poorest states were not privileged in the allocation of Solidarity funds; rather it was the middle tier of states (on most indices of poverty and underdevelopment) that benefited most.[22] It is possible, however, that a more disaggregated analysis would show that, within states, Solidarity programs have successfully targeted extreme poverty, at the individual and local community levels.

Whatever their underlying political rationales or consequences, PRONASOL and PROCAMPO were explicitly intended by the Salinas administration to ease the transition from heavy-handed state interventionism to an economy driven primarily by market forces. The two programs represented a recognition by the technocrats in power that some compensatory measures would be needed to maintain social peace and permit the consolidation of the neoliberal economic reforms as well as the implementation of new, potentially disruptive changes such as the privatization of *ejido* (communally held) land, made possible by 1992 amendments to Article 27 of the Constitution (see Chapter 3).

But did these programs effectively address the root causes of poverty and income inequality, or were they mere palliatives, capable perhaps of improving living conditions but not of helping the poor to generate wealth? A summary index of well-being constructed from such indicators as quality of housing construction materials, the number of persons per room, access to basic services such as water, electricity, and sewerage, and children's school enrollment shows significant progress during the 1989–1992 period,[23] an outcome explicable only by the National Solidarity Program's success in delivering government resources to low-income urban neighborhoods and rural communities.

Such quality-of-life improvements should not be dismissed too casually by critics seeking more fundamental reductions in poverty. Infrastructure projects like street paving, installation of potable water and sewage lines, and electrification often respond to deeply felt needs in the low-income population. Such improvements can dramatically ameliorate household health conditions, ease women's work in the home, increase personal safety for women and children, contribute to a sense of human dignity in poor communities, and even create modest (though mostly temporary) employment opportunities. And they can improve the life chances of today's generation of children when they become adults.

But neither are these kinds of projects likely to be accepted, even by their immediate beneficiaries, as long-term substitutes for the kinds of public programs and investments that would have a greater, more direct impact on poverty and income inequality.[24] Given the magnitude of Mexico's accumulated social deficit (poverty, unemployment and underemployment, malnutrition[25]), programs like Solidarity cannot reasonably be expected to solve these problems, especially in a context of slow economic growth.[26] In specific communities and among certain segments of the population, however, Solidarity-type investments can alleviate some of the worst symptoms of Mexico's uneven development.

In establishing PRONASOL, the Salinas administration made it clear that it wanted to avoid the traps that it saw embedded in the U.S. experience with so-called "welfarist" programs. With the exception of the Children in Solidarity initiative, described below, Solidarity includes no transfer payment schemes and therefore does not directly address problems of current income and consumption, except through the short-term, localized, employment-creating effects of urban infrastructure projects.

## Requisite Next Steps

For the National Solidarity Program (or some variation thereof, in the next presidential administration) to have a greater impact on absolute poverty and income inequality, it would have to complement other types of policy interventions. Foremost among those interventions would be programs focused on regions and economic sectors that would create new, permanent employment opportunities; efforts to upgrade public education (especially preschool, elementary, and secondary education) and to make job training more accessible to both the urban and rural poor; and the creation of new financing and technology transfer mechanisms for small and medium-sized businesses. In sum, Mexico's macroeconomically oriented policymakers cannot afford to overlook the opportunities for socially beneficial microeconomic intervention by the state in a liberalized economy.[27]

Beginning in December 1991, with the establishment of the National Fund for Solidarity Enterprises, there has been a gradual shift of emphasis within the Solidarity program toward supporting more production-related projects that directly raise incomes and multiply employment opportunities. The government seemed to have recognized the limitations of the program's initial focus on urban services and infrastructure improvements.[28] Similarly, several proposals by PRI presidential candidate Zedillo—particularly to create job banks and to promote completion of primary schooling in rural areas by awarding 1.5 million scholarships by the year 2000—indicate an awareness of the need for a social policy that more directly attacks the structural roots of poverty in Mexico.

Much remains to be done, however, to assure that this nascent emphasis is reflected consistently and effectively in government policy. Take, for example, the plight of small and medium-sized businesses in a liberalized and "opened" economy. While averaging only seven employees per firm, small businesses in Mexico provide 60 percent of all employment opportunities.[29] And while many larger enterprises continue to shed labor in order to become more competitive exporters, small businesses continue to absorb most of the new entrants to the labor force. Nevertheless, Mexico's rapid trade liberalization since 1986 has severely reduced the sales and survival chances of small businesses, especially in Mexico's traditional manufacturing industries such as textiles, apparel, and shoes.[30]

If small and medium-sized enterprises are to play the key role in Mexico's future social and economic development that is ascribed to them in the plans and rhetoric of government officials, the human capital they employ must be developed more fully. A 1992–1993 survey of small and mid-sized manufacturing businesses in Mexico's northern border region—where workers' average skill levels exceed those elsewhere in Mexico, except the Mexico City metropolitan area—found that although most owners of those businesses had some university training, the vast majority of production workers had only an elementary school education.[31] Worker training should not take a backseat to technology transfer as a means of increasing the productivity of such enterprises.[32] As Gary Gereffi, drawing upon the experiences of East Asian exporters of manufactured goods, has pointed out, the worker training that is needed can be done with relatively small groups in specific industries, as well as through more generalized vocational education programs.[33]

Worker training and vocational education can not only provide small and medium-sized businesses with the human capital needed to increase the firms' competitiveness, they may also help reduce the extremely high dropout rate among school-age children in Mexico. Although 78 percent of the nation's school-age children were enrolled in primary school in 1990, only an estimated 54 percent of those who start elementary school finish it, according to Secretariat of Public Education statistics analyzed by the Mexican Center for Child Resources (CEMDIN). Moreover, a large proportion of elementary school graduates lack easy access to a secondary school—a major disincentive to continuing their education.[34]

A large body of educational research done in countries around the world has demonstrated that students' perceptions of their likely economic opportunities after finishing school are a crucial determinant of their (and their parents') willingness to continue investing in education. Recent field research in three Mexican cities (Guadalajara and Arandas, Jalisco; Tijuana, Baja California Norte) has found that students enrolled in government-run vocational schools had higher educational aspirations than students in regular secondary schools, because of their greater confidence in their ability to find a job upon graduation.[35]

A much heavier emphasis on worker training and vocational education may require future Mexican governments to reallocate some of the resources that have been channeled to postgraduate and technical education during the Salinas sexenio.[36] Nevertheless, even the World Bank, which has been subsidizing key elements of Mexico's development strategy, has become increasingly critical of "the low and disparate quality of the educational system, and especially of basic education," as well as the failure of Mexican companies to train their workers sufficiently. According to the bank's analysts, inadequate public *and* private investment to upgrade the quality of the labor force is a major factor holding back productivity growth in Mexico.[37]

## Political Constraints on Government Responsiveness

There is a strong consensus among academic specialists on Mexican politics that the ruling party's alliances with its traditional constituencies (to say nothing of still-unorganized groups like workers in the informal economy) have been weakened significantly by economic restructuring and internationalization.[38] The state-shrinking pursued so vigorously by presidents De la Madrid and Salinas, together with the creation of new federal government programs like Solidarity that intentionally bypassed the entrenched PRI machines in the states and municipalities, have deprived the old corporatist structures of much of the patronage and other resources that for decades were channeled through them. It could be argued that, at this juncture in history, the PRI's nearly 60-year-old labor and campesino organizations are too ossified and discredited, its leadership too divided on issues ranging from labor law reform to democratization, and the party too dependent on local caciques and other agents of exploitation and repression to be of much help to the government in containing the social tensions that threaten to overwhelm the newly established macroeconomic model.

The social explosion that shook Chiapas and the nation as a whole in 1994 provided ample proof that even generously funded federal social programs like National Solidarity—which had invested (U.S.) $192 million in Chiapas in 1993 alone—can be sabotaged by state and local elements of the PRI-government apparatus in ways that not only fail to buy time for the consolidation of neoliberal economic reforms but also create new popular grievances against the state. In the case of Chiapas there was a pattern of gross misuse of Solidarity program funds by state and local officials to serve their own political ends.[39] Between 1990 and 1992 state governor Patrocinio González (subsequently promoted to secretary of the interior in the Salinas cabinet, a post that he held until shortly after the Chiapas rebellion erupted) dismissed and jailed several regional Solidarity program representatives who had attempted to support projects proposed by campesino organizations that were independent of his control. He also manipulated a Solidarity program for subsistence farmers in ways that strengthened the power of municipal presidents and local caciques who were loyal members of the governor's political machine.

González and many other "elected" officials in Chiapas, where vote fraud by the PRI was more blatant and more deeply institutionalized than in any other state,[40] never had to show any responsiveness to general public needs or preferences in order to remain in power. In league with large growers and cattle raisers Chiapas's political class for many years had been able to operate the state as a private fiefdom, while Mexico City turned a blind eye to the obvious abuses of authority. Thus, the Chiapas case, while extreme in many respects, illustrates the importance of well-functioning, truly representative political institutions—in a word, democracy—to an effective social policy in Mexico.

Another relevant example lies in the efforts of the Salinas government, especially through the Secretariat of Agriculture and Water Resources (SARH), to create "agroindustrial corridors" of small and medium-sized food processing enterprises throughout the country. Government-affiliated labor union leaders have resisted the program, which might have weakened their control over substantial segments of the labor force.[41]

The experience of Mexico under Salinas shows that distributive and redistributive programs, however carefully designed and well funded, can work only where powerful political and economic interests do not prevent them from reaching their target populations. Even though debilitated, the old corporatist structures, the entrenched state-level PRI machines, and closely collaborating caciques at the local level are still alive and functioning in many parts of the country. Those traditional structures and agents of political control coexist uneasily, if at all, with the kinds of social programs that Mexico requires as it approaches the end of the twentieth century. At worst, the result of such "cohabitation" is the cannibalization of federal government programs—even those, like National Solidarity, that were supposed to operate under tight central controls—when they reach the local level.[42]

In sum, a broader political opening, including a willingness by the federal authorities to break long-standing symbiotic alliances with sectoral and subnational power brokers, will be necessary in the next sexenio. Otherwise, the state will be hobbled constantly in its attempts to implement the kinds of "softening" measures that could make Mexico's market-driven economic policies socially tolerable and politically sustainable in the long term.

## Notes

1. Quoted in Juanita Darling, "Chiapas Revolt Puts Mexico's Economic Future on Hold," *The Los Angeles Times,* January 25, 1994.

2. After five consecutive years of nearly balanced budgets or budget surpluses, deficit spending during the last year of the Salinas sexenio was expected to equal 2 percent or more of GDP. Spending on social services was increased by 14.5 percent during the first quarter of 1994 alone.

3. Ernesto Zedillo, "Crecimiento económico para el bienestar familiar: Diez propuestas," *Examen* (official PRI magazine), vol. 6, no. 62 (July 1994): 5.

4. In per capita terms GDP actually declined by 0.9 percent in 1993.

5. The government's inflation target for 1994 was 5 percent.

6. Recent estimates range from 23.5 percent (National Population Council—CONAPO, and National Institute of Statistics, Geography, and Information—INEGI) to 45 percent of the country's labor force (Autonomous Metropolitan University), depending on the definitions and methodological assumptions employed. A pioneering study by the Center for Economic Studies of the Private Sector (CEESP), a leading private sector think tank, estimated that the underground economy comprised between 25.7 percent and 38.4 percent of the official gross domestic product in 1985, again depending on the method of calculation; see CEESP,

*La economía subterránea en México* (Mexico City: Editorial Diana, 1987) Table
10. In a study of seven Mexican cities surveyed in 1989, the informally employed
(small-scale entrepreneurs, self-employed workers, workers in microenterprises,
and unpaid workers) represented about 32 percent of the labor force; see Bryan R.
Roberts, "The Dynamics of Informal Employment in Mexico," in U.S. Department
of Labor, Bureau of International Affairs, *Work Without Protections: Case Studies of the Informal Sector in Developing Countries* (Washington, D.C.: U.S. Department of Labor, 1993), p. 123, n. 4.

    7. Nora Lustig, "Mexico: The Social Impact of Adjustment, 1983–89"
(Washington, D.C.: The Brookings Institution, October 1991), p. 14.

    8. As reported in *El Financiero Internacional,* May 2–8, 1994.

    9. "La pobreza en México," *Este País,* (July 1994), p. 54, based on data com-
piled by the National Population Council (CONAPO).

    10. See Guillermo Trejo and Claudio Jones, eds., *Contra la pobreza: Por una
estrategia de política social* (Mexico City: Cal y Arena, 1993), especially chap. 3;
and Eric Van Young, ed., *Mexico's Regions: Comparative History and Development* (La Jolla: Center for U.S.-Mexican Studies, University of California, San
Diego, 1992), especially chap. 2.

    11. As measured by the Gini coefficient. See Fernando Cortés and Rosa María
Rubalcava, "Cambio estructural y concentración: Un análisis de la distribución del
ingreso familiar en México, 1984–1989" (paper presented at the conference
"Socio-Demographic Effects of the 1980s Economic Crisis in Mexico," University
of Texas, Austin, April 23–25, 1992, p. 11; and José Córdoba, "Mexico," in *The
Political Economy of Policy Reform,* ed. John Williamson (Washington, D.C.: Institute for International Economics, 1994), p. 272.

    12. The Federal Economic Competition Act, passed in 1992, allows the gov-
ernment to impose fines of up to (U.S.) $1.6 million per company and/or 10 per-
cent of the company's annual sales or assets. Penalties imposed in 1994 averaged
(U.S.) $300,000 per firm.

    13. United Nations Economic Commission on Latin America (CEPAL) and
National Institute of Statistics, Geography, and Information (INEGI), "Informe
sobre la magnitud y evolución de la pobreza en México, 1884–1992" (Mexico
City: INEGI, October 24, 1993).

    14. Córdoba, "Mexico," p. 271.

    15. The cuttoff point between urban and rural areas in this study was 15,000
inhabitants.

    16. Personal correspondence, December 27, 1993.

    17. See Rolando Cordera and Enrique González Tiburcio, "Crisis and Transi-
tion in the Mexican Economy," in *Social Responses to Mexico's Economic Crisis of
the 1980s,* ed. Mercedes González de la Rocha and Agustín Escobar Latapí (La
Jolla: Center for U.S.-Mexican Studies, University of California, San Diego, 1991).

    18. Even so, Mexico's level of public investment in social welfare does not
compare favorably with that of other middle-developed countries in Latin America.
In Brazil, for example, the share of GDP allocated to social expenditures has fluc-
tuated around 15 percent in recent years.

    19. For evidence on the historical pattern, see Bruce Nord, *Mexican Social
Policy: Affordability, Conflict, and Progress* (Lanham, Md.: University Press of
America, 1994); and Peter Ward, *Welfare Politics in Mexico: Papering Over the
Cracks* (Boston: Allen & Unwin, 1986).

    20. Córdoba, "Mexico," p. 269.

    21. See Wayne A. Cornelius, Ann L. Craig, and Jonathan Fox, eds., *Trans-
forming State-Society Relations in Mexico: The National Solidarity Strategy* (La

Jolla: Center for U.S.-Mexican Studies, University of California, San Diego, 1994), p. 20 *et seq.*

22. Data from Mexican government sources, analyzed by World Bank researchers, as disclosed in Rossana Fuentes-Berain, "Dan más PRONASOL a los estados ricos," *Reforma,* August 20, 1994, p. 2A.

23. Córdoba, "Mexico," pp. 270–271.

24. For evidence that Mexico's urban poor—especially women—may have reached the limits of their "survival skills" in an increasingly unfavorable economic environment, see Mercedes González de la Rocha, *The Resources of Poverty: Women and Survival in a Mexican City* (Cambridge and Oxford, England: Blackwell, 1994).

25. A study conducted by researchers at the National Autonomous University of Mexico (UNAM) found that 20 percent of children in Mexico City showed some sign of malnutrition and that between 1985 and 1990 cases of severe malnutrition among children had increased by 66 percent; see Ignacio Rodríguez Reyna, "Lower Classes Fail to Benefit from Economic Growth: INEGI," *El Financiero Internacional,* April 20, 1992. Data are not yet available to determine whether this trend was reversed during the second half of the Salinas sexenio.

26. See Nora Lustig, "Solidarity as a Strategy of Poverty Alleviation," and Carol Graham, "Mexico's Solidarity Program in Comparative Context: Demand-Based Poverty Alleviation Programs in Latin America, Africa, and Eastern Europe," both in *Transforming State-Society Relations in Mexico: The National Solidarity Strategy,* ed. Wayne A. Cornelius, Ann L. Craig, and Jonathan Fox (La Jolla: Center for U.S.-Mexican Studies, University of California, San Diego, 1994), pp. 79–96 and 309–327.

27. For a general survey of evidence from a number of Latin American countries, see Carol Liedholm, "The Impact of Government Policies on Microenterprise Development: Conclusions from Empirical Studies," in *Contrapunto: The Informal Sector Debate in Latin America,* ed. Cathy A. Rakowski (Albany: State University of New York Press, 1994), chap. 5. On the Mexican case, see Carlos Alba Vega, "La microindustria ante la liberación económica y el Tratado de Libre Comercio," *Foro Internacional* 33, no. 3 (July–September, 1993): 453–483.

28. See Cornelius, Craig, and Fox, *Transforming State-Society Relations,* pp. 24–25. Statistics show, however, that by late 1993, the massive Solidarity program had barely begun to shift gears. President Salinas reported that the establishment of 9,210 Solidarity-funded companies had created only 42,000 jobs nationwide; Carlos Salinas de Gortari, "Fifth State of the Nation Report" (Mexico City: Office of the Press Secretary to the President, November 1, 1993), p. 68.

29. As reported in Clemente Ruiz Durán (Faculty of Economics, National Autonomous University of Mexico), "The Future of Small and Medium-Sized Business in Mexico," presentation at the Research Seminar on Mexico and U.S.-Mexican Relations (La Jolla: Center for U.S.-Mexican Studies, University of California, San Diego, February 23, 1994).

30. Alba Vega, "La microindustria."

31. Ruiz Durán, "The Future of Small and Medium-Sized Business."

32. This is not meant to diminish the importance of technological backwardness as an impediment to small firms in Mexico, especially in establishing profitable linkages with larger, export-oriented firms. The same survey of more than 1,000 such enterprises, reported by Ruiz Durán (ibid.), found that only one-quarter were using "modern" manufacturing technologies. See also the illuminating case studies reported in Patricia A. Wilson, *Exports and Local Development: Mexico's New Maquiladoras* (Austin: University of Texas Press, 1992), pp. 96–119.

33. Gary Gereffi, "Mexico's Maquiladora Industries and North American Integration," in *North America Without Borders?—Integrating Canada, the United States, and Mexico,* ed. Stephen J. Randall (Calgary, Can.: University of Calgary Press, 1992), pp. 135–151.

34. Findings of the CEMDIN study, as reported in InterPress Service (PeaceNet), "Millions of Children Out of School Despite Laws," May 27, 1994; reprinted in *Mexico NewsPak* 2, no. 9 (May 23–June 5, 1994), 9.

35. Reported in Melissa Binder, "The Impact of Economic Crisis on Family Decisions Regarding Children's Education and Labor Force Participation in Mexico" (Ph.D. diss., Columbia University, in progress).

36. The principal exception to this generalization has been the Children in Solidarity program, a major component of the National Solidarity Program that has provided scholarships to students in the first three years of primary school. Targeted to students from low-income families who are the most at risk of dropping out of school, the support dispensed through Children in Solidarity has included a small cash stipend, packages of food and other household goods for the child's family, and medical care. For a detailed analysis of this program, see Alec I. Gershberg, "Distributing Resources in the Education Sector," in *Transforming State-Society Relations in Mexico: The National Solidarity Strategy,* Cornelius, Craig, and Fox, pp. 233–253.

37. From a restricted-circulation report on Mexico's economic challenges in the 1990s prepared by World Bank staff, as reported in Damian Fraser, "Trying Hard But Could Do Better, Says World Bank," *Financial Times* (London), February 22, 1994.

38. See, for example, the essays by María Lorena Cook et al., Denise Dresser, Jorge Alcocer, Joseph Klesner, Enrique de la Garza, Jonathan Fox, Paul Haber, and Laurence Whitehead in *The Politics of Economic Restructuring in Mexico,* ed. María Lorena Cook, Kevin J. Middlebrook, and Juan Molinar Horcasitas (La Jolla: Center for U.S.-Mexican Studies, University of California, San Diego, 1994); Spanish edition published in Mexico City by Cal y Arena, 1994.

39. For specific examples, see Neil Harvey et al., *Rebellion in Chiapas,* Transformation of Rural Mexico Series (La Jolla: Center for U.S.-Mexican Studies, University of California, San Diego, 1994).

40. Among all Mexican states Chiapas could be counted upon to deliver the highest percentage of its votes to the PRI, despite abysmal social and economic conditions that would suggest the potential for a large opposition party vote. In Ocosingo, the largest of the four municipalities in which the 1994 rebellion was centered, official statistics show that 105 percent of the total population eligible to vote in the 1991 midterm elections had actually done so—indisputable evidence of large-scale ballot stuffing. Moreover, less than three years before Ocosingo residents took up arms against the government, 72 percent of them supposedly voted for the PRI, according to official vote tallies.

41. Ruiz Durán, "The Future of Small and Medium-Sized Businesses." On the political and economic circumstances affecting the development and socioeconomic impacts of the *agroindustrias* in one state, Jalisco, see the following case studies: Agustín Escobar Latapí and Mercedes González de la Rocha, *Cañaverales y bosques: De hacienda a agroindustria en el sur de Jalisco* (Guadalajara, Jal.: Editorial Unit, General Secretariat, Government of Jalisco, 1987); and Javier Orozco Alvarado, "Desarrollo agrícola y agroindustrial en Jalisco," in *Economía, agroindustria y política agraria en Jalisco,* ed. Orozco Alvarado et al. (Zapopan, Jal.: El Colegio de Jalisco, 1992), pp. 17–75.

42. J. Manuel Marroquín, "The Politics of Redistribution and Poverty Alleviation in Mexico: The Solidarity Experience" (Ph.D. diss., London School of Economics and Political Science, in progress). Marroquín's 1993 field research on Solidarity projects in the states of Oaxaca, Puebla, and Veracruz revealed that local
political elites were likely to respond to the infusion of Solidarity funds into their
domains in one of three ways: outright rejection or resistance; insistence on operating the programs themselves, so that they could control all resource allocations;
or enthusiastic promotion of the programs, to curry favor among government officials at higher levels.

# 9

# Civil-Military Relations and Internal Security in Mexico: The Undone Reform

## Martin Edwin Andersen

To discuss civil-military relations and internal security in Mexico using the assumptions underlying studies published even only a few years ago is like trying to navigate a moon landing using a sextant once owned by Christopher Columbus. Shopworn certitudes about the durability of Mexico's civilian supremacy over the armed forces—in this century the longest-running experience of its kind in Latin America—are today not only misleading or irrelevant but also dangerous.[1]

In 1994 public security became a leading issue in the presidential campaign. The Mexican people, long used to the stability lent by the hegemony of the Institutional Revolutionary Party (PRI), were reacting in horror to a series of spectacular, and tragic, acts of violence: the murder a year earlier of the bishop of Guadalajara by narcotics traffickers, the unexpected New Year's uprising by Mayan peasants in Chiapas, the assassination of front-running presidential candidate Luis Donaldo Colosio (together with the questions raised by revelations of a bodyguard composed of former policemen accused of murder, torture, and corruption, and by the violent death of a police chief investigating the "magnicide"), and the dramatic upsurge in kidnappings of Mexican businessmen, crowned by the abduction of billionaire Alfredo Harp Helú.

The traditional strengths of Mexico's civil-military relationship must be viewed in the light of fast-changing circumstances. Inheriting a society whose decades-long transformation from a revolutionary national project to industrial capitalism has not been accompanied by the development of the democratic institutions of a modern capitalistic state, the next presidential administration will face crucial decisions regarding civil-military relations and law enforcement.

Indeed, the specter of chaos present during the early 1990s has brought into sharp relief the inability or unwillingness of the government of Carlos Salinas de Gortari (1988–1994)—otherwise heralded for its economic reforms and linking of Mexico with the North American market—

155

to assure continued civilian control of the military and to encourage professionalization of the police. Although Mexico has enjoyed a longer reign of civilian supremacy than any other country in Latin America, with no successful coup by the military since 1920 or even a serious threat since the late 1930s, it is difficult to portray the nation in the aftermath of the Chiapas uprising as, in the words of one expert writing before the Mayan revolt, "a model of civil-military tranquility."[2] The following analysis will demonstrate the degree to which recent events cloud pioneer military historian Edwin Lieuwen's view of the Mexican army as, "disciplined, professional . . . shun(ing) political activities."[3]

Even the fact of Mexico's comparatively low military expenditures—an estimated (U.S.) $1 billion, or less than 0.6 percent of the gross domestic product—has become insufficient to lull worries about discontent in the barracks. Inappropriate roles and missions, together with a history of financial independence, not its size, is what makes the Mexican army a potentially dangerous actor outside of civilian control. The role of the 130,000-strong army in the maintenance of internal security, as well as the subordination of the judiciary to the executive branch (and the perception of it as extraordinarily corrupt), means that any discussion of public security issues must include an understanding of both the armed forces and the police.[4]

Mexico's historic one-party dominance made the terms *nation* and *government* almost indistinguishable. The hegemonic role played by the PRI and its earlier incarnations for almost seven decades has kept civilian opponents from knocking on the barracks door in an effort—so common in other Latin American countries—to seduce the armed forces into the role of arbiters of political conflict or allies in the seizure of power. Can the same confidence be maintained in the Mexican military's good behavior as the nation moves, kicking and screaming, toward authentic multiparty rule? The armed forces, like the rest of Mexico, may face the choice of support for stability or support for democracy. The narrowest of election victories by Salinas in 1988 and the travails facing the PRI in the 1994 contest suggest that the time has come to review the strength of Mexico's civil-military relationship.

As one scholar of the Mexican military has noted:

> The most influential element in retaining military loyalty is the officer's belief in the civilian leadership's ability to maintain order. As long as the government demonstrates that ability and retains at least limited popular respect, the military will support civil authority.[5]

Demands for greater public safety, the inevitable strains arising from electoral competition on what is perceived to be a less-than-level playing field, and a growing government credibility gap—evidenced by survey results indicating that fully a third of the Mexican populace believed that the PRI itself was behind Colosio's assassination—suggest serious strains on the armed forces' faith in the ability of the civilian elite to maintain order and muster popular respect.

To these must be added the military's unprecedented willingness to publicly criticize its civilian leaders in the wake of the Chiapas uprising. The army's own uncertainty about its role in a changing Mexico—perhaps an academic issue in times of relative stability—becomes a festering complaint in the face of a security crisis like the Chiapas rebellion. Recent changes in Mexican politics and economics have stripped away the protective curtain of civilian lack of interest and the military's own hostility ("secrecy and suspicions" in the words of one sympathetic observer) to outside scrutiny.[6] At the same time, it has become woefully evident that although civilian control of the armed forces has, in times past, been fortified by the existence of a strong civil society—represented by the hegemonic PRI—today there are neither effective democratic institutions nor entrenched independent entities, such as a vigorous and widely disseminated opposition mass media, to provide the oversight needed in the turbulent times ahead.

This chapter seeks to provide a framework for the study of questions emerging from the new debate over security issues in Mexico. It will demonstrate the ongoing confusion in Mexico over definitions of "national defense" and "internal security," and the dangers inherent in the army's currently ill-defined mission. It will trace the history of civil-military relations in a one-party state and offer insights into why past institutional frameworks for assuring civilian control of the military may not only no longer work, but also contribute to a growing unrest within the barracks. The toll taken on the armed forces' prestige, discipline, and internal cohesion by its involvement in the so-called drug war will also be addressed. Finally, the chapter will review recent developments during the Salinas *sexenio,* when the otherwise reformist president used the military to an unprecedented degree for internal security, while only half-heartedly attempting to clean up and professionalize Mexican law enforcement. Answers to some of these questions are necessarily tentative, in part because the Mexican military openly discourages scholarly examination and, perhaps more importantly, because even today issues encumbering the armed forces frequently vanish into the recesses of public policy discussion, to the point that in recent years analyses of Mexican domestic politics often do not mention the military at all.[7]

### Getting It Straight: Internal Security or National Defense

Law enforcement in the United States and many other modern democracies is primarily civilian and local. In the United States, for example, the military has been forbidden, except in the most dire circumstances, from taking on the law enforcement responsibilities of civilian police. Set down in the principle of *posse comitatus* (18 U.S.C. 1385), the separation of the roles of internal security and national defense was designed to prevent the military from developing into a praetorian guard through illegitimate use of the tools of a police state.[8] This clear legal distinction has lent an important measure of political stability to the nation, successfully checking any open intervention of the armed forces in partisan politics—even during the Cold War, when the military grew to be the largest and best prepared in the world. That law enforcement is largely local has also helped to ensure community support and limit official corruption.

Although both the military and the police wear uniforms and carry guns, in a modern democracy their roles and philosophies are different. The military officer is trained to view any threat as an "enemy" that must be destroyed. A military chain of command is hierarchical, as it must be in times of war. Unable to see the "big picture" in the sound and fury of battle, the foot soldier must obey—his life and those of his comrades depend on his doing so.

Enjoying greater autonomy and capacity for decision, the police officer lives not on a military base but within a community, and the relationship between the police and that community determines each officer's success, and that of the forces of order. Security threats are met by the minimum force necessary to control them. Well-versed in points of law, the professional police officer in a modern democracy carries out his or her duties within the context of those rules. Instead of the several months needed to form a foot soldier, the education of a police officer may take several years.

Argentine legal scholar José Manuel Ugarte traces the pendular pattern of alternating civilian and military rule that is common in most of Latin America to confusion over the terms *internal security* and *national defense.* Open-ended definitions of *national security* tend to justify the military's encroachment on the political power of civilian authorities and its participation in internal security functions. Militaries that retain active roles as "guardians" of a country's internal order are far more likely to be called upon by civilian elites seeking armed intervention into domestic political or social crises. Stable modern democracies, on the other hand, maintain clear distinctions between military and police functions, as in the United States and Western Europe, including Spain, Italy, and France—three countries that, like those of Latin America, follow the Napoleonic code of justice.[9]

A key element of stable democracy, then, is the eventual transformation of the internal security system in countries in which it is wholly or in part dependent on local militaries. In Latin America only four countries have kept the armed forces out of internal security. Costa Rica, Latin America's oldest democracy, abolished its military in 1948. Panama did the same after the U.S. invasion of 1989. Following bitter debate through-out the 1980s, Argentina—with its long history of military coups—clearly defined law enforcement as a civilian police mission. And the 1992 peace accords in El Salvador also forced the military to circumscribe its mission to national defense, while providing for the creation of the National Civil-ian Police (PNC). Venezuela, despite its long tradition of civilian rule and innovative mechanisms to ensure civilian control over the military, does not make a clear distinction between internal security and national de-fense. Since 1989 it has faced two bloody military coup attempts.

Mexico does not have a guiding principle—such as that of posse comitatus in the United States, the Internal Security Law *(Ley de Seguri-dad Interna)* in Argentina, or the Chapultepec peace accords for El Sal-vador[10]—that shapes and informs its security forces along modern demo-cratic lines. Mexican uses of the terms *national security, internal security,* and *national defense* frequently are imprecise and interchangeable. This in turn has created confusion about the proper role of the armed forces.[11]

According to Olga Pellicer de Brody, national security has not been traditionally an important theme in Mexico and is defined "not in terms of the 'danger of aggression' but rather in terms of the fulfillment or nonful-fillment of the great objectives fixed in the Constitution of 1917."[12] Luis Herrera-Lasso and Guadalupe González have noted that the use of the con-cept "conceptually and operatively subsumed the distinguishably different category of internal security" and that the "merging of the powers of the government and the state in just one person [the president] creates an or-ganic fusion of the security of the state and that of the government."[13]

Oddly enough, it was Mexico's civilian leadership that reoriented the military's mission from national defense to internal security. President Miguel Alemán Valdés (1946–1952) first fused military with police func-tions, a role for the armed forces that was repeated only intermittently until the Salinas presidency.[14] The 1983–1988 National Development Plan—which Sergio Aguayo has called "the first attempt to give an ex-plicit meaning to national security"—defined the armed forces' mission as one of "defense of the territorial integrity, independence, and sovereignty of the nation," while adding that changing circumstances had "recast . . . their original strictly military role to include growing activities related to the well-being of the community . . . [including] complementary tasks in regard to national development, with great impact in the areas of the coun-try with greatest social problems."[15] The 1989–1994 National Develop-ment Plan launched by the Salinas regime went even further. Counternar-cotics, disaster relief, and environmental protection were added to the list of military missions, together with a generic call for modernization, that is, "improvements in its professionalism and efficiency."[16]

Mexico's armed forces, said political scientist William S. Ackroyd, have "professionalized for an internal threat."[17] Similarly, military historian

Roderic Camp has noted that through the 1980s the Secretariat of National Defense had a growing internal security focus and that the military's police mission was considered to be a part of the armed forces' professionalization. The importance of the military's growing internal security mission was also evident in the revised Organic Law of the Mexican Army and Air Force, Article 1, Section 2, promulgated in 1986. "The more civilian leadership relies on the military to carry out politicized, internal police functions," Camp noted, "the more the military itself expects to have a voice in political decision making, and equally important, the more society, including future civilian and military leaders, defines intervention as a legitimate military responsibility."[18]

## Civil-Military Relations in the Postrevolutionary Years

Mexico's postrevolutionary state was ushered into being by the defeat of an established and armed militaristic institution by a force of civilian-soldiers, a remarkable process that later endowed both the political and the military elites with a common revolutionary origin and afforded the military high command an uncommon pool of intellect and experience. After only a decade, however, the ruling elites—weary of the general staff's factionalism and wary of the armed institution's potential for political hegemony—moved to limit the military's power over the state. Nevertheless, for more than 25 years, from 1920 to 1946, Mexico's political leadership emanated almost exclusively from the civilian-soldiers of the Revolution of 1910.

The process by which Mexico's military leadership transformed itself into the country's civilian political elite received its highest degree of articulation and institutionalization during the presidency of General Lázaro Cárdenas (1934–1940). It was Cárdenas who, while uniting governmental and party authority under the figure of the president, also established the armed forces as one of the four component parts of the ruling National Revolutionary Party (PRN, which later became the PRI). As one military historian noted, this identification of the military with the party and government, as well as the state, was a necessary transitional step on the road to professionalization, for, in the words of Cárdenas:

> Such a strategy was essential to civilian control: political passivity or neutrality in the officer corps is a luxury regimes can afford only after they have achieved some minimal level of national integration that promotes an underlying value consensus on the fundamental nature of the regime. This integration was effectively achieved through the centralizing and institutionalizing power of the official party, presided over by a civilianized leadership.[19]

Although short-lived, the military's participation in the PRN helped infuse the party with the martial values of discipline, hierarchy, and institutional loyalty.[20]

General Manuel Avila Camacho (1940–1946), Mexico's last military president, took steps to reverse Cárdenas's decision to incorporate the military into the governing party and further moved to reduce the armed forces' political influence by retiring a number of revolutionary-era generals, cutting the military's share of officeholders to one-fifth of the total, and slashing military expenditures from 21 percent to 15 percent of the federal budget. His successor, Miguel Alemán, went even further, reducing the number of military officers to less than 10 percent of his political appointees. As we have seen, however, Alemán melded military and police functions to carry out internal security tasks, thus making the armed forces an integral enforcement arm of his political and economic policies. In the following years military might was employed primarily to repress isolated protests and uprisings, such as the student occupation of the National Polytechnic Institute in 1956, the communications workers' strike of 1958, and the railroad workers' strike of 1959.[21]

The suppression of student activists in Tlatelolco Plaza on the eve of Mexico City's Olympic Games in the summer of 1968 was the most traumatic experience of the Mexican army in its internal security role. Justified at the time by the "interventions of external agents" in a university demonstration, the repression by the army and state paramilitary forces resulted in the deaths of several hundred people, most of them protesting students. Some analysts have portrayed the tragic events as in the last analysis a victory of presidential control over a glowering military, as the armed forces did not seek to remove President Gustavo Díaz Ordaz. Yet the episode clearly showed the limits of civilian stewardship and the robust internal security role the military can script for itself under certain circumstances. Accounts of the massacre say that when Secretary of the Interior Luis Echeverría Alvarez sought to gain control of troop deployment, he was told by General Marcelino García Barragán, Díaz Ordaz's secretary of defense, to "keep his hands off army matters." In the aftermath of the tragedy García Barragán also reportedly told Echeverría that the interior secretary and Díaz Ordaz had "created this mess, now let me clean it up my way."[22]

Military awareness of the damage the Tlatelolco massacre did to its reputation sparked demands on the government for both structural and material changes. According to Roderic Camp, "The military's perception of civilian fallibility after Tlatelolco caused it to reappraise its role in the internal security decision-making process. . . . It opted for a larger role in preventative measures in regard to civil unrest." After Tlatelolco, he noted, the military became increasingly involved in political intelligence against real or suspected subversives; it undertook greater cooperation with the police, particularly the federal police; and the armed forces became a mainstay of clandestine paramilitary groups, or the Brigada Blanca (White Brigade), in what Aguayo has described as a virtually unknown Mexican "dirty war."[23]

The presidency of Echeverría (1970–1976), whose experience in the Díaz Ordaz government had left him with a deep-seated distrust of the armed forces, was nevertheless marked by its own crisis. Ministerial-level opponents, who backed a paramilitary group called Los Halcones (the Falcons) in a brutal repression of student protestors, fomented a palace intrigue whose resolution came only with renewed military support for the president. Echeverría's sexenio was also marked by increasing military involvement in nonmilitary, civic action (civil affairs or nation building, such as health, education, food relief, and reforestation) programs. Even skeptical civilians often view these types of activities as "safe" pursuits for the military, particularly if its forces exceed rational national defense requirements. But a growing body of literature suggests that these same activities tend to politicize the military, place it in competition with civilian authorities for scarce public resources, and leave it unprepared for its national defense tasks. Beyond the focus on civic action and internal security, the Echeverría regime also gave the military control of customs posts.[24]

Echeverría's successor, José López Portillo (1976–1982), also enlarged the military's role in internal security, particularly antidrug efforts, as well as its influence in the making of national security policy. In addition, since the early 1980s officers have been able to enhance their administrative skills through the National Defense College. In 1983 incoming president Miguel de la Madrid (1982–1988) faced a grave economic crisis that required him to focus on reestablishing the credibility of the office of the presidency. Concerned about the political violence reaching a crescendo in Central America, De la Madrid discreetly increased the military's presence in the southern state of Chiapas and in the southeast, in part to safeguard strategic oil and hydroelectric plants from possible foreign attack and in part to respond to frequent incursions by the Guatemalan army against refugee camps there. De la Madrid did, however, place the Secretariat of the Interior in charge of relief and cleanup after the devastating earthquake that rocked Mexico City in September 1985, despite the fact that once a state of emergency had been decreed, according to the third National Development Plan, those tasks were the responsibility of the armed forces.[25] Camp, among others, suggested that De la Madrid's decision "was expressive of the doubts many civilian leaders entertain in regard to the military's becoming prominent in the public arena: it can place civilian leadership in an unfavorable light and enhance the military's political potential."[26]

## The Military and the Drug "War"

With 2,000 miles of border in common with the United States, Mexico's importance to U.S. antinarcotics efforts far exceeds that of any other drug-producing or -transshipping country. (The importance of the Mexican authorities in stemming the entry of illegal substances into the United States is particularly striking given that, until recently, the number of U.S. Border Patrol agents stationed along the U.S.-Mexican frontier was only about the same as the number of police stationed on the New York City subway system.) From the period of quiet cooperation in the 1960s through the stepped-up efforts at crop eradication and interdiction of the 1970s, anti-narcotics efforts rested largely with civilian law enforcement agencies and the justice system. However, as initiatives in the 1970s against the "French Connection" heroin traffic through Turkey and France and in the 1980s against the drug smuggling operations in the Caribbean bore fruit, Mexico became the major transshipment point for most of the cocaine as well as significant amounts of the marijuana and heroin entering the United States.[27]

In 1973 the Federal Security Bureau (DFS), which had been created in 1947 by presidential order and which was autonomous from Congress and the judicial system, was given the task of "analyzing and notifying about any acts related to the security of the nation." The DFS, noted Aguayo,

> was more than an intelligence organization, it was an operational structure with considerable autonomy from the Ministry of Defense and, in some moments, from the Ministry of the Interior with which it was formally associated. The impunity enjoyed by the DFS fostered corruption, as it protected gangs involved in the production and trafficking of drugs.[28]

Although an assiduous customer of DFS intelligence, the U.S. Central Intelligence Agency noted as early as 1951 that "some of the unscrupulous chiefs" of DFS were "actually conducting illegal activities such as narcotics smuggling." The killing in 1984 of investigative journalist Manuel Buendía while he was probing narcotics activities, a crime that later led to the conviction of ex-DFS director José Antonio Zorrilla Pérez and four others, and the brutal murder in February 1985 of Enrique Camarena, a U.S. Drug Enforcement Administration agent, shed light on the drug-trafficking activities of DFS agents and officials and led President De la Madrid to close the bureau later that year, without consultation with or comment by Congress. "This official agency, in charge of safeguarding national security," wrote Aguayo, "contributed to what is now considered to be the main threat to security." Witnesses in a subsequent murder trial in Los Angeles placed ex-defense secretary Juan Arévalo Gardoqui among the coconspirators in the Camarena case.[29]

Since 1977 the internal security role of the Mexican military has been largely dedicated to counternarcotics policing. Under De la Madrid the armed forces' antidrug role grew significantly, even at the expense of the civilian authorities. Following the lead of the United States in elevating the drug issue beyond the realm of law enforcement (by means of the promulgation in 1986 of National Security Directive 221), the De la Madrid administration's insistence on U.S. noninterference in Mexico's internal affairs flagged, particularly after the Camarena case revealed the extent of drug-related corruption among public officials. The Mexican president ordered the creation of a new National Office for Information and National Security and gave wider berth, at Washington's behest, to the military's counterdrug initiatives.[30]

A truly new era of cooperation was initiated under Salinas, who gave even fuller voice to De la Madrid's characterization of narcotics trafficking as a national security threat. Among the initiatives Salinas sponsored were the creation of a formal national security council (which included narcotics issues as part of its brief and folded part of the old DFS's operational functions into its purview), the development of a new national intelligence agency, and a new army staff section for special antinarcotics operations. By the midpoint of the Salinas term an estimated 25,000 of Mexico's 105,000 active-duty soldiers (and some 1,500 police officers) were taking part in the fight against drug trafficking. Those operations gave the armed forces supreme control over parts of the states of Oaxaca, Sinaloa, Jalisco, and Guerrero, at the expense of local civilian authorities and at the risk of whetting officers' political appetites.[31]

The antinarcotics mission of the Mexican military has left the institution exposed to internal rifts and public discredit. Unconfirmed allegations surfacing before a California grand jury linking two serving generals, Juan Poblano Silva and Arturo Cardona, the latter President Salinas's chief of staff, to narcotics corruption shook the army. The discharge in 1990 of the secretary of the navy, Admiral Mauricio Schleske Sánchez, and other top naval officers accused of possessing "inexplicable wealth" overshadowed other drug corruption scandals that wracked that service and resulted in the discharge and conviction of dozens of navy men.[32]

"The security agencies' unsavory reputation, especially [that of] the DFS and the federal judicial police, with whom the military has associated, taints the military," noted Camp.[33] The corruption carries with it not only worries about the armed forces' public prestige, but also concerns that the operationally hermetic military services will be subject to greater civilian scrutiny. Internal intelligence efforts—including wiretapping—within the armed forces concerning drug corruption has reportedly inhibited discussions about military matters as well. Army zone commanders reportedly were rotated with increasing frequency to prevent senior officers from having protracted contact with citizens. According to Herrera-Lasso and González, the military's participation in the drug "war" weighed heavily on the armed forces' structure and functions in other ways too. The military services found their counterdrug activities frequently needed to be financed using nonreimbursable operational funds; interinstitutional coordination remained a problem; and contacts with foreign actors, such as their U.S. military counterparts, increased.[34]

## Expanded Internal Security Roles Under Salinas

The Salinas government came to power in the aftermath of a tightly contested election in which a former PRI dissident, Cuauhtémoc Cárdenas Solórzano, won a large number of votes from within the barracks despite his leftist program and the officer corps' supposedly monolithic conservatism. Salinas's anemic electoral showing was institutionally ameliorated by the new president's broadened mandate for the armed forces. In 1989 he created a National Security Cabinet with military participation and a pronounced internal security bias. And, as noted earlier, counternarcotics, disaster relief, and environmental protection were added to the official list of military responsibilities, together with a program of armed forces modernization. Rather than combat, "the average soldier's experience," wrote *Washington Post* correspondent Tod Robberson in the aftermath of the 1994 uprising in Chiapas, "is more likely to have been providing disaster relief or refurbishing dilapidated public facilities." The armed forces' exemplary courage and loyalty, Salinas said in a January 1991 speech to military officers, represented "the ideology of sovereignty and justice that is the basis for the country's modernization program."[35]

In 1989, brandishing claims of "national security," the Salinas regime used the army to arrest oil union boss Joaquín "La Quina" Hernández Galicia and other PEMEX labor chiefs, accused of corruption and seen by the government as stumbling blocks to necessary administrative reforms of the state oil industry. Herrera-Lasso and González argue that while the government used the union barons' stockpiling of arms to justify military means, it was Hernández Galicia's political capital and ties to important sectors of Mexican society that were the real reason for use of the armed forces.[36]

Labor gangsterism was not the only target for tough (and in a modern democratic state, inappropriate) action by the Salinas government. As Mexico moved by fits and starts toward political pluralism, government violence against political opponents ratcheted upward, with army troops often deployed to maintain order. According to figures cited by Wayne A. Cornelius, from 1988 through April 1993, 207 militants of the opposition Party of the Democratic Revolution (PRD) were murdered, apparently at the behest of local PRI bosses. And in April 1990 the army imposed a state of siege and began to eject PRD militants from a number of official buildings in Michoacán. The military's custody of ballot packets during elections also suggests that members of the armed forces frequently either acquiesced to voting fraud or were directly a party to it.[37]

The policy of using military troops in counternarcotics enforcement, and claims by the government of coordination and support between the army and the police, came in for greater scrutiny in 1991, after army troops guarding a landing strip in Veracruz that was used as a drop site for 1.6 tons of cocaine ambushed federal antinarcotics agents attempting to seize the illicit cargo, killing seven policemen. When the shooting stopped, several federal agents who had identified themselves were beaten up and threatened. The drug traffickers managed to escape. After the firefight Sixth Region Commander General Alfredo Morán Acevedo refused to lift a military blockade of the area to allow the dead and wounded to be removed. A deputy attorney general was later brought into the area by helicopter to meet with Morán Acevedo. Six hours after the incident the bodies were removed by military ambulances and taken to a local forensic facility, where troops and casualties were surrounded by Federal Judicial Police agents. Autopsies were performed under the observation of both military and police physicians. The results of the probe showed that the army soldiers had fired at point-blank range. An investigation was later launched concerning allegations by a former aide that then-Attorney General Ignacio Morales Lechuga participated in the plot, a charge the official, who resigned in 1993, denied.[38]

Earlier, in 1990, responding to public outrage over the murder by federal police of a human rights activist in Sinaloa, Salinas created a government human rights commission. The gesture was viewed as half-hearted, however, when rights advocates sought to use the murder of a Tijuana newspaper editor as a leading case. After it was established that the alleged assassins worked at a racetrack owned by Jorge Hank, a prominent businessman, frequent target of critical columns by the journalist, and the son of Salinas's close associate Carlos Hank, the case was brought to an abrupt close even though one of the alleged murderers, a former federal policeman, reportedly cashed a $10,000 check on the day the editor was killed.[39]

According to the Miguel Agustín Pro Human Rights Center, acts of abuse against poor peasants doubled from 1991 to 1992, with 1,139 cases of assault and battery, 442 illegal arrests, 401 threats, 150 murders, and 122 cases of torture reported in the latter year. More than 63 percent of the cases took place in Chiapas, followed by Oaxaca (7.1 percent) and Veracruz (5 percent)—all states heavily populated by indigenous peoples. The rights group said the state security police and local political bosses were responsible for about 20 percent of the cases of abuse, followed by hired gunmen (13 percent), the State Judicial Police (13 percent), the Federal Judicial Police (12 percent), and the army (5.5 percent).[40]

Other rifts in Mexico's solid civil-military façade came in 1993. A bitter scandal erupted when Secretary of Education Ernesto Zedillo Ponce de León approved the publication of a new history textbook that laid responsibility for the 1968 bloodbath at Mexico City's Tlatelolco Plaza—a taboo subject—at the feet of the army. Although the text was withdrawn, the military found itself in the midst of a politicized debate raging throughout the country. In October the army was shaken again by the declarations of Brigadier General José Francisco Gallardo Rodríguez, voicing a public secret that the army was systematically violating human rights. Gallardo, who proposed the need to create the post of military ombudsman, was arrested the following month and charged with breaching military discipline by, in the words of Defense Secretary General Antonio Riviello Bazán, "spreading negative ideas about the Mexican military, with the object of dishonoring, offending, and discrediting the military in the eyes of the public."[41]

While using the military to an unprecedented degree for internal security tasks, the Salinas government made only half-hearted attempts to clean up and professionalize law enforcement agencies. Not only is the justice system subordinate to the president, but it suffers from deficiencies in both human and financial resources. Cash-strapped antinarcotics police have had to buy their own ammunition, despite the fact that the salaries of most local police do not exceed (U.S.) $200 a month.[42] The police, said rights advocate and federal attorney general for the state of Chihuahua, Teresa Jardi,

> operate like a crime organization, in which everyone is an accomplice. This complicity in the behavior of the various officials of the institution guarantees impunity. The officials know that the agents are torturing, that the officials of the public prosecutor offices are torturing. . . . There is no possibility of changing a police department unless you change the entire apparatus of the administration of justice.[43]

According to a U.S. Border Patrol officer with long experience with the Mexican police, local law enforcement officials tend to be "Barney Fife types. They'll just give the guy a gun and tell him, 'You're the law around here.'" The Federal Police force, while far more professional, was rife with corruption. Its use of local vigilantes, or *comadres,* as bodyguards "and to do the dirty work . . . such as extralegal operations and brutal interrogations," he said, was of particular concern to the Mexican government. The number of comadres in an officer's bodyguard is for many *federales* a sign of prestige.[44] In 1993 Mexican police officials ordered the use of the comadres stopped, after one vigilante killed four people in Sonora.

Public expressions of horror at police brutality and corruption appeared to reach a crescendo with the assassination on May 24, 1993, of

Cardinal Juan Jesús Posadas Ocampo by gunmen linked to the Tijuana-based Arellano-Félix drug cartel. According to eyewitness testimony, federal police officers helped the hitmen flee the parking lot at Guadalajara's international airport and board an Aerovías de México flight to Tijuana. Upon their arrival in Baja California no attempt was made to arrest the assassins, nor were they detained in the following months, despite their frequent appearances in public. Although church authorities continued to voice doubts about the official version of the murder, the government maintained the point-blank attack on the prelate (his heavily armed assailants were less than three feet away) was due to a case of mistaken identity during a firefight between rival drug lords. Nevertheless, Attorney General Jorge Carpizo used the tragedy later to purge from their jobs some 70 federal agents and 250 state officers linked to the drug trade.[45]

A 1993 report by Minnesota Advocates for Human Rights noted that the Salinas government's insistent militarization of the antinarcotics effort was, "in large measure, a result of [its] inability or unwillingness to pursue serious reform of the police." In a prophetic passage, the advocacy group found:

> troubling signs of renewed involvement of the military in civilian affairs during the administration of President Salinas de Gotari. . . . Another disturbing development is the deployment of the army among the indigenous populations of southern Mexico—especially in Chiapas—where long-simmering land conflicts have been aggravated by the government's agrarian policy. Lawless practices of the Mexican military have become increasingly tolerated at the highest levels of the Mexican government. The growing acceptance of lawless military involvement in detentions and searches among civilians is a dangerous development.[46]

### El Grito de Chiapas

The 1994 New Year's rebellion by the Zapatista National Liberation Army took modern Mexico by surprise and shook its self-image to the core, reminding revelers of another national reality, that of lawlessness, poverty, and racism. The insurgents lashed out at targets representing the power of the government and the military, including army posts, municipal buildings, and a prison. Absalón Castellanos, a retired army general and former governor of Chiapas between 1983 and 1988, was taken hostage.[47]

The Chiapas uprising had been long in coming. For years the indigenous communities had been repressed by wealthy landowners allied with the PRI-controlled state government and the security forces. Five major protests had been put down with force in the past three years, and two demonstrations—which included children—were met by troops who opened fire. Hundreds of Mayans were imprisoned without trial. In late

1992 and throughout 1993 the army was engaged in a low-profile but brutal counterinsurgency campaign, which itself contributed to popular support for the rebels. Despite media efforts to link the uprising to the New Year's debut of the North American Free Trade Agreement (NAFTA), guerrilla *subcomandante* "Marcos" admitted having headed for the hills nearly a decade earlier with hopes of extending the Central American conflict to Mexico.[48]

Faced with a military threat unprecedented in modern times, the government moved to crush the rebellion, mobilizing 15,000 army troops against the estimated 2,000 insurgents. The army, its combat prowess dulled by nonmilitary tasks such as civic action and counternarcotics work, proved incapable of crushing the revolt quickly and, according to one account, may have lost control of its field operation. In a rare admission of failure, after initial efforts to impose a military solution and to ridicule the Zapatistas as "criminals" led by foreigners and non-Mayan "professionals of violence," Salinas reversed course and admitted the insurgents had a political basis for their demands. He fired Interior Secretary Patrocinio González Garrido, who as Chiapas governor between 1988 and 1993 was allied to powerful timber and ranching interests, jailing hundreds of indigenous activists on trumped-up charges, and replaced him with Attorney General Jorge Carpizo, the former government human rights ombudsman. Salinas also offered the rebels an amnesty and authorized a probe of charges that the army was responsible for torture, summary executions, and indiscriminate aerial bombing and rocket attacks on the indigenous villages ringing San Cristóbal de las Casas.[49]

Embarrassed by Salinas's about-face and criticism from domestic and international human rights groups, the army took the unprecedented step of going public, to the point of what in other circumstances would have been considered insubordination. At a press conference the military officer in charge of putting down the rebellion, General Miguel Angel Godínez Bravo denied the accusations of torture and summary executions. Military spokesmen privately claimed the military had been shut out of the civilian decisionmaking process regarding Chiapas, then forced to take blame for a "mess," a situation some likened to the 1968 repression of students in Mexico City. They pointed out that after warning the government of the presence of the guerrillas in 1993, civilian officials—preoccupied with the debate in the United States over the ratification of NAFTA—not only prohibited a crackdown on the incipient insurgents but publicly denied their existence. "There are no guerrillas in the state," Chiapas Attorney General Joaquín Armendáriz claimed following a report in the news magazine *Proceso* that said armed indigenous groups were receiving military training in the state. "This alarm is definitely false and comes from people who are trying to discredit the government and foment unrest among the citizenry." As negotiations between the government and the rebels began, the region's powerful cattle ranchers—locked in a decades-old struggle over land rights with the indigenous communities—demanded army protection. "By providing protection to the Chiapas civilian population, the Mexican Army and Air Force have carried out their constitutional responsibilities," Salinas said in a February 19, 1994, Army Day message, in which he also stressed the armed forces' role in public health, disaster relief, counternarcotics, and public safety.[50]

Concern about the military's new assertiveness was not allayed when the newspapers *Reforma* and *El Norte* reported that army intelligence agents were spying on the negotiations led by Peace Commissioner Manuel Camacho Solís and the Zapatistas' Marcos. Daily reports of the conversations, elaborated from the information received through highly sensitive listening devices, were then sent to the Seventh Military Region in Tuxtla Gutiérrez and to Defense Secretary Antonio Riviello Bazán, *Reforma* said. According to the newspaper, a Mexican army officer claimed that "not even Camacho himself is aware that we know everything he said."[51]

The importance of the administration of justice, particularly police reform, was evident by the prominence the issue received in the preliminary peace agreement and suggested the absolute lack of protection by the state for Mexico's twenty Mayan peoples, represented in Chiapas alone by a population of more than 900,000. The accord promised reform of the state's organic police law and the selection of law enforcement agents working in indigenous communities from a list proposed by the communities. Judicial districts would coincide with the communities' boundaries to ensure that judges "may be indigenous people, or professionals respected by them."[52]

The kidnapping of Alfredo Harp Helú, president of the Banamex-Accival financial group, on March 14, 1994, underscored another fast-growing public security concern: the kidnapping of Mexican business executives. (Harp was released after 106 days in captivity and the payment of some U.S.$30 million.) According to one estimate 2,000 extortive kidnappings occurred during the first five and one-half years of the Salinas presidency, a phenomenon that had begun to affect investor confidence. One security expert consulted by *The Wall Street Journal* said that twelve of the abductions in 1993 were for ransoms of more than a million dollars. The newspaper went on to say:

> The problem is also complicated . . . because policemen and former policemen—the type of men who generally act as bodyguards in most countries—are reputed to be the kidnappers in many . . . cases. Partly because of the alleged involvement of the police, security experts say they don't think any of the kidnappers involved in a big money case have ever been caught.[53]

The same month that Harp Helú was kidnapped, an attempt by federal police to arrest Tijuana drug cartel lieutenant Ismael Higuera Guerrero, an associate of the Arellano-Félix crime organization responsible for the murder of Cardinal Posadas, was foiled when the federales were ambushed by the Federal Judicial Police who were guarding the narcotics kingpin. The Federal Judicial Police commander and three others were killed. Higuera escaped. A drug lieutenant detained at the scene was later released after a Baja California Norte attorney general intervened on his behalf. Mexico, charged federal deputy attorney general Eduardo Valle Espinosa as he resigned in May 1994, was a "narcodemocracy," where "nobody can outline a political project in which the heads of drug trafficking and their financiers are not included. Because if you do it, you die."[54]

The assassination of PRI presidential standard-bearer Luis Donaldo Colosio in March 1994 raised questions about a government that would allow its political favorite son to be guarded by former policemen accused of murder, torture, and corruption. Tijuana police chief Federico Benítez, an anticorruption crusader and a member of the opposition National Action Party (PAN), was quietly probing the role of the forty-five-member PRI security force in Colosio's death when he was ambushed and killed in his pickup truck. Just two days before, Benítez had told a *Washington Post* correspondent that records on the local PRI boss who organized Colosio's bodyguard—a former chief homicide investigator for the Baja California State Judicial Police who was linked in the press to the murder of his own ex-wife—had been burgled from Benítez's office. A poll of wealthy Mexico City residents conducted shortly after the assassination revealed that only 7 percent believed the man detained at the crime scene acted alone; 32 percent believed that the PRI itself was behind the murder; and 70 percent said they did not trust the government to be honest about its investigation.[55] After a special prosecutor's report released in July concluded that the assassination was the work of a lone twenty-three-year-old mechanic, the subsequent public outcry caused Salinas himself to publicly reject the findings and announce that another team of investigators would reopen the case.[56]

In May 1994 Salinas named his fourth attorney general—Mexico's chief law enforcement officer—in seventeen months, an inauspicious way of keeping faith with promises to crack down on corruption and crime. Government supporters as well as critics, noted the *Washington Post*, were increasingly worried "the public confidence in the nation's crime-fighting apparatus is rapidly eroding while an image of lawless chaos is being projected abroad." Salinas's newest pick for attorney general, Víctor Humberto Benítez Treviño, quickly fired five Federal Judicial Police commanders, eliminated the force's office of investigations, and ordered a reorganization of the force. A deputy warned federal police chiefs around Mexico that if they did not begin to crack down on the drug mafia bosses, they themselves should prepare to be brought up on charges of complicity and obstruction of justice. Meanwhile, the five members of a Salinas-appointed independent citizens' commission to investigate the Colosio assassination resigned en masse, claiming they lacked the authority to investigate.[57]

In the final months before the August 21 presidential election, national defense and public safety issues continued to dominate the news. Like Salinas, the new PRI presidential candidate Ernesto Zedillo (the former education secretary) proclaimed narcotics trafficking to be the most serious national security threat facing the country. Meanwhile, former federal justice official Eduardo Valle Espinosa released a letter he sent to Salinas that complained of having been impeded in many cases from investigating drug cases by other officials, who balked at antinarcotics raids and who allowed major traffickers to go free. According to the pro-government magazine *Epoca,* what were once five powerful drug cartels operating in the country had grown to nineteen, and all were engaged in bloody territorial warfare. The army was chosen by the Federal Electoral Institute (IFE) to safeguard ballots and other election materials prior to the voting, rather than the police. The military also bought eighteen thirteen-ton water cannons and four unarmed Black Hawk helicopters, normally used to ferry troops into battle, from the United States for riot control in the face of threats of civil unrest if free and fair elections were not held.[58] In the final days before the election *The New York Times* reported that in the west coast city of Coyuca de Benítez:

> Observers reported the sort of scene that has continued to blur the lines between the PRI and the Government, new laws and all. As heavily armed policemen surrounded the town plaza and military helicopters and planes buzzed overhead, hundreds of peasants lined up to receive subsidy checks from a Government agricultural program. . . . Carlos Arévalo, 30, a truck driver who lives near the western city of Guadalajara, said he had heard Mr. Salinas promise to hand over power to whoever won a fair vote but put more stock in reports of the army getting new helicopters, of big troop deployments in the countryside, and of 500 assault rifles disappearing from a stockpile in the coastal city of Puerto Vallarta.[59]

Amidst reports of the beginnings of insurgencies in the states of Hidalgo and Veracruz and the existence of armed groups in at least eight other states, the army moved troops and equipment into the mountains of Guerrero. U.S. business executives availing themselves of opportunities under NAFTA reported increasing incidences of threats, extortion, and violence along the U.S.-Mexican border. In July the PRD candidate for governor of Chiapas, himself close to the Zapatistas, was severely wounded in a suspicious car accident. The growing sense of public insecurity was reflected in a proliferation of private security firms, which in June numbered some

2,156 nationally. These firms are frequently staffed by low-level former police, and 80 percent operate illegally. (Jesús Contreras, head of the Contreras Detective Agency, said that so many ex-police have such checkered pasts that his agency will not hire former security force agents.)[60]

## Civilian Strengths or Civilian Weaknesses?

Although the Mexican military has shown a singular reluctance to open itself for study from the outside, a growing body of literature has yielded a number of explanations for the durability of civilian supremacy over the armed forces, arguments that are still brandished to suggest why events such as a military coup would be unlikely. In 1991 Ackroyd offered what might be described as the classic formulation for the endurance of civilian control:

> The superior position of the state vis-à-vis the military is reinforced by the ideological fusion of nation and state created by the revolution. . . . The mythology of the revolution encourages officers to think of nation and government as one. An attack on the government therefore would be an attack on the revolution.[61]

While not portraying this as a strength of the system, Aguayo has pointed to the vast agenda-setting powers of the Mexican president, who can "decide what is and what is not national security . . . decide what the threats are, which threats should receive priority, what resources might be allocated, which institutions will participate, and what methods will be used."[62]

Pellicer de Brody has argued that Mexico's proximity to the world's remaining superpower and the high degree of state control by the PRI strongly condition civil-military relations. Among the safeguards perceived in the Mexican model, Herrera-Lasso and González wrote, are "the nationalistic, institutional character" of the military; the "sophisticated means" developed by civilians to control the armed forces; the lack of experience of most officers exercising political power, thereby limiting the armed forces' capacity to hold and maintain power; the military's lack of ties with institutions outside of the government; and lastly, the political culture of Mexico, which "is not conducive to military political power."[63]

Other aspects of strength in Mexico's civil-military relations have been noted. The military educational system, largely closed to civilian instructors, is said to offer little political content in the curriculum, thus discouraging interest or involvement in politics, while at the same time screening officers and restricting political knowledge to the highest ranks. The unequal quality of education received by civilian and military elites is also seen as helping to consolidate civilian control. Miguel Basáñez has argued that the military is not coup-prone because it lacks strong ties to Mexican entrepreneurs.[64]

In *Generals in the Palacio* Camp advances several other safeguards for civilian control, some unique to Mexico: a strong antimilitary bias on the part of the general public; the "declining . . . military representation in political affairs since 1946," the "extreme emphasis on subordination in officer formation courses," the armed forces' autonomy from civilian intervention in its internal affairs, and the high degree to which Mexican defense journals promote subordination to civilian authority. In this highly presidential system even the lack of legislative oversight—crucial to U.S. and other democratic models of civil-military relations—is seen in a somewhat favorable light, given that "an attempt to carry out oversight" (which challenges executive branch omnipotence) "might, in some respects, destroy rather than strengthen one of the foundations of civilian supremacy," the unquestioned power of the presidency.[65]

Against the backdrop of these bulwarks of civilian, although not necessarily democratic, control of the armed forces are other practices and trends that might not in and of themselves create a challenge to political control of the military—unless the PRI's hegemony were threatened. These factors will become increasingly relevant as Mexico moves toward a more pluralistic political system, especially if the distinction between internal security (police) and national defense (military) roles remains blurred.

One such factor is that the "mythology of the revolution" referred to by Ackroyd may no longer "encourage officers to think of nation and government as one." On the contrary, in a country in which state leadership derived a great deal of its legitimacy from popular and revolutionary ideology, important sectors of Mexico's population (among them leftists, nationalists, and even PRI *dinosaurios*) interpret the "modernizing" initiatives of the Salinas government as a betrayal of elements of the country's revolutionary legacy. (It is no accident that the Chiapas rebels took the name of the country's most revered rebel leader, Emiliano Zapata, and that the head of one of the country's two most important opposition parties is named Cárdenas.) In other words, the legitimacy the Revolution gave to one-party rule has been severely and probably irremediably damaged.

Moreover, given Mexico's traditionally sympathetic view of Latin American revolutions, the New Year's uprising in Chiapas calls into question a key element for retaining the military's loyalty: in Camp's formulation, "the officer's belief in the civilian leadership's ability to maintain order." The social and professional isolation of the armed forces (neither the navy nor defense secretariats fill decisionmaking or advisory posts with civilian experts, unlike in the United States where civilians abound in the command structure) can readily lead to a caste mentality. That the military's budget and role are not part of public discourse, that legislative oversight is extraordinarily weak, and that security issues have traditionally not been of interest to the opposition parties suggest that in a highly presidential system, a failure of a chief executive's policies may quickly and irreparably tarnish the generals' loyalty to the civilian leadership. The results of the 1994 elections, together with projected reforms in the Senate, could thrust the legislative body into a more activist role.[66]

The armed forces' role in civic action not only violates the Mexican Constitution, but can foster competition for scarce public resources between the armed forces and civilian political leaders. (According to Ackroyd, "civic action" has been the largest category in the contents of the *Journal of the Mexican Army and Air Force.*) Experience in other countries has shown that civic action tends to politicize the armed forces and, when combined with other factors, such as an army's social isolation, can lead to their feeling "different and better" than their civilian counterparts —the antechamber of militarism.[67]

The Salinas government's incorporation of the military as a virtual enforcement arm of the PRI's political and economic policies is nothing less than a return to the practices of Mexico's first postrevolutionary civilian president, Miguel Alemán. Today that policy has not only exposed the military to the danger of corruption by the drug lords, but it also may serve to further discredit the armed forces in the eyes of a populace desirous of change. The "extreme importance placed upon discipline and obedience" in military education, its creation of a caste mentality, along with the tradition of hazing of army cadets, including physical and mental punishment, make for a type of instruction antithetical to the internal security needs of a modern democratic state, namely, law enforcement officers who are sensitive to community concerns and who respect the rights of individuals. Although the literature on the subject in Mexico is scarce, other nations' experiences with law enforcement agencies sharing internal security roles with the military show that such joint operations, beyond politicizing the military, tend to humiliate and corrupt the police.[68]

## Conclusion

The political uncertainty in Mexico at the time of the 1994 presidential campaign portends what necessarily will be a new chapter in civil-military relations and in the administration of justice. In some respects the remarkable stability of Mexico's civil-military relationship has been undermined by the positive changes undertaken during Salinas's stewardship: the opening to political pluralism, the structural changes within the economy, and the willingness—as a result of NAFTA—to be more receptive to foreign influences and trends. But just as clearly, the Salinas regime also introduced innovations and reinforced existing trends that have themselves placed both civil-military harmony and public safety at risk. In simplest terms the military's involvement in policing undermines efforts to win community support for law enforcement, an essential component of fighting crime and maintaining public order.

The issue, however, goes beyond military intervention in public safety. Police corruption and inefficiency, together with a generalized perception of law enforcement as the front rank of a system of state repression, demand a concerted effort to help the public overcome its historic disdain for forces of law and order, whose image reflects Mexico's authoritarian past. As it moves toward participatory democracy, Mexico faces what Richard Millet has called the "Gordian knot" of internal security reform: the professionalization of the police will be expensive, and even a reformed security force will not work unless the judiciary is also reformed. The police lack community support, a corporate mystique of service, and the technical skills and tools needed for effective functioning in a world in which crime has become increasingly sophisticated. But in Mexico personal insecurity is a matter of both the law and law enforcement and therefore will require an extended commitment for the reform of the administration of justice. This includes the creation of an independent judiciary, beyond the reach of the president and the state governors who now pick and fire judges at will. Judicial procedures need to be streamlined and commercial laws dating back sixty years brought into the 1990s. In a country eager to prove its First World credentials, a creaky and corrupt legal system needs the same attention given during the past decade to improving Mexico's economic competitiveness.[69]

Salinas's heirs, from within the PRI family or from without, need to set the Mexican state on a more democratic course, toward civilian control of the military within the context of political pluralism and the checks and balances of competing institutions, and toward a refoundation of the administration of justice. Modern democracy—if that is to be Mexico's destiny—requires policymakers to draw a clear distinction in practice between national defense and internal security. And that must include a demilitarization of the nation's internal security apparatus, by professionalizing the police and effectively placing them at the service of the people they are supposed to protect.

## Notes

1. I would like to thank Robb Kurz and Richard Millet for their helpful comments on an earlier draft and, as always, Riordan Roett for his invaluable counsel and support.

2. William S. Ackroyd, "Military Professionalism, Education, and Political Behavior in Mexico," *Armed Forces & Society* 18, no. 1 (Fall 1991): 81; see also

Roderic Ai Camp, *Generals in the Palacio: The Military in Modern Mexico* (New York: Oxford University Press, 1992), p. 3.

3. Edwin Lieuwen, *Arms and Politics in Latin America* (New York: Council on Foreign Relations, 1960).

4. Martin Edwin Andersen, "Mexico's Bristling Army," *The Christian Science Monitor,* February 18, 1994; Andrés Oppenheimer, "Mexican Army Chafes at Salinas' Action," *Miami Herald,* January 23, 1994.

5. Camp, *Generals in the Palacio,* p. 45.

6. Ackroyd, "Military Professionalism," p. 82.

7. See, for example, the otherwise excellent analysis contained in Wayne A. Cornelius, "Mexico's Delayed Democratization," *Foreign Policy,* no. 95 (Summer 1994): 53–71.

8. See the useful study by Charles Doyle, "Use of the Military to Enforce Civilian Law: Posse Comitatus Act and Other Considerations," *CRS Report to Congress* (Washington, D.C.: Congressional Research Service, July 20, 1988).

9. José Manuel Ugarte, *Seguridad Interior* (Buenos Aires: Fundación Arturo Illia, 1990).

10. On the Salvador peace accords, see William Stanley, "Police and Political Change: Lessons from the Demilitarization of Internal Security in El Salvador" (paper presented at the Congress of the Latin American Studies Association, Atlanta, Georgia, March 1994).

11. Sergio Aguayo Quezada, "The Uses, Misuses, and Challenges of Mexican National Security: 1946–1990," in *Mexico: In Search of Stability,* ed. Bruce M. Bagley and Sergio Aguayo (New Brunswick, N.J.: Transaction Publishers, 1993), pp. 104, 106, 111, 129.

12. Olga Pellicer de Brody, "National Security in Mexico: Traditional Notions and New Preoccupations," in *U.S.-Mexico Relations: Economic and Social Aspects,* ed. Clark W. Reynolds and Carlos Tello (Stanford: Stanford University Press, 1983), pp. 181 and 188.

13. Luis Herrera-Lasso and Guadalupe González, "Reflections on the Use of the Concept of National Security in Mexico," in *Mexico: In Search of Stability,* ed. Bruce M. Bagley and Sergio Aguayo (New Brunswick, N.J.: Transaction Publishers, 1993), pp. 346–347.

14. Camp, *Generals in the Palacio,* pp. 25–26 and 87.

15. Aguayo, "The Uses, Misuses, and Challenges," p. 106.

16. Herrera-Lasso and González, "Reflections," p. 349.

17. Ackroyd, "Military Professionalism," p. 84.

18. Camp, *Generals in the Palacio,* pp. 49 and 88–89.

19. Quoted in ibid., p. 21.

20. Ibid., p. 22.

21. Ibid., pp. 23–24, 26–27, and 68; and Pellicer de Brody, "National Security in Mexico," p. 189.

22. Herrera-Lasso and González, "Reflections," p. 346; and Camp, *Generals in the Palacio,* pp. 27–28.

23. Camp, *Generals in the Palacio,* p. 29; Aguayo, "The Uses, Misuses, and Challenges," p. 105.

24. Camp, *Generals in the Palacio,* pp. 30–31 and 85; Martin Edwin Andersen, "The Military Obstacle to Latin Democracy," *Foreign Policy,* no. 73 (Winter 1988–1989); and Harry Summers, "When Armies Lose Sight of Purpose," *Washington Times,* December 26, 1991. For a fascinating historical perspective, which shows how the quest for social relevance during peacetime left the Canadian officer corps unprepared for service in World War II, see John A. English, *The Cana-*

*dian Army and the Normandy Campaign: A Study of Failure of the High Command* (New York: Praeger, 1991).

25. Camp, *Generals in the Palacio,* pp. 31–33; Aguayo, "The Uses, Misuses, and Challenges," p. 109; and Herrera-Lasso and González, "Reflections," pp. 347 and 350.

26. Camp, *Generals in the Palacio,* p. 48.

27. Dale E. Brown, "Drugs on the Border: The Role of the Military," *Parameters* (Winter 1991–1992): 52.

28. Aguayo, "The Uses, Misuses, and Challenges," p. 111.

29. Ibid., pp. 111–112 and 114; William Branigan, "With Friends Like These, Who Needs Enemies?" *Washington Post* Weekend Edition, July 23–29, 1990, p. 31; U.S. Department of State, *Country Reports on Human Rights Practices for 1993* (Washington, D.C.: U.S. Department of State, 1994), p. 490; interview with Sergio Aguayo Quezada, Mexico City, July 1994; and Andrew Reding, "Hold Mexican Military Accountable for Human Rights Abuses," *Christian Science Monitor,* July 20, 1994.

30. Camp, *Generals in the Palacio,* pp. 32 and 91; Kate Doyle, "The Militarization of the Drug War in Mexico," *Current History* (February 1993): 83–85.

31. Doyle, "The Militarization," p. 84; Aguayo, "The Uses, Misuses, and Challenges," p. 127; Tod Robberson, "Mexican Army Short of Funds and Combat Experience," *Washington Post,* January 19, 1994; and Camp, *Generals in the Palacio,* p. 92.

32. Camp, *Generals in the Palacio,* p. 59.

33. Ibid., p. 88.

34. Ibid., pp. 58–59 and 92; and Herrera-Lasso and González, "Reflections," p. 350.

35. Camp, *Generals in the Palacio,* p. 33; Aguayo, "The Uses, Misuses, and Challenges," pp. 112 and 128; Robberson, "Mexican Army," *Washington Post;* Herrera-Lasso and González, "Reflections," p. 349; and Foreign Broadcast Information Service—Latin America (FBIS-LAT), January 3, 1991, p. 8.

36. Aguayo, "The Uses, Misuses, and Challenges," p. 110; Wayne A. Cornelius, "Mexico's Delayed Democratization," *Foreign Policy,* no. 95 (Summer 1994): 64; and Herrera-Lasso and González, "Reflections," p. 344.

37. Cornelius, "Mexico's Delayed Democratization," p. 63; and Camp, *Generals in the Palacio,* pp. 33–34 and 83–84.

38. Tod Robberson, "Job Security Lacking for Mexico's Attorneys General," *Washington Post,* June 1, 1994; FBIS-LAT, December 9, 1991, p. 12; FBIS-LAT, December 13, 1991, pp. 20–23.

39. Andrew Reding, "Colosio: Victim of Mexico's Lawless Politics," *Christian Science Monitor,* April 19, 1994.

40. FBIS-LAT, May 26, 1993, pp. 6–9.

41. Oppenheimer, "Mexican Army"; Reding, "Hold Mexican Military Accountable."

42. Herrera-Lasso and González, "Reflections," p. 345; Alan Weisman, "The Deadly Harvest of the Sierra Madre," *Los Angeles Times Magazine,* January 9, 1994, p. 33.

43. FBIS-LAT, April 7, 1992, p. 33.

44. Confidential interview, May 1994.

45. Robberson, "Job Security"; FBIS-LAT, May 26, 1993, p. 6; Tod Robberson, "How Mexico Brewed a Rebellion," *Washington Post,* January 9, 1994.

46. Minnesota Advocates for Human Rights, *Civilians at Risk: Military and Police Abuses in the Mexican Countryside* (Minneapolis: Minnesota Advocates for Human Rights, 1993).

47. Robberson, "How Mexico."

48. FBIS-LAT, February 22, 1994, p. 15; David Scott Clark, "Chiapas Ranchers Vow to Take Law into Their Own Hands," *Christian Science Monitor,* January 27, 1994; Robberson, "How Mexico"; Tim Golden, "Jungle to Peace Talks: Mexican Chronicles Revolt," *The New York Times,* February 22, 1994.

49. Tod Robberson, "Mexican Cabinet Shake-Up Called Sign of Willingness to Talk with Rebels," *Washington Post,* January 12, 1994; Robb Kurz, "Narcoinsurgency in Mexico," in *Narco-Insurgent Nexus* (paper prepared for U.S. Department of Defense, Office of the Assistant Secretary of Defense for Special Operations and Low Intensity Conflict, by Booz-Allen & Hamilton, March 30, 1994).

50. David Clark Scott, "Mexican Army Presents Its Case on Chiapas," *Christian Science Monitor,* February 2, 1994; Oppenheimer, "Mexican Army"; Tod Robberson, "Bloody Indian Revolt Continues in Mexico," *Washington Post,* January 4, 1994; Kiernan Murray, "Mexican Ranchers Say They're Victims of Peasant Rebels," *Washington Times,* February 1, 1994; FBIS-LAT, February 22, 1994, p. 13.

51. FBIS-LAT, March 25, 1994, pp. 19 and 21.

52. "Compromisos para una paz digna en Chiapas," mimeographed document in author's possession. The lack of effective state protection has put a number of indigenous communities, such as the Tarahumara in Chihuahua and the Yaquis of Sonora, at risk. See, for example, Alfredo Acedo, "Vigilan agentes de la Policía Judicial el acceso a Potam," *La Jornada,* July 10, 1994; and Weisman, "The Deadly Harvest."

53. Rosa Icela Rodríguez, "Han ocurrido 2 mil secuestros en México durante este sexenio," *La Jornada,* July 10, 1994; Paul B. Carroll, "Mexicans Discover Kidnapping Is a Growing Part of Business Risk," *Wall Street Journal,* March 18, 1994.

54. Reding, *Christian Science Monitor,* April 10, 1994; *Unomásuno,* March 10, 1994, p. 13; Tod Robberson, "'Narcopolitics' Runs Rampant in Tijuana," *Washington Post,* May 15, 1994.

55. Reding, "Colosio"; Tod Robberson, "Police Chief's Death Rocks Tijuana," *Washington Post,* April 30, 1994; Robberson, "New Murder in Mexico Deepens Assassination Mystery," *Washington Post,* May 1, 1994; and Robberson, "'Narcopolitics.'"

56. Tod Robberson, "Confusion Spreads in Mexican's Killing," *Washington Post,* July 16, 1994; Tim Golden, "Mexican Ends Investigation into Shooting," *The New York Times,* July 14, 1994; and Andrés Oppenheimer, "Mexico Agrees to New Probe into Candidate's Assassination," *Miami Herald,* July 15, 1994.

57. Robberson, "Job Security"; Andrew Reding, "For Mexico's Rulers, Reform Is Risky," *Washington Post,* August 7, 1994.

58. Tim Golden, "Mexico's Drug Fight Lagging, with Graft Given as Cause," *The New York Times,* August 4, 1994; Reding, "For Mexico's Rulers"; *Miami Herald,* June 17, 1994; Jesús Belmont Vázquez and Ernesto Zavaleta Góngora, "El narco se reproduce: Ahora existen 19 carteles," *Epoca,* July 11, 1994; and Rosa María Méndez and Gerardo Mejía, "'Desplaza' ejército a policía," *Reforma,* July 31, 1994.

59. Tim Golden, "To Change or Not to Change? Mexicans Are Voting Today," *The New York Times,* August 21, 1994.

60. Anthony DePalma, "Mexico Crash Badly Injures a Candidate," *The New York Times,* July 26, 1994; Miryam Hazán and Miguel Badillo, "'Charlatanes y expolicías,' en la mayoría de las empresas de seguridad e investigación," *El Financiero,* July 11, 1994.

61. Ackroyd, "Military Professionalism," pp. 86 and 91.

62. Aguayo, "The Uses, Misuses, and Challenges," p. 113.

63. Pellicer de Brody, "National Security in Mexico," p. 181; and Herrera-Lasso and González, "Reflections," pp. 351–352.

64. Ackroyd, "Military Professionalism," pp. 86 and 88; Basáñez cited in Camp, *Generals in the Palacio,* p. 75.

65. Camp, *Generals in the Palacio,* pp. 6, 10, 16, 48, 53, and 85.

66. Pellicer de Brody, "National Security in Mexico," p. 15; Camp, *Generals in the Palacio,* pp. 10, 45, 50, 76–77, and 184; Herrera-Lasso and González, "Reflections," p. 342; Aguayo, "The Uses, Misuses, and Challenges," p. 114; and Cornelius, "Mexico's Delayed Democratization," pp. 55–56.

67. Camp, *Generals in the Palacio,* p. 85; and Ackroyd, "Military Professionalism," pp. 87–88.

68. Ackroyd, "Military Professionalism," pp. 89–90; and Martin Edwin Andersen, *Dossier Secreto: Argentina's Desaparecidos and the Myth of the "Dirty War"* (Boulder, Colo.: Westview Press, 1993), pp. 311 and 338.

69. Interview with Richard Millet, August 1994; Carlos Díaz Abrego, "Justicia injusta," *Epoca,* July 11, 1994; Damian Fraser, "Mexican Legal System Puts Progress in Fetters," *Financial Times,* July 15, 1994.

# — PART 3 —
## Conclusions

# 10

# The Politics of Institutional Reform in Mexico and Latin America

## Riordan Roett & Guadalupe Paz

It was the 1982 debt crisis that set Mexico on its course toward economic change and adjustment. Today, we are witnessing a subsequent process of social and political adjustment not unlike that in other Latin American countries, one that is both historic and profound.

The shift from a *dirigiste* or statist economy to an open, modernizing, and increasingly competitive economy, seen throughout most of Latin America over the past decade (Chile, the exception, began liberalizing its economy in the previous decade) reflects the failure of the old corporatist state model in a changing international environment. Economic development strategies require a certain level of consensus in both the policymaking levels and the various other sectors of society. Because the costs of economic structural reform are quickly felt while the benefits materialize in the medium to long term, building social consensus and engaging in active dialogue with labor, the peasantry, and business are necessary steps to maintain stability in political and civic life.

In some Latin American countries the most successful reform programs have come under authoritarian regimes, such as those in Brazil in 1964 and in Chile in 1973. The Chilean case is particularly interesting, because although import substitution and protectionism formed the prevailing economic model in Latin America at that time, Chile was able to institute a radical program of economic liberalization. Whether Chile was able to implement the reforms solely because of the near-absolute power of the military regime, or whether the skilled economic team assembled by General Augusto Pinochet (1973–1990), was the real key to their success, Pinochet had the vision to consult closely with leading business executives, lawyers, and economists. It was the economists, opposing the others, who suggested an open-market policy to stabilize the economy. Pinochet listened to the economists.

The special interests in Chile had no choice but to accept the economic reforms, given that Pinochet's economic team enjoyed the support of the military. Once the economy began to grow, then-Minister of Labor José Piñera extended the reforms to the social sector by introducing a pension privatization plan, first to business and trade union leaders—unsuccessfully—and finally directly to the people through a mass media campaign. The pension privatization plan was approved some weeks later.

Minister Piñera understood the importance of reform in sectors other than the economic, as well as the government's need for enough social consensus to maintain its power. He recently stated, however, that "one final, crucial ingredient in the political economy of any country making the difficult transition to a free, open economy is the presence at the top of people who are real leaders rather than politicians," pointing out that this element is equally necessary in military regimes as it is in parliamentary democracies.[1] This type of leadership is just as crucial in promulgating institutional reform in other sectors of society.

The changing roles of different sectors of Latin American societies, in light of the new economic realities of the 1980s and 1990s, are important factors in not just which reforms are carried out, but how. In Colombia, for instance, amidst rapid economic liberalization, the César Gaviria government (1990–1994) successfully reformed labor legislation, in spite of the traditional political strength the labor force derived from its ability and willingness to threaten the government with strikes. Two decades of complaints from employers regarding the burden Colombia's job security legislation imposed on their businesses had not sufficed. Employers began to fire workers before they obtained any rights to job security, and as a result Colombia went from having a high level of job stability in the 1960s to having the highest labor turnover rates in the world in the 1980s.

Just as the Mexican *ejido* system was a failure for restraining peasants rather than, as was originally intended, protecting them, the Colombian job stability legislation seemed to have had an effect opposite to that desired. What made the job security reform politically possible was the argument that economic liberalization required labor market flexibility to prevent the failure of certain industries, which in turn would create unemployment. Furthermore, the drug-related and guerrilla violence that plagued the country in the late 1980s and early 1990s captured the attention of both government and society, thus weakening the labor sector and its threats. This shift in power in the state-labor relationship in Colombia will require a redefinition of the role of workers in the new economic environment as well as the role of the government in responding to the demands of organized labor, as the country continues its drive toward modernization.

In the case of Mexico, as has been demonstrated in the previous chapters, political stability or "governability" is rapidly gaining importance and is becoming increasingly challenging in a system that has been under the leadership—and control—of the Institutional Revolutionary Party (PRI) for over six decades. The series of economic, political, and social reforms that Mexico has engaged in especially since 1988 has had the dual nature of maintaining governability and deepening the democratization process. Maintaining governability, however, may require a true democratic transition, which, in the eyes of many, means a transfer of power from the PRI to another party.

In 1992 Antonio Camou concluded in his analysis entitled "Eleven Theses about the Mexican 'Transition': Governability and Democracy"[2] that the Salinas de Gortari administration had reached "renovated conditions of governability" through real economic improvement, thereby gaining political legitimacy for the PRI in a "passive consensus for results." Although economic success did defuse social discontent in the first years of Salinas's *sexenio,* the Mexican people are no longer content with "passive consensus," and the events marking the end of the Salinas administration have driven the PRI to accelerate political and social change as economic stability and the status quo are being threatened by civil unrest.

The North American Free Trade Agreement passed in 1993 has increased external pressures on the Mexican political system to achieve a peaceful transition to democracy. Civil society in Mexico is demanding more than a political voice—it is *engaging in* political mobilization—as the economic reform continues to stimulate a change in values and expectations in both the political and social arenas. The greatest challenge in implementing successful institutional reforms in Mexico lies in the timely recognition of this changing zeitgeist, and in accepting it—and adopting it—as part of the modernization and democratization process.

U.S.-Mexican as well as hemispheric relations are entering a new era of increased trade and cooperation and growing common interests. Even Mexico's powerful neighbor to the north is undergoing significant pressures to reform not only the health, education, and welfare systems, but also the very rules and procedures for making and carrying out public policy. In Mexico the state is seeking political reconciliation and a reassessment of the social agenda, while the people are demanding true democratic change. The United States is promoting exports and becoming more competitive. Mexico is inserting itself into the global economy. Similar agendas, as described by the National Security Council's Richard E. Feinberg in his *Substantive Symmetry* approach to hemispheric relations, "can and should translate shared values into concrete work plans."[3]

The challenge of institutional reform in Mexico will require both wise political leadership and determined social participation in the transition process. But Mexico is not alone. Mexico is, in fact, a leader in economic and political reform in Latin America and the world. Reaching a social consensus should include recognition of the need to maintain economic stability, not at the cost of democratic freedom or social well-being, but as one necessary element in the process of overall reform.

## Notes

1. José Piñera, "Chile," in *The Political Economy of Policy Reform,* ed. John Williamson (Washington, D.C.: Institute for International Economics, 1994), pp. 230–231.

2. Antonio Camou, "Eleven Theses about the Mexican 'Transition': Governability and Democracy," *Nexos* (February 1992).

3. Richard E. Feinberg, "Substantive Symmetry and Hemispheric Relations" (address to the Latin American Studies Association, Atlanta, Georgia, March 10, 1994).

# About the Contributors

*Jorge Alcocer V.* is founder and coordinator of The Center for Studies for a National Project, a nonprofit research institution in Mexico City, and is director of *Voz y Voto,* a monthly magazine of political news and analysis. He served as federal deputy from 1985–1988 and as representative of various parties before the Federal Electoral Commission from 1987–1990. Since January 1994 he is a personal advisor on electoral issues to the president of the General Council of the Federal Electoral Institute.

*Martin Edwin Andersen* is senior consultant at the Center for Democracy in Washington, D.C., and a consultant to the John Jay School of Criminal Justice of the City University of New York and to the International Criminal Investigative Training Assistance Program (ICITAP) of the U.S. Department of Justice.

*Roberto J. Blancarte* is academic coordinator at the Colegio Mexiquense, A.C., in Toluca, Mexico. He is president of the Center for the Study of Religions in Mexico (CEREM) and a columnist in the national newspaper *La Jornada.*

*Ruth Berins Collier* is associate professor of Political Science at the University of California, Berkeley.

*Wayne A. Cornelius* is the Gildred Professor of Political Science and director of the Center for U.S.-Mexican Studies at the University of California, San Diego.

*Merilee S. Grindle* is the Edward S. Mason Professor of International Development at the John F. Kennedy School of Government at Harvard University. She is also a fellow at the Harvard Institute for International Development.

*Matilde Luna* is Research Associate at the Institute for Social Research of the National Autonomous University of Mexico (UNAM). She teaches in the Political and Social Sciences Department at UNAM as well as in the José María Luis Mora Institute in Mexico City.

*Guadalupe Paz* is coordinator of the Program on U.S.-Mexican Relations at the Paul H. Nitze School of Advanced International Studies at the Johns Hopkins University.

*Riordan Roett* is the Sarita and Don Johnston Professor and director of Latin American Studies at the Paul H. Nitze School of Advanced International Studies at the Johns Hopkins University.

*James G. Samstad* is a doctoral student in the Department of Political Science at the University of California, Berkeley, and a 1993–1994 fellow at the Center for U.S.-Mexican Studies at the University of California, San Diego.

*Guillermo Trejo* is research associate at the Development Research Center (CIDAC), Mexico City, and a Ph.D. candidate at Columbia University.

# Index

# About the Book

The Salinas administration's reforms in Mexico generated both widespread attention and a host of questions. This book addresses those questions, examining the impact of the recent reforms on the state's relations with key social and political actors—labor, the peasantry, business, political parties, and the church—and assessing reform initiatives in the areas of education, human rights, and social welfare.

The authors consider the external, as well as the domestic, impetuses for reform, discuss the challenges ahead, and compare the path of reform in Mexico to that in other Latin American countries.

**Riordan Roett** is Sarita and Don Johnston Professor of Political Science and director of the Latin American Studies Program of the Paul H. Nitze School of Advanced International Studies, Johns Hopkins University. He also serves as founding director of the SAIS Center of Brazilian Studies and as director of the SAIS Program on U.S.-Mexican Relations. Dr. Roett is editor of *Mexico's External Relations in the 1990s* and *Political and Economic Liberalization in Mexico* and author of numerous books and articles on Latin America.